GREAT BRITISH CHEFS

GREAT BRITISH CHEFS

KIT CHAPMAN

PHOTOGRAPHY   MARTIN BRIGDALE

PYRAMID BOOKS

.... oh! yet
Stands the Church clock at ten to three?
And is there honey still for tea?
Rupert Brooke

In memory of my brother Gerald
for whom afternoon tea was most important

First published in 1989 by
Pyramid Books
an imprint of the Octopus Publishing Group,
Michelin House,
81 Fulham Road,
London SW3 6RB

ISBN 1 871307 89 9

Produced by Mandarin Offset – Printed In Hong Kong

Editor Isobel Greenham
Senior Art Editor David Rowley
Design The Image and Pauline Bayne
Sub-editor Diana Vowles
Cookery Consultant Jane Suthering
Production Controller Alyssum Ross

CONTENTS

PREFACE

This book was born out of a curious emotional entanglement with food from the earliest years of my childhood. It is part envy and part admiration for the chef's talent – a state of mind which once prompted Chris Oakes to accuse me of being a 'frustrated cook' when he ran the kitchens at the Castle. Cast in the fourth generation of a family of hotelkeepers and restaurateurs, I grew up over the shop and so my mother had no need to cook. Indeed our flat at the top of the hotel did not even have a kitchen because our dining room table was admirably served by a dumb waiter. Good food appeared like magic at the press of a bell. Did this make me pitifully deprived or disgustingly privileged? Either way, it has made me oddly timid of my own abilities in the kitchen – I have a passionate interest muted by a detached involvement which has turned me into something of an armchair chef and gastronomic voyeur.

Nevertheless, some of the happiest and most painful moments of my youth are drawn from a vast collection of vivid memories of tastes, smells and food-related experiences which seem to have filled my upbringing. At school I could not eat the tapioca at lunch and was forced to take my plate back to the classroom. At tea, tinned spaghetti melted into toast like corrugated card sodden by rain. And at breakfast, sadistic prefects ladled porridge from cauldrons, slowly dribbling its scalding lumps over thumbs which dared to protrude around the edges of plates. My parents were so worried by my loss of weight that they embarrassed me with tuck parcels of Stilton, Hungarian salami and Radio Malt.

Holidays and family outings to restaurants, on the other hand, were my greatest joy. In Grindelwald on New Year's Eve we would eat roast suckling pig at the Grand Hotel Regina and at a simple *bistro* in Verbier I recall the heady, pungent aroma of a cheese fondue. On our train journeys across Europe to Greece, I remember the operatic calls of the platform vendors in Austria shouting 'Heisse Würstel!' And in Thessaloniki my grandmother would greet us with a spoon of large preserved cherries glistening in syrup which we would wash down with a glass of iced water. I remember also the fish of the Aegean islands – *synagritha* and *barbouni*, eaten simply with a little olive oil, herbs and lemon juice.

In England, in the late Fifties, my first recollection of a really good restaurant was the Hole in the Wall in Bath and I can still see George Perry-Smith, sandals on his feet, standing by his bounty-laden cold table. But, generally, eating in this country was a singularly miserable affair in those days and even in 1976 when I returned to the Castle to join the family business, it did not seem much better. My first introduction to a wine merchant took place in a rather dreary steak house where we ate a gunmetalled rump with our bottle of Château Léoville-Barton 1929.

However, Britain's gastronomic depression is lifting and this book is a celebration of that change. Over the past ten years a quiet revolution has been spreading through the kitchens of this country and a new force of native Brits is beginning to assume a supremacy which, traditionally, has been held by a brigade of brilliant expatriate Europeans.

The 18 chefs whose stories I have chosen to tell are my own personal selection from the best in the land. Omissions are inevitable but I stand by my choice. The only rules governing the list were that they be British born and bred and that each in their own way must have made a significant contribution to the advance of gastronomy in the United Kingdom. I make no apology for the book's inherent chauvinism. At last British nationals are shaking off the culinary image which has blighted this country in the perceptions of a mocking world.

My introduction attempts to sketch the development of restaurants and eating out over the past 40 years and to discuss British attitudes to food in our social and cultural environment. This is necessary because if, indeed, there is a revolution in our kitchens, its expression is valueless without the popular support of an enthusiastic audience. And that audience is the customer.

Lastly, if my title – *Great British Chefs* – strikes a somewhat brazen note in the mind of the sceptic, so be it. Here are 18 courageous and highly gifted pioneers who are leading the way in a land which, in its provinces anyway, still remains largely inimical to the civilized pleasures of eating out.

Kit Chapman 1989

INTRODUCTION

The revival of the fortunes of British cuisine is a bit like the story of Adam and Eve. The Garden of Eden was the Mediterranean but the fruit of the tree of knowledge was less forbidden and more forgotten or ignored in a country which was still emerging from the deprivations and austerity of war. For in the beginning – and for my purposes this must be 1950 – two people lit a tiny flame which has grown to light, guide and influence profoundly British cooking and restaurants in the second half of this century. The first was Elizabeth David, a well-travelled and scholarly diplomat's wife, whose first book – about Mediterranean food – appeared at the time and has continued to be republished since, most recently in 1988. Her writings inspired a new generation of cooks and her name is invoked frequently in the chapters which follow in this book. The second was an historian and political commentator called Raymond Postgate who appreciated his food and wine but who was outraged by the sheer gastronomic poverty of most British restaurants. He decided to take action by launching an informal club of like-minded individuals whose members were invited to file reports on their experiences and in 1951 he published the first edition of the *Good Food Guide*. Adopting the attitude that, to raise standards, it would be better to reward careful cooking rather than to condemn idleness and malpractice, Postgate's *Guide* sold 5,000 copies and listed 500 places which could be recommended with confidence. Today, the *Good Food Guide*'s campaigning spirit and the principles laid down by its founder still remain firmly intact, and the influence it has achieved far exceeds its annual sale of 65,000 copies.

The educated amateur

Historically, dining out in Britain has been – and for the most part remains – a middle-class pastime. The great pre-war eating places were found principally in the grand hotels and restaurants of London but in the Fifties and early Sixties a new and more informal style of eating took root. The movement was led by a small band of educated amateurs who had travelled abroad and who took a fancy to becoming *patrons* of their own intimate and often cramped little bistro-cum-restaurants in and around the fashionable streets of Chelsea and Kensington. Dr Hilary James, a psychotherapist, opened Le Matelot

and La Bicyclette in Elizabeth Street. Walter Baxter, a novelist whose books landed him in court, opened the Chanterelle. Nick Clarke, an Old Etonian, opened Nick's Diner. These, with a handful of other enthusiastic visionaries, and not the professionals of the large established kitchens, seemed to touch the popular imagination of the day and invariably their menus echoed the recipes of Elizabeth David. For the first time, Londoners encountered the tastes of *soupe de poisson, aïoli, ratatouille* and tarragon with their chicken.

From Ray Parkes to the Roux brothers

However, perhaps the most notable forerunner of today's breed of young British chefs at the end of the Fifties was Ray Parkes – a man who abandoned his architectural studies to cook. His work included spells at La Bicyclette and the Chanterelle before opening his own restaurant in Beauchamp Place in 1960. Parkes's cooking was a revelation because, in effect, he introduced *nouvelle cuisine* to London at a time when Anton Mosimann was barely out of short trousers and 13 years before the French food critics, Henri Gault and Christian Millau, coined the expression. The source of Parkes's inspiration was Fernand Point, the proprietor of La Pyramide in Vienne, one of the greatest restaurants in France, and the father of *nouvelle cuisine*. Egon Ronay described Parkes as a genius and culinary surrealist, noting in the 1962 edition of his guide: 'My wife's choice (melon in Yquem) would have certainly looked as smart on her head (at a masked ball) as it was appetizing.' Sadly, Ray Parkes died in 1963 which meant that he left no lasting culinary legacy.

Outside London, the gastronomic map looked hopelessly barren. However, in the Fifties one man emerged as a key figure and was to become a seminal influence on the next generation. This was George Perry-Smith, who opened the Hole in the Wall in Bath in 1951. He became the spiritual leader of Britain's culinary renaissance and his pupils are now well scattered about England and even abroad (see the chapters on Joyce Molyneux and Stephen Ross). Like his fellow *patrons* in London, Perry-Smith was an Elizabeth David-inspired amateur but his legacy reached beyond a reputation as an outstanding cook and restaurateur. Above all, he was a teacher. He came out of Cambridge with a degree in French and German and, after taking a diploma in education in Paris, his love of food led him to Bath where the initials M.A. after his name gave the Hole an air of respectability in a trade which enjoyed little popular esteem. It was a small but significant gesture which began the slow and tortuous process of raising the chef's public image from that of skivvy to star.

There were, of course, a number of other pioneering spirits who attracted Raymond Postgate's attention in those early years and whose influence can still be felt today. The great Eighties boom in luscious hotels created by the rescue and restoration of many of Britain's beautiful country houses had its origins in the Fifties. The owners' motto was rural peace and comfort as well as excellent food, and the leading protagonists included people like Francis Coulson and Brian Sack at Sharrow Bay on Ullswater, Gerard Harris, a solicitor, at the Bell at Aston Clinton and William Heptinstall at the Fortingall Hotel in Perthshire.

Nevertheless, in the country at large, these were still pretty bleak times and a decade after the launch of the Good Food Club, Postgate's report in the 1961/62 edition of the *Guide* offered only qualified praise. 'Food in Britain is nothing like as bad as it was ten or so years ago. But then, it was intolerable in those days. There is still a lot of dreadful food served in this island,' he wrote.

With the rapid growth of Britain's immigrant population in the Sixties, a major dynamic of post-war eating out has been what Christopher Driver, Postgate's successor as editor of the *Good Food Guide*, has called the rice-bowl revolution. Indian, Chinese and the ethnic cuisines of a wide variety of other oriental and eastern Mediterranean cultures have made almost as great an impact on the shape of the modern British chef as the culinary traditions of France and Italy. The eclectic repertoires of Shaun Hill, Alastair Little and Simon Hopkinson are notable examples in this book. Their innate curiosity to explore some of these exotic themes is a natural expression of the Briton's long-standing love affair with spices, an attachment which was encouraged particularly by the trade of the British East India Company in the 17th century.

The Sixties, therefore, saw the first signs of another new dimension to restaurant cooking and the start of the break from the awfulness of the Windsor soup-meat 'n' two veg syndrome or the French classical formality of the grand hotel dining room. In the library of definitive literature in the British kitchen, Claudia Roden joined Elizabeth David.

However, it was Robert Carrier who set out to liberate food in the minds of a guilt-torn public by suggesting that the marvellous diversity of the cuisines of the world could be beautiful, fun and sexy.

Carrier, an American of Irish and German parentage, oozed all the credentials of star quality which endowed him with the ability to communicate with and enthuse an audience. He was an actor turned PR man turned writer and TV chef who opened London's first eclectic restaurant of note – Carrier's in Camden Passage – where he fed the yuppies of the Sixties and Seventies off a globe-hopping menu which ranged from Indonesian lamb with satay sauce to an ever-so-English lemon posset with things French, Spanish and Greek in between.

A less flamboyant landmark of the time but the one which was to grow into arguably the most powerful force for raising standards, lifting the status of the craft and mobilizing the training of aspirant young chefs, was the arrival of the Roux brothers on the London restaurant scene with the opening of Le Gavroche in Lower Sloane Street in 1967. These two Frenchmen – Albert and Michel – now stand among the leaders of a tiny expatriate community of luminaries whose influence in the Eighties has been beyond calculation.

Meanwhile, in the countryside, there was little movement in the Sixties. The markers laid down by the likes of George Perry-Smith and Francis Coulson did not inspire a host of imitators, although the spotlight did fall upon a few illustrious newcomers. Kenneth Bell, a Scottish student of the Lausanne Hotel School who graduated top of his year, made the Elizabeth in Oxford *vaut le voyage* 20 years before Raymond Blanc's arrival in Summertown. 'Gastronomically remarkable,' noted Postgate of Bell's cooking in 1961. But for Bell the Elizabeth was just the curtain raiser for his rise to celebrity which mushroomed after he bought Thornbury Castle near Bristol in 1966. Every culinary decoration was showered upon him subsequently and the *Good Food Guide* crowned him 'the monarch of British restaurateurs'.

Catalyst years and cooking's 'Big Bang'

It was also at about this time that Patrick and Sonia Stevenson bought the Horn of Plenty near Tavistock in the West Country while at the other end of England, at the Box Tree Cottage in Ilkley, Malcolm Reid and Colin Long, two ex-rag traders with tastes as astute in the aesthetic as they were in the gastronomic, had already established a remarkable restaurant which was far ahead of its years. Here were two more amateurs who had eaten their way around France and who, in effect, introduced *nouvelle cuisine* to Yorkshire before it took root in London. Trail-blazers in their day, by 1977 they had won two Michelin stars – a distinction which they shared only with the French-run kitchens of the Connaught, Le Gavroche and the

Waterside Inn at Bray. Moreover, the Michelin double, let alone the triple, is a culinary Holy Grail which has persistently eluded every other Brit-run restaurant since.

There is one other notable provincial restaurant of the period whose pre-eminence in Wales today remains as unchallenged as it was in the Sixties when it was first opened by Franco and Ann Taruschio. Wales seems oddly out of sync with progress in the rest of Britain for, with the exception of the Taruschios at the Walnut Tree Inn at Llandewi Skirrid, the country still offers little that compares remotely with the best in England and Scotland. The Walnut Tree is a Welsh country pub with an exuberant Italian chef-proprietor who offers wholesome and interesting fare prepared from unimpeachable ingredients on a par with Richard Smith at the Royal Oak in Yattendon. And for that achievement alone Taruschio merits an honorary place in this book because, like Smith, he is trying to democratize eating out in this land by appealing to his customers through the social institution they feel most at home in. His principles are noble and need to be emulated in a country which still suffers from an appalling absence of good eating at prices which are affordable by the majority.

The 1970s proved to be the catalyst years for the decade to follow. At last there were stirrings in the countryside as a handful of new pace-setters emerged to demonstrate that Britain had a major asset to offer its rising tide of foreign tourists, particularly those from North America. In the event, the country house hotel developed into a multi-million pound genre in the Eighties and, significantly, it became the principal stamping-ground for ambitious young chefs who were eager to make their mark. Inverlochy Castle, Miller Howe, Maison Talbooth, Gravetye Manor and Chewton Glen were all major movers and shakers of the time. Their proprietors revolutionized attitudes to provincial hotelkeeping by redefining standards of comfort and service and by dictating style and tone.

With the exception of people such as John Tovey at Miller Howe and Stephen Ross at Homewood Park, few of the owners of these handsome houses are chefs. However, with the splendour of their surroundings and their meticulous attention to the quality of the fabric and the hospitality, they demanded cooking to match. And so, guided and encouraged by their patrons, many of the new boy-wonders of the stove who came to prominence in the 1980s found a natural stage upon which to perform.

Of course, as much as this book celebrates the rise of the indigenous chef, Britain's culinary superstars of the past 15 years are still the foreign-born descendants of Carême, Soyer and Escoffier in the 19th and early 20th centuries. It will be for the history books of the next century to decide the relative greatness of the Roux brothers, Anton Mosimann, Michel Bourdin, Nico Ladenis, Raymond Blanc and Pierre Koffmann. But the kitchens of this brigade of giants have become seedbeds for the young British chef — the recognized élite 'academies' which have supplied many of our country house hotels and some of the new wave of chef-proprietors. Ian McAndrew is a Mosimann graduate. David Adlard studied under Bourdin. And John Burton-Race was apprenticed to Blanc.

However, the culinary 'Big Bang' of the Seventies came with the apotheosis of that hopelessly misread label *nouvelle cuisine* — or what the *Good Food Guide* once described as the *trompe-l'oeil* school of cookery. So much has been written about the subject that I do not intend to enter any pleas for its defence or its prosecution other than to offer the opinion that, either way, *nouvelle cuisine* was a very good thing. Without it, I fear that the body politic of the British restaurant scene might still be languishing in the Dark Ages. The point, surely, is this. Before *nouvelle cuisine*, food and eating in Britain was not considered, anyway on a wide scale, to be a matter of serious public interest. Wine was quite a different story. For ever since the reign of Henry II and that king's good fortune to number Bordeaux among his possessions, we British have venerated the grape and our newspapers employed an erudite bunch of sniffers who could be counted on to promote our devotion. The cookery column, thanks to Elizabeth David, Jane Grigson, Margaret Costa and others, was also suitable subject matter for exercising keen home cooks in the privacy of their own kitchens. But then we have an honourable tradition of cookery writers — Hannah Glasse in the 18th century and Eliza Acton and Isabella Beeton in the 19th. Before Raymond Postgate, however, we had no gastronomes of the order of Grimod de La Reynière, Brillat-Savarin or Curnonsky whose influence on French tastes in the past 200 years has been enormous. In London in the 1970s, the only restaurant critics of note were Quentin Crewe and Fay Maschler.

Nouvelle cuisine put a pin in all this apathy and disinterest because it made food trendy. French masters like Michel Guérard, Roger Vergé and the Troisgros brothers started to write books and in this country they were followed by Anton Mosimann and his contemporaries. Their creations, presented visual images that were breathtakingly artistic, elevating cuisine from the functional to the sensual. It was the start of a whole new industry in food journalism and photography as publishers and picture editors fell over themselves to devote sections of their newspapers and colour supplements to this exciting new dimension in modern lifestyle.

The post-*nouvelle* age

The media's discovery that food made good copy transformed the image of the chef in British society. Cooking for a living shed its tag as a menial and sissy occupation; indeed it began to acquire the glamour and trappings of show business and, inevitably, it fired the imagination of young home-grown talent which had lain dormant until then. The great London kitchens which, in the past, had had to import their brigades from the continent, now found an able and enthusiastic pool of domestic recruits.

When *nouvelle cuisine* became a dirty word, engendered by an army of opportunistic charlatans who abused its principles and methods, the whole foodie movement had travelled beyond the point of regression. The media bandwagon was hooked – often seduced by the colourful personalities of some of the chefs as much by the brilliance of their food – and television, the most powerful medium of all, produced stars like Keith Floyd who injected a new *joie* into the craft.

Now that the *nouvelle* hype has died down, the post-*nouvelle* age is bringing in its harvest. Chefs today, and not least the British new wave, have been reassured, not gulled, by the public spotlight which has charged their self-confidence. It has encouraged them to reassess the fundamentals of good cooking as a necessary discipline to fuel their inquisitiveness and will to experiment. In essence, the artistic licence of *nouvelle cuisine* is being realigned with the basic tenets of classical practice, from which point our chefs are evolving in a variety of exciting directions. What seems to be emerging is an approach to cooking and a range of styles which can be ascribed more to the British chef than to his French opposite. The difference between the two is essentially one of pedigree. The culinary traditions of France have made her chefs thoroughbreds who, in the modern era, are for the most part either direct or, at least, spiritual disciples of Fernand Point. The cooking of the modern British chef, on the other hand, assumes the shape of a scruffy but canny mongrel which has looked itself in the mirror, re-groomed its coat and said: 'Well, I know I'm a bit of a hybrid, but I look pretty good after all.' There may be common threads running through some of the 18 chefs described in this book, but few are alike. What is striking is the wonderful diversity of their themes and ideas. Where some recipes may use the same main ingredient, its treatment will vary from chef to chef. Similarly, individual menus are not necessarily monogamous in their provenance. Old and new, regional food, English nursery favourites and ethnic derivatives are often woven together on one carte. In the kitchen, stir-frying and braising are methods which are being deployed across the same range.

Producers and patrons

However, the most significant development is the underlying thrust of the modern British menu which has been revolutionized in the past decade. Before 1980, menus tended to be dictated by an establishment's tried and tested listings on the à la carte. Frozen vegetables were commonplace. Menus today are invariably shorter, change more regularly and will often present meals at a fixed price. Above all, the chef of the Eighties and Nineties is led by the availability of fresh produce and not by his repertoire – a positively life-enhancing side-effect of *nouvelle cuisine*. The demand for good quality raw materials has grown in harmony with the rebirth of culinary talent and whereas in the past chefs would passively accept the deliveries of their indolent suppliers, the boot is now on the other foot. As a result, Britain has suddenly come alive with producers, growers and merchants who are not only providing us with goods of outstanding quality but who are also tempting us with a vast inventory of new and rediscovered varieties for our pleasure. Rocket, lolla rossa, lamb's lettuce and oak leaf are brightening up our salads. Fresh herbs are available on a scale unheard of ten years ago. Samphire, calabrese, kohlrabi and Swiss chard have entered into regular usage in the kitchen's vocabulary. And monkfish, John Dory and gurnard are appearing on menus alongside salmon and plaice. Specialists like Anne Petch at Heal Farm in Devon have become famous for putting the flavour back into pork, beef and lamb. And *affineurs* like Patrick Rance and James Aldridge have transformed the dreary face of British cheese. Where once you could count the varieties on the fingers of two hands – with difficulty – now they run into their hundreds. Britain's restaurants are better served today than they have ever been and the supply industry is better organized – not least by the assistance of a national grapevine which has been codified into its own guide books. New publications like *British Food Finds* and the *Good Food Directory* have become as valuable to chefs as their recipe books.

The story so far may appear to be one of undiluted enthusiasm. Certainly, progress has been dramatic, standards have risen and the media continue to bow before the chef's toque. Good eating in Britain is no longer an international joke. But nirvana still lurks beyond the gastronomic horizon and it is unlikely to come into view for a generation or two, or maybe even three. The issue is not one of quality because that is now present, but the numbers, anyway by European measures, are not. For Britain's kitchen revolution remains a phenomenon which is predominantly trade-led rather than consumer-driven. The problem is one of patronage and the habit of eating out in this country which trails way behind food-loving nations like France and the United States. Tom Jaine, the new editor of the *Good Food Guide*, is even more pessimistic than me. He believes the British palate 'may take hundreds of years to change'.

What has sustained and invigorated our restaurants in recent times, therefore, has been the patronage of artistic virtue rather than that definition which relies exclusively on the commercial support of the customer. The most obvious example is the influence of the guide books – notably the *Good Food Guide*, Michelin and Egon Ronay among many others. The carrot and stick psychology embodied in their systems of stars, awards and grades has been a very effective method of raising the quality of our restaurants. But although it would be naïve to suggest that the customer has not responded, if the sales of these powerful publications is contrasted with, say, France whose population is comparable with our own, their penetration in Britain stands at about one quarter of the French market.

There are, however, a number of other motivating forces which, though more benign than the guides, are making a profound mark on the status of the craft. Since 1980, the trade has been reorganizing itself into bodies which have become efficient lobbyists and vigorous self-publicists. Organizations such as the Restaurateurs Association of Great Britain, the UK chapter of the Académie Culinaire de France and the British Culinary Institute are advancing the public persona of the profession by launching campaigns, competitions and events aimed at improving trading conditions, educational standards and product quality. The Roux brothers – an industry in themselves – now run their own well-publicized scholarship scheme for young chefs. But initiatives taken by well-known people like the Roux have also reached outside the parish of the trade. What is encouraging is that other distinguished, high-profile personalities in British society have entered the field as powerful patrons of the culinary arts and, more importantly, the mere fact of their presence has had a salutary effect on customer interest. Witness the aura shed by Sir Terence Conran and Paul Hamlyn upon Bibendum, Michael Caine over Langan's Brasserie and Sir David Napley at L'Ortolan in Shinfield. Lord Lichfield, with his restaurants, is another patrician example.

Of grub and guilt

While patronage of this order is undoubtedly helpful, its influence across the wider brush of our culinary landscape remains isolated and superficial. It does not flow through the veins of our culture as it does in France. When President Giscard d'Estaing presented Paul Bocuse with the Légion d'Honneur in 1975 and threw a lunch at the Elysée cooked by the country's greatest chefs, the whole world sat up in awe. Given the dietary preferences and gastronomic disinterest of our own Royal family and Prime Minister, it is impossible to imagine the Queen allowing a similar bash to take place at Buckingham Palace, never mind the idea of bestowing a knighthood or the Order of Merit on one of our chefs. In fields like the arts, theatre and fashion, royal approval has helped to establish Britain as a world leader. British gastronomy, it seems, still has to wait its turn.

That wait, as I have already suggested, may be protracted. As long ago as 1971, Christopher Driver's preface to that year's edition of the *Good Food Guide* noted that the art and craft of cooking 'is still the most despised ingredient of our national culture'. His observation would merit some qualification today, but in essence his sentiments remain pretty well true – particularly in the provinces. More recently, Jonathan Meades, *The Times* restaurant critic, remarked in his column that 'provincial cities are the graveyards of ambitious restaurants'. I should know, because I run one and the only reason we have held off the grave-digger is because our bedrooms enable us to import our customers from beyond Taunton's frontiers. Indeed, of the 13 country chefs listed in these pages, only four are displaying the courage to manage their places without the financial palliative of crisp bed linen after dinner.

In moments of despair, I often ask myself why the British are so odd about their food. Why the inherent guilt, meanness and hypocrisy? Why do we prefer to mess about in our boats on the Solent or chase foxes across the countryside where drink, not food, is an essential ingredient of social convention? Why do we revel in that perfidious word 'grub' as a term of endearment for good food? Eating for pleasure still carries notions of naughtiness which is to be resisted. It is an attitude which I encounter regularly and it manifests itself in all kinds of ways. With my injunction to satisfied guests to return next year, popular calls include: 'It's been such a *sinful* weekend, it wouldn't do to return too soon.'

Long live the prawn cocktail

Dissatisfied guests complain, but too often it is a cover for ignorance and social insecurity or a device for expressing self-disgust. I still hear people say that going to a restaurant is like eating pound notes. Attitudes to children are as repugnant, mean and hostile among some British hoteliers as they are among their customers. Where one will bar the admission of children below a certain age, the other's refrain is: 'I wouldn't waste good food on my kids.' What hope is there for the future, if we actively conspire to deprive our young of one of life's most noble joys? And then there is our apparent, and hugely publicized, obsession with health, diet and vegetarianism. The good old British 'blow-out', however, gets no publicity but all the customers. The nation's favourite restaurant meal remains prawn cocktail, steak and Black Forest gâteau. At this level, gastronomy becomes as confused a definition as the difference between a chocolate bar and the Milky Way in the night sky. For the palate takes on the role of gateway to a heaped plate. Satisfaction is a loaded belly. And value-for-money is measured by the degree of your indigestion.

Politics and an impoverished diet

In this age of plenty, the British have yet to resolve their historical hang-up of needing food merely to fuel the body over the virtue of food as a sensory pleasure which deserves to be appreciated with as much respect as music on the ear or art on the eye. Interestingly, many of my chosen chefs have music or art deeply ingrained in their backgrounds. But out there in the trenches, the philosophical war between the 'eat-to-live' and 'live-to-eat' camps is being waged as furiously as ever. However, unlike food, wine appreciation is accepted as a serious pursuit – a pleasure touching the intellect and worthy of debate among the educated middle classes. It has even acquired a 'tasting' language of its own – but no such vocabulary exists to the same degree in food criticism because, relatively, this is a newer phenomenon. Of course, again like anything artistic or musical, food as a sensory and emotional human interest does not have to demand intellectual attention. Its place in our community is as important as a civilized background to social or business contact as architecture is on the street or taped music in the home.

Why, then, the hang-up? I am not persuaded by the argument which often invokes our puritan heritage because our eating and drinking habits have, in history, been governed more by prevailing political and economic factors than by the acceptance of any puritan morality. As it is, the puritans were beer drinkers who despised wine as papist poison and in the 18th century and Regency times, Britain was on a gastronomic high. No, it is rather the sacrifices of fighting wars and defending an empire which seem to have instilled into us the notion of food as fodder. We are a cold island nation stuck in the North Atlantic and our will to survive any predatory incursion has encouraged a siege mentality. While food had to sustain the body, alcohol at least fuelled the spirit. Our climate and geography have not helped us to nurture that greater sense of balance enjoyed in the warmer countries of southern Europe, where good food and good wine taken together are more naturally part of the rhythm of life.

It is hardly surprising, therefore, that since the last war government food policy has been coloured by national instinct. Food had to be cheap and it had to be plentiful. The result of these policies has been to make the British diet the most impoverished in Europe but, mercifully, the fallibility of modern agricultural methods and food science is now being exposed and food has suddenly become a 'green' issue.

The gradual recognition of the importance of honest, natural food offers British gastronomy hope for the future although, at present, a pathetically negative atmosphere hangs limply over the country casting the impression that there are few foods which are not stamped with a government health warning. Producers and politicians, hell-bent on promoting cost efficiency at the expense of quality, have a lot to answer for in the wake of the effects of land sprayed with pesticides and nitrogenous fertilizers and intensively reared animals which have had their bodies pumped with antibiotics and anti-stress drugs. Proud chefs are not economists or scientists; they are instinctive creatures with a natural feeling for food which has led them to seek out well-husbanded produce and animals and poultry which have been raised happily and healthily. For the chef, common sense dictates that to do otherwise is to court an inferior product just as a craftsman or artist would refuse to work with lousy materials. Almost 20 years ago, Jane Grigson's call in her introduction to *Good Things* was prophetic: 'The encouragement of fine food is not greed or gourmandise,' she wrote. 'It can be seen as an aspect of the anti-pollution movement in that it indicates concern for the quality of environment.' While the Prince of Wales may fall short of being labelled a foodie patron, his moves to turn his own farmland over to organic agriculture could just make him the British chef's best friend.

A nation that has become accustomed to cheap and degraded food from the supermarket or fast food counter is also a nation that has had its palate deprived of the real thing. Tastes have become forgotten or debased or homogenized. Convenience suppers – cook-chilled, canned, dried or frozen – with EastEnders on TV have devalued the sanctity of the family's evening meal. 'We're back to the primitive idea of eating to keep alive,' to quote Jane Grigson again.

Yet how primitive are we today? What of the supermarket? After all, it is the emporium of the nation's larder and, as such, must be a serious barometer of the national palate. It is a fair measure for there is nothing altruistic about these places. They have shareholders to satisfy and not the pedantic demands of a gastronomic minority. Every square foot of the shop floor must pay its way. Like restaurants, supermarkets are a mixed bag but the evidence would suggest that over the last ten years they also have come a long way. The cheap stuff is still well represented but at least there are now clear signs of a growing will to revive interest in the old-fashioned tastes of wholesome foods. Affluence is inciting a little experiment. Water and polyphosphate-pumped frozen chickens share space with fresh maize-fed birds, fresh fish and meat is being better handled, a wider variety of fresh fruit and vegetables is being displayed and companies like Sainsbury's are actively promoting new tastes and even indulging in gentle campaigns of re-education. The British consumer is discovering a taste for mango and the Pink Fir Apple potato and labels are being more explicit. Alongside those perfectly sculpted but utterly tasteless little tomatoes, wrinkled monsters from Provence are flagged with the message, 'Selected for flavour rather than appearance.'

The new dawn of British gastronomy

Although we are beginning to learn that food produced in its most natural state is not only more healthy, but tastes better, it does not lead to an automatic connection between the progress of the domestic larder and the advance of an eating-out culture in Britain. Historical hang-ups aside, a major part of the problem is price because good eating out in this country is still beyond the reach of most people. It is a situation which is both tragic and unnecessary. Outside the home, cheap eating means mostly fast food, and most fast foods are unnourishing, technologically reprocessed junk yards which have devastated the palates of a predominantly young and impressionable mass market. Tastes acquired in youth affect our attitudes to food, if not for life, for a very long time unless we are fortunate enough to be weaned off a bad habit or preconception. I hated school food – dishes such as steak and kidney pie and bread and butter pudding revolted me. It took me 15 years to learn just how good these dishes were when they were cooked properly. How much more difficult is it, therefore, if a young person *likes* junk food, to be persuaded to pay the same or a little more for the pleasure of honest-to-goodness fresh food?

The battleground must be the pub which, for the British, has all the social allure of the bistro or café in France. At present, that great British institution makes some effort to serve a decent pint of real ale but its own brand of microwave gastronomy holds as much appeal as the high street hot dog. Yet the pub is where the revolution can be won or lost. What is needed is more chefs of the order of Richard Smith and Franco Taruschio to take up popular feeding with the same passion and enthusiasm as their confrères in the glitzier places.

The difficulty is the story of the chicken and egg. Eating out in Britain has not penetrated our social fabric to the same degree as the continent and, in the trade, we still do not have an established artisan culture. In France, Italy and Spain, there is a great tradition of restaurant-keeping where kitchens have been held in one family for generations. In Britain, no such tradition exists – fathers want their sons 'to do better'. Meanwhile, until we see a wider and more sophisticated restaurant habit, what are the chances of a British tradition taking root?

I do not believe that I would have had the energy to write this book if I did not think there was very real hope for the long-term prosperity of British gastronomy. The heat being generated by a whole body of dedicated individuals and organizations – as I have already described – is now so intense that it would not be too romantic or fanciful to conclude that a new dawn is in sight – even if it does take another generation or two for the sun to reach its zenith.

War, plague and pestilence excepted, the mediocre will fall out in larger numbers. Greater affluence and competition will stimulate demand and higher standards. Pubs are slowly improving and the middle ground will be filled. Indeed, several of our top chefs are already beginning to open cheaper eateries as support vessels to their flagships. I see this as a vital development for the future. Christopher Driver, writing about the cultural value of gastronomy in his book *The British at Table 1940–1980* again draws upon artistic analogy when he says that 'high art depends on the quality of what is held in common.' Now, education, that much neglected catalyst of cultural progress, is being grabbed by the scruff of the neck by formidable forces like the Académie Culinaire de France in Britain and a rising swell of young chefs is leaving our master kitchens better trained. Their talent is every bit as impressive as anything in Europe – the only difference being that, as yet, the domestic engine is not big enough to generate them in equivalent numbers. It must come. In the meantime, how good it would be if we could find our own idiom for that cordial imperative 'Bon appétit!'

Kit Chapman 1989

FRANCIS COULSON

At the top of Hallin Fell the air is like a perfectly chilled glass of crisp Sancerre. But it is the view that is intoxicating. To the south, Beda Head divides the marbled landscape into two giant wok-like valleys – with a magnificant patina of greens, greys, burnt orange and creamy yellow – and on the lower slopes, the hill farmers have stitched their enclosures with miles of rugged dry-stone walling. Far below, to the west, the north and the east, Ullswater snakes lazily from Patterdale to Pooley Bridge. In the early morning, fast ribbon swirls graze the smooth silver surface of the lake and in the middle distance Sharrow Bay is a pearl-pale brush stroke sharply mirrored in the water and set against the dark green of the shoreline woodland.

One sunny April morning in 1948, Francis Coulson sat on a boulder by the water's edge and stared at the perfect reflection of the house in the lake. He was clutching a two-inch square estate agent's notice cut out of the *Manchester Guardian* but he had arrived an hour early for his appointment. 'The beauty of the place enthused me beyond measure and I knew that I had to share this wonder with the world,' he recalls. Two months later, Francis returned with his father who also fell in love with Sharrow Bay and agreed to pay the first year's rental. In October the same year, Francis moved in. He arrived at about 6.30 in the evening carrying with him his pans, a kettle, a pair of gumboots, a torch, a few candles and some groceries. The taxi driver dropped him at the lodge and asked the young stranger what he was going to do at the 'mansion'.

'Turn it into an hotel,' said Coulson. The man roared with laughter. 'Best of luck, m'boy,' he said and sped off.

As Francis walked down the long drive towards the house, the moon was beginning to rise and he felt the chill of the lake wind on his face. He turned the key in the lock and the iron-studded oak door heaved open with a slow, eerie creak: 'Then I smelt the air of Sharrow and it gave me the most glorious feeling.' That night, after he had cooked his first meal, he laid a mattress by the open range in the kitchen and slept like a top.

Forty years on the emotion of those first hours remains as stirring in the memory and he still tells the story with a wistful shine of tears in his eyes. Sharrow Bay is a love story at the heart of which lies the unselfish inspiration of two men – Francis and his partner Brian Sack – who have devoted their lives to the happiness of other human beings in a manner which makes the phrase good hospitality inadequate as a suitable definition. Their motto is 'to cosset, to nourish and to nurture'. But their beneficence and charm – saintly in Francis, avuncular in Brian – run deeper. They are blessed with the genuine gift of raising the spirit and soothing the soul. Here are two people who have touched the hearts of thousands.

From his earliest years, Francis Coulson learned the importance of giving and sharing in life. The son of a Quaker and youngest of five children, he was born in Bedford where his father owned a drapery business. At home his mother cooked and administered a household which played host to a permanently extended family. In the 1930s their comfortable home welcomed groups of Jewish refugees who had fled persecution in Nazi Germany and on Sundays Mrs Coulson always cooked an aitchbone of beef, fresh vegetables and a pudding which the children distributed on their bicycles to the less fortunate in the neighbourhood before the family sat down for their own lunch.

Francis adored his mother and he soon began to share her love of good food by working alongside her in the kitchen. Her great forte – as is Francis's at Sharrow – was pastry work. 'I feel happy today, so my pastry's going to be light,' she would say, and her son still insists that you need a light heart to bake a light cake. His sister Bessie also inherited mother's gifts and during the school holidays Francis added

to his seminal preparations for an as yet unknown future by submitting to Bessie's strict tutelage at the Loom and Teapot, her small hotel in Wonersh near Guildford. 'I made my first omelettes there but she threw them out until I got them right.'

Francis was educated at Bedford Modern School, an institution governed by the ethos of gamesmanship and the cane. He hated it. The oppression and intimidation of the place affected his gentle and artistic disposition which only found escape in his talent as a musician. Towards the end of his schooling, he came under the influence and teaching of Marshal Palmer, the Duchess of Bedford's organist at Woburn Abbey, who inspired his longing to enter King's College Cambridge as a music scholar. But war intervened.

Like his father, Francis was a pacifist although later his beliefs were to change. He registered as a conscientious objector and was assigned to forestry duties in Gloucestershire – work for which he was completely unfitted. So he returned home and joined TOC-H, an Anglican foundation which was setting up a network of canteens-

cum-billets for the forces in a number of towns across the country. With an army of 180 volunteers, Francis suddenly found himself in charge of the Bedford unit – a makeshift hotel accommodating up to 80 people and turning over 300 meals a day. He was in his element – caring for people, cosseting them and cooking aitchbones of beef with all the trimmings for Sunday lunch. The Church of England also required him to conduct evening prayers, a task which he undertook enthusiastically because it kept him in Communion wine.

As the war drew to its end Coulson was transferred, with the less pleasant brief of ministering to enemy prisoners. His pacifism evaporated when finally he witnessed the horror of Nazi brutishness in a POW camp in Northamptonshire. The sight of a pet dog being tortured and mutilated with hot cinders and the sheer strain of the last few years took its toll. He was discharged and sent home.

As he lay recovering in the peace of his own bed, his mind began to sketch the picture that he sought for his future. He yearned to bring beauty, love and caring into people's lives. Sharrow Bay was to

become the outward expression of his innermost feelings about life and when he spotted the advertisement in the *Manchester Guardian*, his convalescence came to a swift end.

Sharrow opened its big oak door to the world in time for Easter 1949 and Francis, joined by a team of five helpers, set about fulfilling his dream. Post-war austerity imposed a do-it-yourself regime and provoked a spirit of improvisation. Curtains and loose covers were made on Bessie's old sewing machine and branches cut from the woods made do as substitutes for vases of fresh flowers. At night Francis read himself to sleep: 'I went to bed with my goddesses – Constance Spry and, soon after, Elizabeth David.' But before long he made friends with a French Cordon Bleu cook called Renée Atkinson who, with her husband, owned the Kirkstone Pass Inn. Mrs Atkinson, whose reputation with pastry had earned her a commission with Fortnum and Mason, came to Sharrow for a while and taught Francis her secrets and her recipes.

The benefit of that early teaching is particularly apparent at Sharrow today where breakfast croissants and brioches and afternoon tea cakes, scones, shortbreads and sponges make temptation irresistible. The same uninhibited generosity and brilliant sleight of hand appear at dinner time in the form of a rich montage of exquisite

desserts displayed at the entrance to the dining room – a pastry-art gallery eclipsing any notion of the ubiquitous sweet trolley. Indeed, Sharrow's puddings are as famous and as decorous as some of their admiring consumers. There was one notorious occasion when Francis honoured Joan Sutherland as Escoffier had once complimented Melba. On the opening night of Bellini's *Norma* at Covent Garden, Brian and Francis travelled to London and presented the prima donna with an apricot and brandy bavarois in her dressing room. She was so charmed by the gesture that she ate the eponymously christened confection instantly and with a relish which paid no favour to her substantial constitution. As she launched herself into the opera, she was struck by an acute attack of wind – much to the discomfort of the tenor. Ever since the dessert has been affectionately presented on the menu as La Stupenda Bavarois.

However, the repertoire's most celebrated dessert remains Francis's sticky toffee sponge. If I were a condemned man, this would be my final wish. Deceptively light and airy, it is the ultimate English nursery pudding accompanied best by a spoon of vanilla ice and dash of cream. A sublime state upon which to approach the gallows.

English tradition then is the foundation of Sharrow's kitchen and Francis Coulson is the defender of the faith: 'To a point, I think we are going sadly astray. While I admire the work of the great modern chefs, I still believe that we need to rediscover the wonderful recipes of our ancestors so that we can pass them on to future generations.'

He deplores the demise of the word 'gravy' from our culinary vocabulary and he is suspicious of gimmicky sauces which do little to reflect the true flavours of the main ingredient: 'What is the point of serving roast grouse if the gravy does not correspond with the natural goodness of the bird?' He is equally sceptical about modern fads like *al dente* vegetables and pink meat which again do not necessarily do justice to the raw materials: 'Vegetables are difficult to cook well – to catch the flavours and textures at just the right moment. Similarly, the degree of cooking in a piece of lamb depends on the cut, the age of the beast and how long it has been hung.'

Although he is a traditionalist at heart, Coulson has not ignored the developments of the past 20 years. He has been quick to exploit the rising availability of exciting new ingredients and his style can often be strikingly modern – even with old favourites like cabinet pudding, which comes with a raspberry sauce beautifully feathered into the egg custard surround. However, irrespective of styles ancient or modern, in the end cooking for Francis is like playing his piano at home: 'It is a gentle art which comes as much from the heart as it does from the hands. You are giving of yourself.'

Nowadays the main burden in the kitchen falls to Sharrow's head chef Juan Martin, although Francis still cooks breakfast every morning and continues to keep a benign eye on both detail and culinary principle. This he achieves without any loss of freedom of expression in a youthful team which he encourages with the same loving care he and Brian lavish on their guests.

If Francis was Sharrow Bay's creator, Brian Sack, who joined him in 1952, has been its mainstay. Francis's virtues as a human being – his infinite generosity, his modesty and his great love of people – have also been his shortcomings as a businessman. He never counts the cost of his hospitality and he still hates giving guests their bills: 'I can't help wondering whether we are worthy of the money,' he says. While both men share the same beliefs and outlook, it is Brian who ensures that Sharrow has the wherewithal to continue its mission of human nourishment.

With George Perry-Smith, Francis Coulson and Brian Sack were the first pioneers of Britain's culinary renaissance and Sharrow Bay was the model for the British 'country house hotel' movement.

Indeed, it was Brian Sack who originally coined the expression. They have been showered with honours and Sharrow is the only hotel and restaurant ever to receive both Egon Ronay's Gold Plates – 'Hotel of the Year' in 1974 and 'Restaurant of the Year' in 1980. Characteristically, Francis has never believed that he deserved any award and whenever Sharrow is honoured he pins a sharp memo on the staff noticeboard saying: 'Just because we have won an award, do not think that we are supreme. We are not.'

Certainly, these two remarkable people did not create Sharrow with a burning ambition to achieve a particular goal. Their simple concern has been to bring joy to their guests, not to build glorious self-monuments. Success for them has been a by-product achieved through an unfashionable capacity for humility, love and hard work. And it has made Sharrow Bay into a living legend.

AVOCADO MOUSSE WITH DRESSED PRAWNS

2 ripe avocado pears, skinned and stoned
6 tbls water
150 ml (¼ pt) mayonnaise
300 ml (½ pt) double cream
1 tbls lemon juice
1 tbls onion juice (from finely grated onion)
10–15 g (¼–½ oz) gelatine
salt and pepper
sugar to taste
dash of Worcestershire sauce

For the garnish
225 g (8 oz) whole peeled prawns
cucumber slices
avocado slices
tomato slices
sprigs of fresh parsley
French dressing

Liquidize the avocado pears with 3 tablespoons of water. Place in a bowl and add the mayonnaise, cream, lemon juice and onion juice. Dissolve the gelatine in the remaining water over gentle heat.

Season the avocado mixture to taste with the salt, pepper, sugar and Worcestershire sauce, then add the gelatine. Put the mixture into six small china ramekins and cover with cling film. Place in the refrigerator to set.

Turn out on to a serving plate and garnish with prawns, cucumber, avocado and tomato slices and a sprig of fresh parsley. Pour a little French dressing around and serve immediately.
Serves 6

Right: *Avocado mousse with dressed prawns*
Far right: *Chicken livers with fresh marjoram*

CHICKEN LIVERS WITH FRESH MARJORAM

450 g (1 lb) chicken livers
a little vegetable oil
salt and pepper

For the sauce
½ onion, chopped
3 rashers bacon, chopped
6–8 button mushrooms, thinly sliced
¼ clove garlic, crushed
25 g (1 oz) unsalted butter
25 g (1 oz) plain flour
600 ml (1 pt) single cream
2 tbls chopped fresh marjoram
1 tbls chicken jelly (reduced chicken stock
or a little chicken bouillon)
salt and pepper

For the garnish
12 cherry tomatoes
6 sprigs fresh parsley
6 crescent-shaped puff pastry fleurons

To make the sauce, heat a frying pan and cook the onion, bacon, mushrooms and garlic in the butter for about 3–4 minutes. Add the flour and cook for 2–3 minutes. Add the cream, 1 tablespoon marjoram and the chicken jelly. Cook gently over a low heat for about 5–10 minutes or until a coating consistency is reached. Strain thorough a very fine sieve and set aside the bacon and mushrooms. Add the remaining marjoram to the liquid and season to taste with salt and pepper. Keep warm.

Remove any sinew and green or yellow parts from the chicken livers. Cut each liver into two or three pieces. Preheat a heavy-based frying pan over high heat and add enough vegetable oil just to cover the bottom of the pan. Add the livers to the pan and season, then toss for about 2–3 minutes over a high heat.

Remove any excess fat from the livers and add the reserved bacon and mushrooms. Toss over a gentle heat for about 1 minute. Cover with sauce and serve garnished with cherry tomatoes, parsley and a crescent-shaped pastry fleuron.

Serves 6

FRESH PRAWNS COOKED IN WHITE WINE AND CREAM WITH TARRAGON AND VEGETABLES

½ small onion, finely sliced
1 small carrot, finely sliced
1 stick celery, finely sliced
½ small leek, finely sliced
50 g (2 oz) unsalted butter
1 bay leaf
1 bouquet garni
2 tbls tarragon vinegar
150 ml (¼ pt) dry white wine
450 ml (¾ pt) double cream
salt and pepper
1 tsp chopped fresh dill
1 tsp chopped fresh tarragon
1 tsp chopped fresh chervil
dash of lemon juice
30 large uncooked whole prawns
600 ml (1 pt) court bouillon

Cover the vegetables with water, add 15 g (½ oz) butter, and the herbs. Bring to the boil and simmer until the vegetables are just tender. Drain and reserve the cooking liquid.

Pour the vinegar into a pan with the wine and reduce by two-thirds. Add the stock from the vegetables and reduce by three-quarters, add the double cream. Reduce until it reaches a coating consistency.

Pour over the vegetables and season. Add the chopped herbs and lemon juice. If you require a stronger sauce, add more vinegar.

Remove the heads from the prawns. Simmer the prawns gently in the court bouillon for 2–3 minutes. Refresh in cold water and remove the shells.

Gently reheat the prawns in the remaining butter for 2–3 minutes. Add the sauce to the prawns. Simmer gently until the butter is infused and serve immediately.

Serves 6

FILLETS OF LEMON SOLE IN PUFF PASTRY

175 g (6 oz) fresh spinach leaves
salt and pepper
2 young carrots
2 courgettes
2 dessert apples
6 lemon sole fillets
75 g (3 oz) unsalted butter
4 tbls dry white wine
6 cooked puff pastry rounds or squares
about 7.5 cm (3 inches) in diameter and
2.5 cm (1 inch) deep
sprigs of dill, chopped

For the sauce
3 shallots, chopped
100 g (4 oz) unsalted butter
20 cardamon pods, bruised
20 coriander seeds, crushed
a pinch of ground ginger
1 bay leaf
150 ml (¼ pt) fish stock
150 ml (¼ pt) dry white wine
300 ml (½ pt) double cream
salt and pepper
½ tsp lemon juice

Preheat the oven to 180°C/350°F/Gas
Mark 4.

Plunge the spinach leaves into boiling salted water for about 2 minutes then drain and place straight away into iced water until cool. Leave to drain.

Using a small Parisienne cutter, shape the carrots, courgettes and apples into balls. Cook in boiling salted water until *al dente* and refresh in cold water. Drain.

Remove any bones from the lemon sole fillets and poach in the oven in 50 g (2 oz) butter and the white wine with seasoning for 5–7 minutes, until just firm to the touch.

To make the sauce, sweat the shallots in 50 g (2 oz) butter and add the spices and bay leaf. Add the fish stock and white wine and reduce by two-thirds. Add the double cream and reduce by half. Strain through a fine sieve and whisk in the remaining butter. Season with salt, pepper and lemon juice.

Cut the puff pastry rounds or squares in half horizontally.

Warm the spinach in 15 g (½ oz) butter. Season and place on the base of each pastry casing. Place a folded sole fillet on top of the spinach with a little of the sauce over and around the fish and around the pastry casing.

Place the pastry lid on top and garnish with the Parisienne of vegetables which have been warmed in 15 g (½ oz) butter, seasoning and chopped fresh dill.
Serves 6

WHITE AND DARK CHOCOLATE MOUSSE

For the white chocolate mousse
175 g (6 oz) white chocolate
4 tbls milk
2 egg yolks
50 g (2 oz) caster sugar
15 g (½ oz) gelatine
8 tbls water
150 ml (¼ pt) natural yoghurt
150 ml (¼ pt) double cream

For the dark chocolate mousse
175 g (6 oz) dark bitter chocolate
4 tbls milk
2 egg yolks
75 g (3 oz) caster sugar
10 g (¼ oz) gelatine
3 tbls water
175 ml (6 fl oz) double cream
150 ml (¼ pt) soured cream

For the crème anglais
300 ml (½ pt) single cream
few drops of vanilla essence
1 tsp strong black coffee
3 egg yolks
25 g (1 oz) caster sugar

To make the white chocolate mousse, melt the chocolate and milk slowly in a pan. Whisk the egg yolks and sugar until pale, then add to the chocolate mixture. Dissolve the gelatine in the water over gentle heat and add to the mixture. Place the mixture over a bowl of ice until beginning to set. Whisk the yoghurt and cream together, add to the mixture and whisk until smooth.

To make the dark chocolate mousse, melt the chocolate with the milk. Whisk the egg yolks and sugar together until pale and thick. Add the chocolate. Dissolve the gelatine in the water over gentle heat and add to the mixture. Whisk the creams together until 'floppy' and fold into the chocolate mixture.

Leave to set over a bowl of ice and then pipe the base and sides of 6 dariole moulds with the dark chocolate mousse and fill the centre with the white chocolate mousse. Leave to set.

To make the crème anglaise, gently heat

the cream in a double saucepan with the vanilla essence and coffee and leave to infuse for 10 minutes. Whisk the egg yolks with the sugar until pale and creamy. Gradually add the warm cream and cook over a low heat until the mixture begins to thicken (do not boil or the mixture will curdle). Cool.

Serve each mousse turned out with coffee-flavoured crème anglaise poured around.
Serves 6

STICKY TOFFEE SPONGE

50 g (2 oz) unsalted butter
175 g (6 oz) caster sugar
2 eggs
175 g (6 oz) dates, chopped
300 ml (½ pt) water
1 tsp bicarbonate of soda
175 g (6 oz) self-raising flour
1 tsp vanilla essence

For the sauce
300 ml (½ pt) double cream
50 g (2 oz) demerara sugar
1 dessertspn black treacle

Preheat the oven to 180°C/350°F/Gas Mark 4.

Cream the butter and sugar until light and fluffy, add the eggs and beat well. Boil the dates in the water until soft and add the bicarbonate of soda. Mix the flour, dates and vanilla essence into the butter mixture and pour into a greased baking tin about 20 × 13 cm (8 × 5 inches). Cook in the oven for approximately 30–40 minutes until just firm to the touch.

To make the sauce, boil all the ingredients together. Pour over the top of the sponge until it is covered (there will be some left over), and place under a hot grill until it begins to bubble. Remove, cut into squares and serve with the remaining sauce.
Serves 6

Above left: *Fillets of lemon sole in puff pasi*
Right: *White and dark chocolate mousse*

NOUGATINE WAFERS WITH APPLE SORBET AND VANILLA SAUCE

For the nougatine wafers
50 g (2 oz) caster sugar
50 g (2 oz) flaked almonds
50 g (2 oz) liquid glucose
150 ml (¼ pt) double cream
pinch of ground cinnamon
finely sliced apples, to decorate

For the apple sorbet
275 ml (9 fl oz) unsweetened apple purée
150 ml (¼ pt) sugar syrup
juice of 1 lemon
40 ml (1½ fl oz) dry cider

For the vanilla sauce
2 egg yolks
25 g (1 oz) caster sugar
150 ml (¼ pt) milk
a few drops of vanilla essence, to taste

To make the nougatine wafers, preheat the oven to 180°C/350°F/Gas Mark 4.

Melt the sugar in a saucepan until golden brown. Add the flaked almonds and spread on an oiled tray to cool. Grind when cool and mix with the liquid glucose to form a paste.

Place 18 teaspoons of the mixture on to bakewell (non-stick) paper, allowing room between the mixture as it tends to spread. Bake in the oven for approximately 5 minutes. Allow to cool then cut into rounds.

To make the sorbet, mix all the ingredients together and process in an ice cream churn, or freeze in a rigid container and then work in a food processor until smooth. Freeze until required.

To make the vanilla sauce, beat the egg yolks and sugar until pale. Boil the milk and pour over the egg mixture. Strain into a saucepan and cook over a low heat until the custard thickens (do not boil or the mixture will curdle). Flavour with vanilla essence.

To assemble, whip the cream and cinnamon. Arrange 3 wafers on each plate sandwiched together with a little of the cinnamon cream. Spoon a little vanilla sauce to the side. Place 2 scoops of the sorbet on each plate and decorate with apple slices.
Serves 6

Above: *Nougatine wafers with apple sorbet and vanilla sauce*
Far right: *Strawberry mousse in wafer thin baskets*

CABINET PUDDING

150 g (5 oz) Madeira sponge cake
40 g (1½ oz) glacé cherries, chopped
40 g (1½ oz) sultanas
300 ml (½ pt) milk
300 ml (½ pt) single cream
1 vanilla pod or few drops vanilla essence
3 eggs
50 g (2 oz) caster sugar

For the raspberry sauce
175 (6 oz) fresh or frozen raspberries
1–2 tbls icing sugar

Preheat the oven to 180°C/350°F/Gas Mark 4.

Dice the sponge cake into 5 mm (¼ inch) cubes and carefully mix with the cherries and sultanas.

Half fill 6 buttered dariole moulds with the fruit and sponge mixture.

In a saucepan gently heat the milk and cream with the vanilla pod, set aside and leave to infuse for 10 minutes. Whisk the eggs with the sugar until pale and creamy. Stir in the warmed milk mixture, then strain and pour into the moulds to fill them. Place the moulds in a baking tin half-filled with hot water and cook in the oven for approximately 30–40 minutes until the puddings are just firm to the touch.

To make the raspberry sauce, liquidize the raspberries and pass through a fine sieve. Add the icing sugar, place in a saucepan and warm gently. Unmould the puddings and serve with the raspberry sauce. Any egg custard sauce remaining may be thickened over gentle heat and served as an additional sauce.
Serves 6

STRAWBERRY MOUSSE IN WAFER THIN BASKETS

For the strawberry mousse
3 eggs
2 egg yolks
175 g (6 oz) caster sugar
just under 15 g (½ oz) gelatine
juice of ½ lemon made up to 65 ml
(2½ fl oz) with water
225 ml (7½ fl oz) strawberry purée
300 ml (½ pt) double cream, whipped
18 fresh strawberries

For the baskets
1½ egg whites
75 g (3 oz) icing sugar
65 g (2½ oz) unsalted butter, melted
60 g (2¼ oz) plain flour, sifted

For the strawberry sauce
175 g (6 oz) fresh strawberries
1–2 tbls icing sugar

To make the strawberry mousse, whisk the eggs, egg yolks and sugar until pale and thick. Dissolve the gelatine in the lemon juice and water over gentle heat and add to the eggs and sugar, together with the strawberry purée. Fold in the whipped cream. Place in a bowl and chill until set.

To make the baskets, preheat the oven to 190°C/375°F/Gas Mark 5. Whisk the egg whites with the sugar until stiff. Mix all the ingredients together to form a smooth paste.

Make a circular stencil from cardboard or plastic 3 mm (⅛ inch) thick and 13 cm (5 inches) in diameter.

Spread the mixture on to bakewell (non-stick) paper, using the stencil. Bake in the oven for 4–5 minutes, until golden brown, but keeping a constant watch as it can catch. Remove from the oven and press each round into a small bowl, to shape. Cool.

To make the strawberry sauce, liquidize the strawberries and pass through a fine sieve. Add the icing sugar.

Remove each basket from its mould and pipe in the strawberry mousse. Decorate with fresh strawberries and serve accompanied with the strawberry sauce.
Serves 6–8

JOHN TOVEY

'Theatre means joy and sorrow, laughter and tears, comedy and drama. Cooking, too, contains all these elements.' These words, used by John Tovey to introduce his first book *Entertaining with Tovey*, apply equally to the life of the man himself although his show at Miller Howe is played to a script designed solely to bring joy and wonder to the evening audiences who have filled his tables since July 1971. For Miller Howe is pure theatre – an exuberant mix of high camp and Hollywood assisted by the natural backcloth of Lake Windermere with the silent majesty of the Langdale Pikes rising like ocean waves above its western shore.

Within, and facing this heart-stopping panorama through arched plate-glass, the auditorium is two-tiered to provide both stalls and a dress circle. Behind, a large internal window tinted in surgical blue gives diners a secret glimpse into the mystery of chefs at work – darting and gliding noiselessly about their kitchen like fishes in an aquarium. Beyond, an adjoining dining room is set amidst whimsical, romantic murals, painted by a Florentine artist, depicting water scenes, snow-capped mountains, hillocks crowned by medieval castles, Roman temples, orange trees and exotic birds. Clouds drift across a ceiling from which hang five enormous baskets of dried flowers and in the centre a chubby-cheeked, tulip-lipped Cupid, with rainbow-coloured wings, clutching a spoon in one hand, and a knife and fork in the other, gazes ethereally down upon the tables.

At 8.30 every evening guests take their seats, the house lights are dimmed, wine is poured and the show begins – a set feast of five courses ending with a choice of six delicious puddings. Miller Howe may be theatrical but Tovey's hospitality and cooking is as genuine, fresh and uplifting as the breezes bouncing off his beloved lakeland landscapes.

John Tovey was born in Barrow-in-Furness in 1933, and the first sixteen years of his life were a mixture of great happiness and shocking misery. Abused by his mother and beaten by his father, he was fortunate that for much of his childhood, during the years his father served in the Indian army, he was under the care of his maternal grandmother. John adored his 'Nan'. She gave him his love of good food and several of his books bear touching references to her influence. Indeed, 'My Nan's Tipsy Trifle' is arguably Miller Howe's most famous dessert. On Sundays, lunch always came with six or seven vegetables. That was Nan's way and still, each evening at Miller Howe, John keeps faith with that tradition every time the main course is served.

In 1970 Nan was put in a home and she died two years later, soon after John had opened Miller Howe. For six days before her death he visited her late at night, leaving the hotel at the end of the service with a small quantity of the evening's food which he had liquidized with a little cream. She was oblivious of her grandson, aware only that she was being loved as he sat by her bedside, cuddled her and fed her.

And so it was to his Nan that John turned in 1949 when, as a troubled and mixed-up teenager, the only thought in his head was an urgent desire to leave home. She encouraged him to apply for a job at the Colonial Office and, having forged his father's signature on a passport form, he went to work in Rhodesia. Young Tovey proved to be a very able civil servant and by the time he was 21 he had been posted to Nyasaland as private secretary to the commissioner for native labour on the princely salary of £1,200 with a car, a government house and four servants all thrown in. However, in 1959, struck down by an evil cocktail of tropical diseases, he was air-lifted to Blighty where he spent eight weeks languishing in hospital.

With riots now heralding the end of Empire, Tovey did not return

to Africa. Instead, it was home to Barrow-in-Furness, Nan and an enthralling but commercially disastrous love affair with an old Victorian theatre which cost him his colonial savings. So in 1960 he persuaded the manager of the Old England Hotel in Bowness-on-Windermere that he needed a secretary.

Within a week Tovey was running the reception office and, 18 months and several promotions later, he became assistant manager before skipping up the road to the Hydro, which he took over as manager in 1963.

The hotel was a monster-pile of Victoriana, churning out meals like toothpaste on a production line and filling beds with coach-loads like chickens on a battery farm. But this was the unlikely and bizarre setting that put Tovey on his launch-pad to fame. It was at the Hydro that the clever administrator gradually metamorphosed into the showman-chef. The Swinging Sixties came alive on Windermere as his parties and dinner-dances established the Hydro as the in-place to be and in 1968 he annexed a corner of the hotel to create 'Tonight at

8.30' – an exclusive 24-seater restaurant serving a set five-course dinner. John wrote the menus and did some of the cooking. The *Good Food Guide* approved and bestowed its decorations. Here was the blueprint for Miller Howe.

It was during the 1960s that Tovey came to know and admire Francis Coulson and Brian Sack at Sharrow Bay and the cooking at 'Tonight at 8.30' drew much of its inspiration from their example. 'Francis and Brian were like gods to everyone,' says Tovey. 'Francis used to cook things like tomato and orange soup which was new and different in those days. It was all very exciting.'

And so at the end of 1970 John left the Hydro for a three-week crash course at the Cordon Bleu School in London before moving into the kitchens at Sharrow Bay in January 1971. It was a disastrous experiment which lasted four months and, although the friendship has since been renewed, the anguish of that memory still haunts Tovey. 'It is the one event in my life which is still on my conscience. It is the one thing which still worries me. I was in a manic-depressive state and probably going through an early male menopause.'

In spite of the trauma, Tovey marshalled his wits and, with the help of his bank and an old Rhodesia friend who became his business partner, he snapped up Miller Howe for £26,000 and spent more than twice as much again embellishing, equipping and rearranging the house into a ten-bedroomed hotel.*

One of the great gastronomic mysteries of our time is how, on rare occasions, a virgin cook rises, as if by magic out of the vapours of the stove, to become an overnight culinary star. With a smidgin of experience at 'Tonight at 8.30', where he attended to the puddings, a rushed stint at Cordon Bleu and his brief spell at Sharrow Bay, John Tovey's only comfort – and in the event a very considerable one – was his friend Margaret Costa at the other end of a telephone line and her *Four Seasons Cookery Book* tied to his apron strings. In 1972, less than a year after opening, the *Good Food Guide* rated Miller Howe amongst the top 20-odd hotel restaurants in the land and declared that Tovey's dishes – like his decor – were 'assembled with similar virtuosity'. Seventeen years on, his position remains as exalted.

Tovey's gift is for marrying an extraordinary panoply of flavours and textures in a manner which has made his cooking style uniquely John Tovey. He is like an interior designer presenting the separate elements of a scheme on a mounted board with the intention of bringing them all together in one room. At first sight the effect is one of a violent clash of colour and form. The result is startlingly successful.

A quiche deploys a curried wheatmeal pastry, its base lined with a date chutney. The filling might be tomato, red pepper and onion – except that Tovey sours the peppers by lightly sautéing them in raspberry vinegar and sweetens the onions by sweating them in brown sugar and oil. Salads are busy and vivacious. Lettuces jostle in a bowl with orange segments, garlic croûtons, bacon bits, toasted pine kernels, buttered herbed eggs and deep-fried curried leek rings. Amazing and delicious, this was one of the most exciting salads I have ever eaten.

Soups are equally irrepressible. A borage-crowned and almond-necklaced carrot and caraway soup is served, not with bread, but with Cheddar cheesey leek and onion scones.

Tovey's genre of gastronomic theatre is the palate-thriller. He

Right: *Miller Howe and its enchanted garden. Stone cherubs, maidens and goddesses hide among the oak trees, firs and shrubs; and a small herb garden is planted with a dozen aromatic species for John Tovey's kitchen.*

Far right: *Act IV – the main course. John Tovey at the hot plate saucing breasts of duck as his assistants assemble the vegetables, the plum purée and the onion and sage sauce.*

loves to surprise, to shock but never to offend, to attack the taste-buds as much as to amuse them. Main courses take on an additional dimension and become voyages of discovery round a plate. A roasted, crisp-skinned duck breast may hide two purées beneath – one of plum, the other of onion – and a glossy rich gravy trickles off the top into a bacon and lemon thyme stuffing. Then, surrounding the duck, there are the seven vegetables, a silent celebration to the memory of Nan: runner beans, carrots with coriander, cauliflower cooked in bacon fat, mangetout, a marrow savoury casserole, baby sweetcorn topped with mustard butter and potatoes with cream, garlic and cheese. At Miller Howe the Englishman's worship of fresh vegetables is elevated to the high altar.

Come the puddings, Tovey's philosophy is straightforward enough: 'If you've got it, flaunt it!' And he does, with a choice of generous offerings prefaced with words like 'rich' and 'squidgy' and suffixed with naughtinesses like butterscotch, Jersey cream, Cointreau and rum.

John Tovey is a one-off. He has brought sparkle and panache to the lacklustre image of English cooking and he is dismissive of the fads and fashions which have made us so self-conscious of our eating habits. He says, 'Nouvelle cuisine left me cold. I just get on with what I'm doing.'

His main concern – and his greatest source of pride – is his staff, 'a nucleus of dedicated, devoted people who I am sure will look after me in my old age'. He has installed some as equal partners in other businesses and he has similar plans for those now running Miller Howe. Since 1974, and with the support of British Airways, he has taken them with him on winter tours of the United States, Japan, South Africa and the Middle East to promote his cooking. And he has written seven books in nine years, dedicating the last, *Eating Out With Tovey*, to his staff in recognition of their help with his BBC TV series.

At Miller Howe today, Tovey's principal role is that of composer and conductor. He writes all the menus, creates and tests new recipes and keeps an eye on his chef's progress along the way. And at the end of the evening performance, he takes a bow at each table. If the slightest thing goes wrong, he moves heaven and earth to put it right. But, equally, he is intolerant of ungracious guests and is never shy to allow his bluff north-country temperament full voice. On one famous occasion, he had greeted every table in the restaurant except one which he deliberately ignored because the client had been rude to his

staff. After dinner, agitated by the omission, the man confronted his host and demanded an explanation. Tovey obliged. 'When you see shit, you don't stand in it,' he replied.

Keen of mind, wit and tongue, John Tovey's achievements are prodigious. Hotelier and restaurateur, businessman and inspirer of youth, entertainer and culinary ambassador, author and television personality, no other British chef has done more to develop and promote English food and distinguish it with such a mark of individuality. All he says of his success is that Nan is sitting on his shoulder at every minute.

For a full account of John Tovey's own story read The Miller Howe Cookbook (Century Hutchinson).

MILLER HOWE GAME TERRINE

450 g (1 lb) duck leg meat
2 eggs
a generous pinch of grated nutmeg
400 g (14 oz) thinly sliced smoked bacon,
derinded
450 ml (¾ pt) double cream
50 g (2 oz) pistachio nuts, skinned and
halved
breasts from 2 grouse marinated for 3 days
in 2 tbls cooking brandy
36 stuffed green olives
breasts from 3 wood pigeon marinated for
3 days in 3 tbls Marsala
18 canned water chestnuts
350 g (12 oz) loin of venison, fat removed,
marinated for 3 days in 300 ml (½ pt) red
wine and 1 tbls olive oil mixed with 1
clove crushed garlic and 4 juniper berries

Mango purée
3 ripe mangoes
150 ml (¼ pt) white wine

On the third day that the meats are marinating blend the duck leg meat with the eggs and nutmeg in a food processor, transfer to a bowl, cover and leave overnight to chill.

The next day, line a terrine measuring 30 × 7.5 cm (12 × 3 inches) with the smoked bacon, allowing the ends to drape over the sides so as to eventually cover the terrine. Return the duck meat to the food processor and slowly blend in the double cream. Remove from the food processor and stir in the pistachio nuts. This mixture is used as the 'cement' between the various layers in the terrine.

Put a little of the mixture on the base of the terrine and then place the drained grouse on top making a single layer. Coat with more mixture then add the olives and the drained wood pigeon breasts. Cover with more mixture, then the water chestnuts and finally place the drained venison on top. Finish with a layer of mixture.

Bring the overlapping ends of the bacon over the filling. Place a piece of greaseproof paper on top and put the lid on.

Preheat the oven to 200°C/400°F/Gas Mark 6.

Above: *Miller Howe game terrine*

Put the terrine in a roasting tray and pour boiling water into the tray to come halfway up the outside of the terrine. Cook for 1¼ hours then remove from the oven but leave the terrine in the roasting tray if you want there to be little sign of blood in the meats. Remove if you prefer a pinkish trait. Chill until required.

To make the mango purée, peel and roughly chop the flesh. Liquidize with the wine then pass through a fine sieve.

Cut the terrine into slices and serve on the mango purée with herb flowers such as borage and thyme, and quartered cucumber slices.

Serves 16

CARROT AND CARAWAY SOUP

100 g (4 oz) unsalted butter
225 g (8 oz) onions, finely chopped
1 kg (2 lb) carrots, scrubbed and trimmed
and roughly sliced
2 tbls caraway seeds
2 tbls caster sugar
150 ml (¼ pt) cooking sherry
900 ml–1.2 litres (1½–2 pt) good homemade stock
salt and pepper (optional)

Melt the butter in a large frying pan and cook the onions until they are soft and golden. Add the carrots, caraway seeds and sugar and mix well with the onion. Pour in the sherry and cover closely with a dampened, doubled sheet of greaseproof paper. Leave to simmer gently, preferably covered with pan lid, for 40–45 minutes. The vegetables will create moisture, but check periodically to make sure that they are not catching on the bottom of the pan.

Add the stock and then liquidize the soup. Pass through a sieve into a clean pan.

Reheat very gently and taste for seasoning. Add salt and pepper if necessary.

I like to use cold, raw, finely chopped contrasting vegetables and fruits for garnishing soups. In this instance I have used toasted flaked almonds, borage flowers and chopped parsley. You could also enrich and decorate by simply pouring in a little twirl of cream or natural yoghurt. And, of course, you could use croûtons.
Serves 6–12

LEEK AND ONION SAVOURY SCONES

225 g (8 oz) onions, finely chopped
150 g (5 oz) butter, softened
1 tbls olive oil
225 g (8 oz) leeks, finely diced
450 g (1 lb) self-raising flour, sifted
50 g (2 oz) caster sugar, sifted
2 tbls curry powder of choice
25 g (1 oz) Cheddar cheese, grated
2 eggs, lightly beaten
a little soured cream, milk or yoghurt

Cook the onions in 25 g (1 oz) butter and the olive oil until they are quite dark and fairly crisp then drain them on kitchen paper. Combine with the leeks.

Place the flour, sugar and curry powder in a bowl and gently rub in the remaining butter and the cheese (draw this up as high as possible to get plenty of air into the mix).

Add the onion and leek mixture then add the beaten eggs and gently combine bringing together with sufficient soured cream to give a firm dough.

Preheat the oven to 200°C/400°F/Gas Mark 6.

Turn the mixture out on to a floured work surface and flatten lightly to about 2.5 cm (1 inch) in thickness. Cut into diamonds, using a palette knife, and transfer to baking trays lined with greaseproof paper. Bake in the oven for approximately 15 minutes. Remove from the oven and serve warm.
Makes 24 scones

Below: *Carrot and caraway soup with leek and onion savoury scones*

TRIO OF SALMON

350 g (12 oz) each of fresh salmon, smoked
salmon and gravadlax
dry white wine
1 tbls olive oil
½ iceberg lettuce, shredded

For the garnish
lemon slices or twirls
salmon eggs
sprigs of parsley
mixed salad leaves

Place a baking tray on your hob. Cover the
bottom with a mixture of half water and
white wine and the olive oil, bring to the

boil, and place the fresh salmon in. Simmer
for 2–3 minutes only. Drain and leave to
cool.

Put the three types of salmon decoratively
on individual plates. Here I have placed the
cooked salmon on a plate and covered it
with a mound of shredded iceberg lettuce
and then draped the smoked salmon and
gravadlax on top. Then arrange a pretty
garnish in the middle of the dish – for
example, use a slice of lemon topped with a
spoonful of salmon eggs and a sprig of parsley
then arrange the mixed salad leaves decoratively. You can accompany each serving with
a small pastry tartlet filled with dill mayonnaise and garnished with a borage flower.
Serves 6

Above: *Roast duck served with plum purée
and rich onion and sage sauce*

Below: *Trio of salmon*

ROAST DUCK SERVED WITH PLUM PUREE AND RICH ONION AND SAGE SAUCE

1 duck, dressed and weighing about
2.75 kg (6 lb)
½ orange
½ onion
1 carrot, roughly chopped
1 onion, roughly chopped
1 stick celery, roughly chopped
salt and pepper

For the onion and sage sauce
225 g (8 oz) onion, finely chopped
100 g (4 oz) butter
3 × 7.5 cm (3 inch) sprigs fresh sage
300 ml (½ pt) single cream
salt and pepper

For the plum purée
350 g (12 oz) Victoria plums, stoned
50 g (2 oz) caster sugar
150 ml (¼ pt) white wine

Preheat the oven to 230°C/450°F/Gas Mark 8. Make sure the skin of the duck is dry and stuff the cavity with the orange and onion. Place on top of the carrot, onion and celery in a roasting tin, season with salt and pepper and roast for 1½ hours, draining off the fat at regular intervals.

To make the onion and sage sauce, sweat the onion in the butter until golden and then add the sage and single cream. Blend in a liquidizer and sieve. Season to taste.

To make the plum purée, simmer the plums in a pan with the sugar and wine When they are soft, either blend in a liquidizer or pass through a sieve.

Serve the duck with the two sauces accompanied by a selection of vegetables such as mangetout, baby corn or new carrots. Serves 4

WHEATMEAL PASTRY QUICHE

100 g (4 oz) wheatmeal flour
100 g (4 oz) plain flour
1 tsp curry powder
a pinch of salt
150 g (5 oz) butter, softened
1 egg, lightly beaten
275 g (10 oz) filling of choice

For the custard
300 ml (½ pt) double cream
2 eggs
1 egg yolk
salt and pepper
a pinch of freshly grated nutmeg

To make the pastry base, mix the dry ingredients together on a work surface and make a well in the middle. Place the butter in the well and then pour the egg on top. Work with your fingertips until the mixture reaches scrambled egg texture, then cut together to a dough with a palette knife. Roll into a ball and chill in a polythene bag.

When chilled, bring out of the refrigerator and leave at room temperature to warm. Roll out and line either six individual 7.5 cm (3 inch) cases or one 20 cm (8 inch) deep-sided flan case. Leave to chill again.

Above: *Wheatmeal pastry quiche with an accompanying salad*

Preheat the oven to 160°C/325°F/Gas Mark 3.

When chilled, cover with foil, fill with baking beans and bake blind for 30 minutes for the large cases, or for 15–20 minutes for the small ones. Remove the foil and beans and, if necessary, return to the turned-off oven for another 5–10 minutes. When cooked remove and set aside to cool.

Raise the oven temperature to 190°C/375°F/Gas Mark 5.

To make the custard, simply beat the ingredients together and pour, in conjunction with your favourite filling, into the pastry case or cases. Bake the small quiches in the preheated oven for 20 minutes or allow 40–45 minutes for the large one. Serve accompanied by a varied, mixed salad.

Fillings:
Broad bean, pepper and bacon: Core and dice 75 g (3 oz) red pepper. Then fry or grill 50 g (2 oz) smoked bacon until crispy. Dice and mix with 150 g (5 oz) lightly cooked baby broad beans then add to the custard.
Smoked haddock and sweetcorn: Poach 225 g (8 oz) smoked haddock, flake and remove any remaining bones. Mix with 50 g (2 oz) sweetcorn and add to the custard which has been flavoured with 1 tsp powdered mustard. Top the quiche with 50 g (2 oz) tasty Cheddar cheese, grated.
Serves 6–8

FARMHOUSE PASTRY FRUIT PIES

350 g (12 oz) self-raising flour
100 g (4 oz) jumbo oats
350 g (12 oz) butter, broken into walnut-
sized pieces and softened
100 g (4 oz) icing sugar, sieved
finely grated zest of 2 oranges
3 egg yolks, lightly beaten

Sieve the flour into a bowl and mix in the oats. Add the soft butter pieces, spreading them all over the dry mixture, and work in lightly with your fingers. Once the butter has been roughly absorbed – it is important that you do not overwork it – it will get rather wet and sticky to the touch.

Fold in the icing sugar along with the orange zest. Zig-zag the egg yolks over the mixture, and then, holding the bowl firmly, shake it vigorously, tossing the mixture up and down and around. The dough will rapidly come together.

Divide the dough into two parts and form into two ball shapes very, very gently. Wrap individually in foil and leave overnight (at least) in the refrigerator to chill. This is a very delicate pastry which requires a lot of chilling.

The next day, allow the pastry to come back to room temperature before rolling out one of the balls of dough. Line a 20 × 28 cm (8 × 11 inch) loose-bottomed, fluted flan tin and put back into the refrigerator to chill for at least 30 minutes while you preheat the oven to 160°C/325°F/Gas Mark 3. Bake the case blind for 30–35 minutes.

Many fillings are quite liquid so I always sprinkle Farola or semolina on the cooked base before adding any filling. I also add a sprinkling after the filling has gone in. This soaks up the liquid a bit, but doesn't alter the flavours. Fill the pie generously with your chosen uncooked filling and sweeten to taste with demerara sugar.

Roll the second ball of dough out gently on a floured board and lift with a rolling pin over the filled pie. Use any leftover pieces to make roses or leaves to decorate the top of the pie.

Chill the pie again before baking, and preheat the oven to 200°C/400°F/Gas Mark

6. Bake for 20 minutes in the oven, then reduce the heat to 180°C/350°F/Gas Mark 4 and bake for a further 25–35 minutes. If it's browning too much, cover the top loosely with aluminium foil.

Fillings:

Apple and orange: Peel, core and slice 6 Granny Smith apples, part-cook and cool them, then arrange in the blind-baked case. Peel and segment 2 oranges and arrange on top of the apples.

Banana, walnut and ginger: Skin and slice about 8 bananas and place in the blind-baked case. Add 2 preserved pieces of stem ginger, chopped, and 18 chopped walnuts.
Serves 8–12

Pear and Stilton: Peel, core and slice 5 pears and arrange in the blind-baked case. Sprinkle the top with 50 g (2 oz) crumbled Stilton.

Above: *Farmhouse pastry fruit pie*
Far right: *My Nan's tipsy trifle*

MY NAN'S TIPSY TRIFLE

As this dish can serve any number of people, there is little point having accurate measurements. So follow your instinct and use as much or as little as you like!

enough sponge cake to cover the base of
your chosen dish or dishes
strawberry jam
double cream, whipped
brandy
Marsala
1 small can apricot halves, drained and
liquidized

For the rich custard
8 egg yolks
50 g (2 oz) caster sugar
600 ml (1 pt) single cream

To decorate
raspberries
mint leaves
150–300 ml (¼–½ pt) double cream,
whipped

Slice the sponge cake and spread with as much strawberry jam and whipped cream as you like. If you are over-generous with the sponge cake at this stage, you will end up with a heavier trifle which will require more 'tipsy' to soften it. Pour over the 'tipsy' which is one-third brandy to two-thirds Marsala. Top the alcohol-soaked sponge with the apricot purèe.

If you are using individual glass dishes you could layer the ingredients starting with the 'tipsy' sponge, cream, strawberry jam, and apricot purée.

To make the rich custard, beat the egg yolks and sugar together while warming the single cream. Add the cream to the egg and sugar mixture and stir. Return the pan to a low heat and stir until the mixture begins to coat the back of a wooden spoon (do not allow it to thicken too much or the eggs will curdle – and remember that custard thickens on cooling). Pour on to the trifle, or trifles and leave in the refrigerator when cold.

Decorate as lavishly as you like with the raspberries, mint leaves and whipped cream.

SONIA STEVENSON

The story of Sonia Stevenson is as much the story of the most celebrated lady chef of our generation as it is a ballad composed and conducted by her husband Patrick and performed by them both. It is a song of old-fashioned love and sacrifice about two accomplished musicians who forsook their careers to open a restaurant in a grey, manse-like, Victorian pile on a steep slope overlooking the Tamar Valley and Bodmin Moor near Tavistock.

To this day, Sonia remains faintly bewildered by her success and Patrick would feel affronted to be described as a restaurateur. Even of her, he insists, 'She is not a cook, she is a violinist.' But to Sonia both pursuits are noble art forms and easily reconcilable: 'Cooking a dish is like playing a violin concerto. Interpretations vary each time you perform and there is a constant striving for perfection. Cooking reflects your personality and tests your technical ability to balance flavours, textures and colour. It is the same with music.'

These are brave sentiments which at first do not seem to square with her childhood. She was born to a Scottish mother and a father who was an American-Argentine-Englishman with a dash of Dutch – 'but basically he was terribly British'. Her upbringing was strict and puritanical and a love of food was not considered good form by the family. Certainly cooking was never a consuming passion, although animal and earthy textures fascinated her from an early age. She loved gutting and dissecting grey squirrels shot by her father and she enjoyed making mud pies, which she used to decorate with toothpaste.

After she had left school she continued her studies at the Royal College of Music and in her final year, when she was still only 19, she met Patrick, a successful opera singer and 20 years her senior. They were married a year later, in 1956, after she had promised her parents to complete her teaching degree and in spite of a paternal

caution that she might be committing herself to an unduly long term as a widow.

The young bride soon learned that her life would be shared with Patrick's three other great loves: music, trains and food. While the first had kindled their passion, the second and third were entirely alien to her. Since his childhood, Patrick had been fascinated by steam trains and before he came to opera he had been a cadet on the Southern Railway. But her greatest trial as a housewife was to satisfy his appetite. Patrick was a hungry man with a sophisticated palate – a bon viveur who owed more in his Homeric frame to gastronomy than he did to grand opera.

The first week of married life was not propitious. Patrick was treated to a diet based entirely on bangers and mash until he summoned the courage to propose a little variation in the menu. Before all else in life, Sonia's principal wish has been to please Patrick. And so it began. They were living in London's Campden Hill and she took the short walk to a butcher's in Kensington High Street where she demanded a leg of beef. She knew that legs of lamb and pork were suitable for roasting and so she felt confident that her request was perfectly sensible. The butcher was somewhat perplexed.

'For how many?' he enquired.

'For two,' she said.

'You've got the wrong cut, love. What do you want to do with it?'

'I want to give my husband roast beef,' she explained.

The butcher was a kind and patient man. He instructed her carefully and sent her on her way. Mrs Stevenson had been given her first cookery lesson.

Sonia's apprenticeship spanned the next ten years. Already infected by Patrick's enthusiasm, she was introduced by him to many

of the best restaurants in London and, in their travels abroad, they soon became friends with some of the great chefs of Europe, including Roger Vergé before the master's arrival in Mougins, a sleepy village of the Midi which he transformed into a gastronomic Mecca. Charmed by her curiosity, they all invited her into their kitchens where she watched, learned and took notes of favourite recipes in a loose-leaf journal which she keeps to this day. At Col de la Luère, near Lyon, she spent two days with Mère Brazier, who taught her to make the quenelles which are still a star feature on the Horn of Plenty's menu.

But Sonia's greatest inspiration and number one pin-up was M. Dertu, one of London's most famous post-war chefs, who kept La Réserve in Gerrard Street. Whenever a recipe failed at home, Patrick swept her off to M. Dertu who promptly put her right.

Invitations to dinner chez Stevenson soon became much sought after and her growing skills were given added substance by an expanding collection of books, including Philip Harben's *The Way to*

Cook and Samuel Chamberlain's *Bouquet de France*. Some of the Horn of Plenty's most enduring dishes were tried and tested on Patrick in Campden Hill, such as her lamb en croûte with a mint béarnaise which she made because everyone else was doing it with beef. Foolishly, I once suggested that Sonia's poached salmon with sorrel sauce might have been inspired by the Troisgros' *escalope de saumon à l'oseille*. Patrick winced: 'Wrong. We were doing it before the Troisgros. Anyway, Sonia's dish is quite different.'

By the middle Sixties, Patrick and Sonia had acquired a family. Sinclair was born in 1959 and Toby arrived five years later. Inevitably, the children imposed new demands on the priorities of their parents which forced them to reorder their lives. As much as Patrick loved his work, separation from home and the uncertainties of life as a professional singer, exacerbated at the time by severe bronchitis, were not ideal ingredients for a secure family existence and their desire to endow the children with a private education.

They consulted their friends, some of whom owned country

restaurants in France, had children themselves and, moreover, were earning a living. But when Patrick first suggested that they should do the same, Sonia was aghast: 'My cooking isn't good enough. It's all right for dinner parties but not for people to pay.'

'Nonsense,' chided Patrick, 'I've been paying for us to eat in restaurants where the food isn't nearly as good.' Finally, their old chum David Wolfe, himself a restaurateur and wine expert, came to dinner, fell in love with Sonia's heavenly quenelles and set the seal on their nervous plan.

Years before, Patrick's days on the footplates of the Southern Railway had spoiled him with views of Devon's striking and seductive landscapes. He decided to return to the source of those spiritual and romantic memories which he now sought to share with Sonia and his two young sons.

They lost no time in their search for a suitable house and they bought the first one they saw in the early months of 1966 — a handsome property which offered all three elements of Patrick's simple brief to the estate agent: a view, a cellar and a walled garden.

Local architects were commissioned to build a restaurant on to the side of the house and the Horn of Plenty opened for business in May 1967, supported by a highly ingenious publicity campaign. Their enthusiastic architects deserted their drawing boards for a while to become amateur marketing consultants and spent hours with Tavistock's electoral roll attempting to identify the town's latent and repressed foodies. The strategy worked but, one suspects, the rush of interest was aroused more to satisfy local curiosity than to quell any gastronomic deprivation.

The menu was a revelation. No-one had seen cooking like this before and Mrs Stevenson was doing some very strange things with her ingredients. Saffron, hitherto used in cakes, was being applied to meat and poultry — witness her *poulet au safran sauté niçoise*. Rice, normally reserved for a comforting nursery pudding, was being offered as a savoury accompaniment to veal. Sonia also had great difficulty finding a dairy to supply her with double cream. This was Devon, where cream was clotted. Eventually she found a supplier who asked her why she wanted it:

'To make my quenelles,' she explained.

'What are quenelles?' enquired the man.

'A kind of fish mousse,' replied Sonia.

'Cream and fish!' he exclaimed. 'Sounds disgusting!'

Nevertheless, the news of Sonia's remarkable cooking soon spread and the business took root. Patrick constantly encouraged her to

Right: *From her large kitchen, Sonia Stevenson cooks to please Patrick and her visitors. It is also the classroom for her regular cookery courses — the most notable being her famous 'Courses for Sauces'.*

Far right: *Early morning mists begin to lift over the valley to reveal the Horn of Plenty with its vine-draped terrace overlooking Bodmin Moor.*

experiment and develop her repertoire. He was the final arbiter and if a new dish passed its audition, he introduced it on the menu. His most successful innovation – and one of the great hallmarks of the restaurant's fame – was to feature a regular series of regional menus which carried a fixed price, including the wines served ad lib throughout the meal. In 1969 the *Good Food Guide*'s first report about the Horn of Plenty noted 'it is their special dinners from Burgundy, the Jura, or the Loire . . . which members applaud.'

Star-shaped garlands followed from the Egon Ronay and Michelin guides. But one of the great mysteries of restaurant life is the immense fortitude of proprietor-chefs with young families who, inevitably, become torn between their children and their customers. For Sonia, a devoted mother, the pressures were particularly intense and both she and Patrick weathered their share of crises, not least when Toby was struck by a suspected case of meningitis.

In spite of the heartaches, their progress continued to be rewarded by critics and customers alike. And in the autumn of 1976, Sonia arrived at her apotheosis. Patrick, hearing the news first, broke into a mischievous recitative:

'Think of the most terrifying thing you would ever have to do.'

'Cook for the Queen?' rejoined Sonia.

'No. It's infinitely worse than that.'

Egon Ronay was celebrating the twentieth edition of his guide and to mark the occasion he had persuaded Maxim's in Paris to open its kitchens to five British chefs who would prepare a feast for 120 members of France's culinary aristocracy – platoons of three-star chefs and notables of the Académie des Gastronomes and Club des Cent.

Sonia was the first woman to cook at Maxim's. Her dish – brioches stuffed with calves' sweetbreads and served with two sauces – was pronounced a triumph and at the end of the luncheon Egon Ronay presented her with his Gold Plate award, naming the Horn of Plenty 1976 'Restaurant of the Year'. In a matter of a morning's work, Sonia Stevenson had succeeded in dismantling one of the great ramparts of French chauvinism.

In May 1988, the Horn of Plenty celebrated its coming of age and it is still going strong. Restaurants come and go, too often blighted by the vicissitudes of fashion or the burnt-out carcases of their owners. Longevity, therefore, is an accolade in itself. Indeed, the Stevensons are listed amongst the *Good Food Guide*'s top 20 longest-serving restaurateurs.

While the menu today keeps faith with the traditions of Campden Hill, Sonia's vitality in the kitchen continues to be fuel-injected by Patrick's highly articulate appetite. Newer dishes include turbot with a melon and verbena sauce which was created specially for the twenty-first anniversary dinner and asparagus in filo pastry, though not highly favoured by Patrick, nonetheless received his grudging approval as a courtesy to vegetarians.

In the universe of British restaurants today, this is a unique partnership. A huge accident of fate turned two professional musicians into amateur restaurateurs whose success was founded on the refreshing – almost homespun – philosophy of treating their customers as an extension of their own family. This was the only way Sonia understood cooking. If it gave Patrick pleasure, she could satisfy the world. And so they have never quite succeeded in taking their business too seriously. Like every good Christian household, you ate up your food and were grateful. Patrick is not a person to subscribe to the dictum that the customer is always right. When you eat at the Horn of Plenty, Sonia is always right. The world has been happy to agree.

Above: *Asparagus tart*

ASPARAGUS TARTS

4 sheets filo pastry
90 g (3½ oz) unsalted butter, melted
20 asparagus stalks, trimmed of all inedible
parts

For the onion purée
450 g (1 lb) onions, roughly chopped
50 g (2 oz) unsalted butter
2 sprigs of fresh basil or chervil
1 tbls double cream
pepper

Preheat the oven to 220°C/425°F/Gas Mark 7.

Using 4 × 10 cm (4 inch) straight-sided individual tins, make the pastry bases by overlapping 5 × 13 cm (5 inch) squares of filo pastry and turning the corners over. Brush each square with 75 g (3 oz) of the melted butter as it is put in place. Make a few slashes in each base to allow steam to escape and prevent them from rising and bake in the oven for 3½ minutes.

Slice off the top 5 cm (2 inches) of each asparagus stalk. Slice the remaining stalk into rounds. Simmer in lightly salted water until just cooked. Drain and reserve some of the liquid to make the onion purée.

Sweat the onions with the butter and a little asparagus water until they are soft and dry. Do not allow them to brown. Purée them with some basil or chervil in a liquidizer. Turn into a saucepan, add the cream and reduce to a thick purée, stirring continuously. Season with plenty of pepper. Add the rounds of asparagus.

Assemble the tarts, filling the cases with the purée and shaping it into a mound in the centre. Build the asparagus tips into a tent shape over the top. Brush with the remaining melted butter.
Serves 4

SALMON QUENELLES

225 g (8 oz) salmon cut from tail end
salt
6–8 egg whites
475 ml (16 fl oz) double cream

For the sauce
4 shallots, chopped
75 g (3 oz) unsalted butter
300 ml (½ pt) dry white wine
1 tsp plain flour
300 ml (½ pt) fish stock
300 ml (½ pt) double cream
salt and pepper

To make the sauce, sauté the shallots in 25 g (1 oz) of the butter until transparent. Add the white wine and reduce until almost dry (until the butter shows again). Stir in the flour and add the fish stock and cream. Simmer very gently for 20 minutes to mature the flavours. Strain and beat in the remaining butter. Adjust the seasoning, peppering generously.

Meanwhile, remove all skin and bone from the salmon and place the flesh in a liquidizer with a little salt. Cover with the egg whites and blend, adding more egg white if necessary, until the mixture is smooth and fairly thick.

Turn into a bowl. Add the double cream, whisk until it thickens slightly, and chill.

Dip a tablespoon into a large wide pan of boiling salted water. Take a large spoonful of chilled mixture and roll it against the edge of the bowl to form an oval shaped quenelle. Alternatively shape between 2 spoons. Make 16 quenelles. Drop them into the pan with the water just at boiling point. Poach the quenelles, ensuring that the water does not bubble. Turn them over halfway through; they take about 8 minutes and should be like poached eggs – slightly soft inside. Drain on a kitchen cloth and arrange on individual plates.

To serve, place 2 quenelles on each plate, spoon the sauce over and serve immediately.
Serves 8

LETTUCE AND BACON SOUP

200 g (7 oz) unsalted butter
6 rashers smoked streaky bacon, rind
removed and diced
1 small onion, chopped
225 g (8 oz) outer leaves of round lettuce
900 ml (1½ pt) chicken stock
1 egg yolk
pepper

Put 100 g (4 oz) of the butter, bacon and onion into a hot saucepan and sauté for 5 minutes or until thoroughly cooked. Add the lettuce and sauté for a further 2–3 minutes (do not overcook or the leaves will lose their colour). Add the stock and bring to the boil and continue cooking for a further 2 minutes. Remove from the heat and liquidize until smooth.

In a separate bowl whisk the egg yolk and gradually incorporate the remaining butter which has been melted. Return the soup to the pan and gradually whisk in the egg and butter mixture. Check the seasoning and serve immediately.
Serves 6

LAMB IN PASTRY WITH MINT BEARNAISE

1 large loin of lamb
225 g (8 oz) shortcrust pastry
salt
grated zest of 1 lemon
a sprig of fresh lemon thyme or thyme
1 egg, beaten for egg wash

For the mushroom duxelles
50 g (2 oz) onion, finely chopped
25 g (1 oz) unsalted butter
100 g (4 oz) mushrooms, finely chopped
a little grated nutmeg

For the sauce
bunch of fresh mint
150 ml (¼ pt) white wine vinegar
375 g (13 oz) unsalted butter
3 egg yolks
1½ tbls water
salt

Ask your butcher to remove the 'eye' of the lamb and the fillet from the loin. Remove any gristle and fat.
· Preheat the oven to 230°C/450°F/Gas Mark 8.

Make the mushroom duxelles by sautéing the onion in the butter until soft and transparent. Add the mushrooms and cook until almost all the liquid has evaporated. Finally add the nutmeg.

Roll out the pastry fairly thinly. Place the fillet alongside the thinner end of the loin and lay on one edge of the pastry. Season the meat with salt, lemon zest and thyme and cover with mushroom duxelles.

Roll the lamb up tightly in the pastry and seal carefully. Brush with an egg wash. Bake in the oven for about 10 minutes until the pastry is brown and cooked. Remove and keep warm so that the meat continues to cook gently and evenly through.

To make the sauce, chop the fresh mint leaves and boil down in the vinegar and 25 g (1 oz) of butter until the mixture has lost its kick. In a clean saucepan, melt the remaining butter. In a liquidizer blend the yolks and water and gradually add the melted butter a little at a time, blending until thoroughly incorporated between each addition. Add the mint mixture to the liquidizer and blend again. Season with salt.

Cut the lamb into 15 slices and pour the sauce around.
Serves 5

Below: *Lamb in pastry with mint béarnaise*

Above: *Ingredients for Salmon and sorrel sauce*

SWEETBREADS IN BRIOCHES WITH TWO SAUCES

150 ml (¼ pt) dry white wine
grated zest of 2 lemons
sprig of lemon thyme
600 ml (1 pt) chicken stock
750 g (1½ lb) veal sweetbreads, soaked
overnight in cold water
1 tsp plain flour and 1 tsp butter mixed
together to make beurre manié
300 ml (½ pt) double cream
½ bottle full-bodied red wine
2 onions, chopped
25 g (1 oz) unsalted butter
600 ml (1 pt) demi-glacé sauce
salt and pepper
150 g (5 oz) unsalted butter, melted and
cooked until it turns brown

For the brioches
1 tsp dried yeast
1 tbls caster sugar
150 ml (¼ pt) warm water
500 g (1¼ lb) strong white flour
5 eggs
375 g (13 oz) unsalted butter
1 tsp salt

Make the brioches 12 hours in advance.

Preheat the oven to 200°C/400°F/Gas Mark 6.

Dissolve the yeast with the sugar in the warm water. Beat the flour, eggs, butter and salt together until well mixed, then gently mix in the yeast liquid. Beat well for 5 minutes. Cover with a damp cloth and allow to stand in a warm room until doubled in volume, about 3 hours. Beat it down. Allow it to double in volume a second time, about 1 hour, beat down and three-quarters fill 12 dariole moulds. Allow to rise again and bake in the oven until brown and cooked through, approximately 15 minutes. Remove and allow to cool a little. Turn out of the tins and let the brioches dry. Cut the tops off as lids and hollow out the centres.

Boil down the white wine with the lemon zest and thyme to half its volume. Add the chicken stock. Drain the sweetbreads, then poach them in the stock for 10 minutes. Lift from the stock and remove any gristle and

GALIA SAUCE FOR TURBOT

2 small ripe Galia melons
a few lemon verbena leaves
1 tbls double cream
1 tsp fresh green peppercorns
1 egg yolk
250 g (9 oz) unsalted butter
juice of 1 lemon
salt
6 × 200 g (7 oz) turbot steaks

Remove the flesh from the melons and liquidize it with the verbena leaves. Transfer to a stainless steel saucepan and reduce until pulpy. Add the double cream and the peppercorns, reduce a little, then add the egg yolk and beat in the butter a little at a time. Season with lemon juice and salt.

Cook the turbot by poaching in simmering salted water for 12 minutes, or until tender. Remove and serve with the sauce.
Serves 6

SALMON AND SORREL SAUCE

2 handfuls of sorrel leaves
350 g (12 oz) unsalted butter
3 egg yolks
1 tbls water
salt
6 × 200 g (7 oz) fresh salmon steaks

To make the sauce, sauté the sorrel in 50 g (2 oz) of the butter for 1 minute until khaki coloured all over. Liquidize the egg yolks and water. Melt the remaining butter to boiling point and pour over the egg mixture in the liquidizer, a little at a time, blending well between each addition. Season with a little salt. Add the sorrel to the liquidizer and purée into the sauce until it is all smooth.

Cook the salmon steaks by gently poaching in simmering, salted water for 8–10 minutes until tender. Serve the salmon with the sorrel sauce.
Serves 6

membrane. Cut into small pieces, return to the stock and simmer for a further 5 minutes.

Drain and set aside. Reduce the liquid to 300 ml (½ pt). Thicken with the beurre manié, add the cream and boil until the sauce reaches coating consistency. Replace the sweetbreads and keep warm.

In a clean saucepan, simmer the red wine, onions and butter until all the wine has evaporated. Add the demi-glace sauce and simmer for a further 5 minutes. Remove from the heat and put through a fine sieve. Correct the seasoning and thickness, it should be coating consistency. Beat in the browned butter.

Fill the hollowed-out brioches with the sweetbreads and a little sauce. Replace each lid. Place two per person on a plate and surround with the remaining white sauce. Pour the brown sauce over and marble the two sauces together.

Serves 6

CREPES SOUFFLES GRAND MARNIER

6 crêpes
15 g (½ oz) unsalted butter
25 g (1 oz) plain flour
150 ml (¼ pt) milk
1 egg yolk
1 tbls Grand Marnier
2 egg whites
50 g (2 oz) caster sugar
a little icing sugar

For the kumquat confit
450 g (1 lb) kumquats
600 ml (1 pt) sugar syrup
2 tbls Grand Marnier
juice of ½ lemon

For the confit, slice the kumquats into rings or in half and poach in the sugar syrup, Grand Marnier and lemon juice for 35-40 minutes. When cooked set aside to cool.

Preheat the oven to 230°C/450°F/Gas Mark 8.

Lay the crêpes out flat on individual heatproof plates. Melt the butter in a saucepan and add the flour. Cook for 1 minute then add the milk. Cook, stirring, until thickened. Remove from the heat and beat in the egg yolk and Grand Marnier. Whisk the egg whites stiffly then whisk in the sugar a little at a time and fold into the sauce.

Cover one half of each crêpe with the mixture and fold the other over. Bake in the oven for up to 10 minutes until fully risen. Dust with icing sugar and mark crosses on the crêpes with a red-hot skewer.

Serve with the kumquats.
Serves 6

Below: *Crêpe soufflé Grand Marnier*

JOYCE MOLYNEUX

At the ferry end of South Embankment, the name given to the quayside promenade at Dartmouth, a huge medieval cannon points straight out to sea. At the other end of the strip, at number two, an exuberantly decorative pseudo-Tudor, mock-tiled and balconied frontage shaded by blue canopies advertises the presence of the Carved Angel. The pleasure within is brought instantly to life by three large plate glass shop windows framed by white tubs which, according to the season, may be planted with fuchsia, petunia, begonia, miniature cyclamen, crocus or hyacinth.

Unfortunately, this living video commercial for one of Britain's finest restaurants is largely ignored by the many thousands of visitors to Dartmouth who, year on year, trip blithely past its threshold. Which is why, every time I lunch at the Carved Angel, I have a wicked urge to turn that cannon through 180 degrees to impress upon these tourists the consequences of their ignorance. Not that it would do much good. The English holidaymaker still prefers to lunch out of cling film and thermos in the comfort of his municipally parked car.

Excellence aside, the Carved Angel is important for another reason. Joyce Molyneux, its *patronne*, is the most distinguished disciple of George Perry-Smith, the patriarch of post-war British chefs – and, indeed, the restaurant still bears many of the classic hallmarks of the Hole in the Wall in Bath which Perry-Smith owned from 1951 until 1972.

Joyce came to the Hole in the Wall in 1959 via domestic science college, a 'desperately unhappy' year in an industrial canteen and nine very good years at the Mulberry Tree in Stratford-upon-Avon, a notable restaurant in its day presided over by Douglas Sutherland, a military intelligence officer turned chef.

She was brought up in Birmingham and, during the war, the family was evacuated to the country near Worcester. Her childhood was simple and frugal – the Sunday joint was always followed by cold cuts on Monday – but her parents dispensed their modest income imaginatively to provide Joyce and her two brothers with an interesting, cultured and scholarly upbringing based solidly on the Protestant work ethic.

She was especially close to her father, a metallurgist with Avery's the scale makers, who shared his love of music, reading and theatre with her and from whom she inherited her love of good food. By the time he died, Joyce had been working at the Hole in the Wall for seven years and had been away from home for 16. But his death affected her deeply and although she was already 35, she suddenly became conscious that she was no longer a child: 'I realized that I had now grown up.' In spite of the shock, she worked right up to the day of the funeral – an indication of the deep sense of duty and self-discipline which has characterized her life.

At the Hole in the Wall, Joyce found fulfilment and purpose under the beneficent tutelage of George Perry-Smith. Even today, as partners in the Carved Angel – although he is not actively involved in the business – his influence and friendship have a paternal quality which has provided her with the foundations for her work.

When Douglas Sutherland left the Mulberry Tree in 1959, Joyce took three months off – her first proper holiday in 10 years. She answered an advertisement in *The Lady* for a job as a general assistant at the Hole in the Wall and was not only invited to attend an interview but was offered lunch first – a gesture rarely made by employers these days, never mind 30 years ago. But Perry-Smith expected his staff to eat and enjoy the same food as his customers.

Her host and future mentor made an immediate impression on her. A handsome, bearded man in sandals and an open-neck shirt, he struck her with his kindness and intelligence. She also remembers

exactly what she ate: onion soup, Dover sole *sur le plat* – the fish baked with a cheese topping – and, finally, *ricotta al caffè*, a delicious confection of finely ground coffee, cream cheese, rum and sugar which Perry-Smith had taken from Elizabeth David's *Italian Food*. Much as she enjoyed her treat, it was eaten in some discomfort caused by an orthodontic brace whose wire clasps seemed to take an equal interest in the food and were particularly greedy about the pudding. Her embarrassment was short-lived and she was soon absorbed into this extraordinary *ménage* –not so much in the spirit of a family business but more that of an industrious family.

Although the work was physically demanding – at its peak the Hole would serve over 100 meals on a Saturday evening – Perry-Smith spun a relaxed and democratic aura about the place. If the staff maintained a pecking order it was undefined, expressed more through approval of a natural discipline suggested by the man who led them and underwritten by their affection and awe for his remarkable personality. Everyone's view was respected and taken seriously.

Indeed, you were expected to have a point of view on things – not at all the normal order of affairs in a trade where tyranny was a well-proven management style.

The menus at the Hole in the Wall, like its *modus vivendi,* were different and a refreshing escape from the classical formulas prescribed by Escoffier in that era preceding the sweep of *nouvelle cuisine*.

Perry-Smith took his cue from the writings of Elizabeth David and his *carte* read like a gastronomic travelogue through the French provinces and the Mediterranean. Although Joyce's menu at the Carved Angel has moved on, some of these dishes were transported from Bath with her and repeat fixtures, like the ballottine of duck and Provençal fish soup, continue to give pleasure to her guests today.

However, the homage to Elizabeth David was characterized by a number of other dishes which were notable specialities at the Hole in the Wall and remain so in Dartmouth. The most famous of these must be Perry-Smith's salmon baked in pastry with currants and ginger, whose origins lie in a late 17th-century recipe discovered in André

Simon's *Concise Encyclopaedia of Gastronomy.*

When, in 1972, the Hole in the Wall was sold, Joyce had already been made a partner in the business but, she recalls, 'It was getting so busy and successful, it was like a devouring animal. The Hole was beginning to run us rather than us running it.'

While Perry-Smith took a year off in France Joyce continued to work at the Hole until, on his return to England, he invited her to renew the old partnership. And so it was that they moved to the greater tranquillity of the deep south-west. He, with Heather Crosbie, opened the Riverside at Helford in the spring of 1974 and Joyce, now joined by George's stepson, Tom Jaine, followed in July that year with the opening of the Carved Angel.

In all but name, it was the Hole in the Wall reborn. The cooks at their stoves and the guests at their tables enjoyed open views of one another. The cooks also shared the tasks of welcoming their guests, serving their food, pouring their wine and clearing their plates. The generous menu offered tarama and salad niçoise among its cold 'beginnings', fish soup and a gratin of courgettes and tomatoes amongst the hot. All the main dishes were available under the familiar menu headings of 'usually' (moussaka, chicken roasted with tarragon) and 'sometimes' (skate with black butter, *carré de porc*

provençale). And the Hole's celebrated cold buffet was reincarnated.

Business that first summer was disastrous. Eventually, the menu had to be pruned severely and the cold table was abandoned. 'We had the arrogance to think that because we had come from the Hole in the Wall, everybody would now beat a path to Dartmouth. It wasn't like that at all.'

However, it was not long before Christopher Driver signed his approval of the Carved Angel and in the 1975 edition of the *Good Food Guide* he ended his report with the injunction: 'More reports, please, before the honours list is thrown open.' When it was, Mr Driver obliged – with the Order of the Pestle-and-Mortar, a badge only conferred upon restaurants 'grudgingly'. Other honours followed – including those of the Michelin – and the Angel took flight.

Helped, indeed challenged, by Tom Jaine – 'a terrific influence' – Joyce's cooking began its metamorphosis and, after almost 15 years' service in Bath, she confesses that, perhaps, she had 'fallen into a rut'. Her menus still remain faithful to that experience but they have evolved to take greater account of her location and the expectations of a new generation, all of which have added a sense of liberation and *joie* to her culinary lexicon.

The imaginative use of fruits, flowers and vegetables has become a

Right: *The timbered façade of the Carved Angel overlooking the Dart estuary.*

Far right: *For sale, olive and hazelnut oil, local goat's cheese in olive oil with fresh herbs, spiced oranges, homemade Seville orange marmalade and Balsamic vinegar.*

provenance of this pudding is intriguing in itself because it points to some of the influences which have come in the wake of Elizabeth David. The peach brioche is Jane Grigson's and the ice cream emerged from a recipe of Roger Vergé for a peach leaf custard.

Coming right up to date, even Raymond Blanc has insinuated himself upon Joyce's most recent menus. Her lobster and parsley ravioli reflect the current rage for pasta and the two-tone parcels filled with a sole mousseline reveal a hint of fun in her food which, she feels, is so much a part of the pleasure and surprise of eating out.

In concert with the other chefs in the provinces, she has also taken advantage of the dramatic improvements in the availability of first-rate local supplies. Her cheeses are now pretty well all Devonian, including her fresh goat's cheese which she drains on towels overnight to extract the excess moisture and then keeps in jars of olive oil and herbs. Again it was Jane Grigson who inspired the idea for a goat's cheese and hazelnut soufflé which Joyce offers as a flexible feast – on its own with a salad for lunch, or as a 'beginning, middle or ending'.

Some of her other sources of supply are endearingly whimsical and, thereby, impose their will on her menu. One lady brings elderflowers which make fritters, syllabub, cordial and vinegar. Another has a morello cherry tree which Joyce harvests for chilled soup with soured cream. And Mrs Hicks, Agatha Christie's daughter, opens her estate near Paignton to the staff of the Carved Angel who pick carrier-bag loads of old-fashioned red roses for petal sorbets and ice cream.

When Tom Jaine moved on in 1984 his place was filled by Meriel Boydon, George Perry-Smith's niece and another graduate of the Hole in the Wall. The sense of family remains intact, therefore, and now its dynamic tradition is approaching its fifth decade. But like any potent and evolving force, perhaps at last Joyce Molyneux has made the Carved Angel her own – shaking loose from the spell of the apostle without breaking entirely free.

She is a very private person – modest, controlled and self-contained. But a simple warmth and generosity shine from her face and they have found expression in her craft. She has devoted her life to giving honest pleasure to others and she seeks nothing in return. For her, a 'thank you' from a contented guest genuinely brings greater joy to the spirit than any icons of merit to remind her of the praise she has received. Perhaps this is why she is such a great cook.

trademark. Salmon caught in the Dart river is paired with samphire, which she gathers herself, or with home-grown rhubarb – even though these workings could never displace the ancient recipe with ginger and currants. Her salad of avocado, strawberries and melon with an elderflower dressing is a delicious, beautifully balanced but impish send-up of the avocado vinaigrette. And her hot peach brioche with peach leaf ice cream contrasts the sensations of hot and cold harmonized by the union of two elements of the same tree. The

GREAT BRITISH CHEFS

Above: *Goat's cheese and hazelnut soufflé*

GOAT'S CHEESE AND HAZELNUT SOUFFLES

50 g (2 oz) butter
50 g (2 oz) plain flour
300 ml (½ pt) single cream
300 ml (½ pt) milk
salt and pepper
1 tsp chopped thyme
a pinch of grated nutmeg
4 egg yolks
225 g (8 oz) soft goat's cheese
6 egg whites
melted butter
2 tbls dried breadcrumbs
2 tbls grated Parmesan cheese
50 g (2 oz) roasted hazelnuts, chopped

Make a roux with the butter and flour, then add the cream and milk. Cook the sauce thoroughly for 4–5 minutes and set aside to cool. Season and add the thyme and nutmeg. Stir in the yolks and cheese. Whip the egg whites until stiff and fold into the sauce.

Preheat the oven to 220°C/425°F/Gas Mark 7.

Brush the inside of 8 × 10 cm (4 inch) ramekin dishes with melted butter. Mix together the breadcrumbs and Parmesan cheese and coat the inside of the ramekins. Fill them about three-quarters full with the soufflé mixture, top with chopped hazelnuts and cook in the oven for 10–15 minutes. They should be well risen but still moist inside. Serves 8

BALLOTTINE OF DUCK

1 large duck, boned out, liver reserved
450 g (1 lb) salted belly pork, rind reserved, cut into 5 mm (¼ inch) strips
225 g (8 oz) chicken livers
50 ml (2 fl oz) ruby port
50 ml (2 fl oz) brandy
salt and pepper
50 g (2 oz) dried apricots, cut into strips
bunch of fresh parsley, chopped
1 clove garlic
a pinch of fresh thyme
120 ml (4 fl oz) dry white wine
1 tbls green peppercorns
50 g (2 oz) pistachios, peeled

For the stock
duck giblets (minus liver)
duck carcase
rind from belly pork
1.2 litres (2 pt) water
1 carrot, chopped
1 onion, chopped
1 stick celery, chopped
salt and pepper
bouquet garni
1 egg white

To make the stock, put the giblets, carcase and rind from the belly pork in a saucepan with the water and add the carrot, onion, celery, seasoning and bouquet garni. Bring to the boil, cover and simmer gently for 1 hour. Remove from the heat and strain. Set aside.

Lay out the boned duck on a flat surface, skin side down; it will form a rough triangle. Slice off about half the breast meat and cut into strips about 5 mm (¼ inch) wide. Put in a bowl with half the belly pork, the duck liver and half the chicken livers all cut into similar size strips. Add to this the port, brandy, a little salt and pepper, the apricots and half the parsley. Marinate for 4 hours.

To prepare the duck farce, remove about half the leg meat from the duck and trim excess fat from the interior of the duck. Mince both finely with the remaining belly pork, chicken livers, the garlic, thyme and remaining parsley. Add the white wine, green peppercorns, peeled pistachios and a little salt and pepper, mix well. Divide this mixture into three.

Put one third of duck farce down the centre of the duck. Arrange half the marinated ingredients on top in neat lines. Spread over the second third of the farce. Then arrange the rest of the marinated ingredients. Finally cover with the rest of the farce. Bring the sides of the duck together and sew up in a neat parcel with button thread.

Preheat the oven to 140°C/275°F/Gas Mark 1. Choose a flameproof casserole which is slightly larger than the duck. Season the outside of the duck and brown gently in the casserole, ending breast side up. Pour over the strained duck stock, bring to the boil and put in the oven for 2 hours, turning over halfway through cooking. Remove and allow to cool overnight.

Next day remove the fat from the top and set aside. Lift out the duck and remove the thread. Wrap in foil and put in the refrigerator. Whisk the jelly in the casserole with a balloon whisk. Add the egg white and whisk thoroughly, then bring gently to the boil on top of the stove. The egg white will clarify the jelly, bringing all the impurities to the surface. Keep at a very gentle simmer for 10 minutes. Put a piece of muslin in a strainer over a bowl and pour the jelly in carefully. Allow to drain through, then put jelly to set in the refrigerator.

Serve the duck in thin slices with some of the jelly.
Serves 10–15

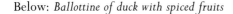

Below: *Ballottine of duck with spiced fruits*

PROVENCAL FISH SOUP

225 g (8 oz) onions, finely chopped
3 cloves garlic, finely chopped
50 g (2 oz) celery, finely chopped
50 g (2 oz) cucumber, finely chopped
2 tbls olive oil
a large pinch of saffron threads
a sprig each of fresh parsley, thyme, fennel or dill and basil, chopped
1 × 397 g (14 oz) can tomatoes
½ bottle dry white wine
1.2 litres (2 pt) fish stock
juice of ½ lemon
100 g (4 oz) smoked fish such as haddock, skinned and diced
salt and pepper

To serve
garlic croûtons
sauce rouille (see recipe below)
grated Parmesan cheese

Sweat the onions, garlic, celery and cucumber in olive oil for 10 minutes then add the saffron, herbs, tomatoes and white wine. Simmer for 5 minutes. Add the stock, lemon juice, smoked fish and seasoning. Simmer for a further 15 minutes. Taste to check the seasoning.

Serve with garlic croûtons, sauce rouille and grated Parmesan.
Serves 6–8

SAUCE ROUILLE

1 × 198 g (7 oz) can pimientos, drained
1 clove garlic
1–2 fresh chillies, seeded
salt
1 tbls olive oil

Put all the ingredients into a liquidizer and blend until smooth. Check for taste — it should be spicy hot, being a condiment to balance the richness of the fish soup.

SALAD OF AVOCADO, MELON AND STRAWBERRIES WITH ELDERFLOWER DRESSING

2 avocados
1 small or ½ large Galia or Canteloupe melon
225 g (8 oz) strawberries
a few roasted hazelnuts, chopped
small bunch of watercress

For the dressing
3 tbls elderflower vinegar or tarragon vinegar
1 tsp caster sugar
150 ml (¼ pt) groundnut oil
salt and pepper
150 ml (¼ pt) single cream

To make the dressing, blend the vinegar, sugar, oil, salt and pepper. Add the single cream and blend again.

To prepare the salad, halve and stone the avocados. Cut the melon into four, peel and seed. Hull and slice the strawberries. Put a little dressing on each plate, slice and arrange the melon, avocado and strawberries on top. Brush with dressing. Finish with hazelnuts and watercress.

Note: To make elderflower vinegar, take a wide necked, 1 litre (1¾ pt) capacity jar, fill three-quarters with elderflowers, loosely packed. Fill up with white wine vinegar covering the flowers by 5 cm (2 inches), cover the jar and leave for 2 months. Strain through muslin and bottle. It will keep well.
Serves 4

LOBSTER AND PARSLEY RAVIOLI WITH SOLE MOUSSELINE

For the parsley pasta
150 g (5 oz) strong plain flour
25 g (1 oz) fresh parsley, finely chopped
1 egg
a pinch of salt

For the lobster pasta
150 g (5 oz) strong plain flour
1 tbls lobster eggs
1 egg
a pinch of salt

For the sole mousseline
200 g (7 oz) fillets of sole
1 egg white
300 ml (½ pt) double cream
salt and pepper

For the garnish
diced tomatoes
sprigs of fresh fennel

Make the parsley pasta by mixing all the ingredients together in a food processor. Wrap and chill for 30 minutes. Using a pasta machine (set one setting below thinnest) roll out into long strips. Cover with a damp cloth to prevent drying. Make the lobster pasta in the same way.

To make the mousseline, work the sole and egg white thoroughly in a food processor. Add the cream. Mix for 1 minute, rub through a sieve and season.

To make up the ravioli lay out a strip of parsley pasta, pipe small mounds of mousseline on to it about 5 cm (2 inches) apart and lay a strip of lobster pasta over the top. Press gently between the mounds to seal. Using a sharp knife cut and separate the ravioli. Put in a pan of boiling salted water and poach gently for 3 minutes. Drain. Continue making the ravioli until all the ingredients are used up. Serve the pasta brushed with melted butter and garnished with diced tomato and sprigs of fennel.
Serves 8–10

Below: *Salad of avocado, melon and strawberries with elderflower dressing*

Above: *Hot peach brioche with peach leaf ice cream*

MERINGUE WITH ROSE PETAL ICE CREAM AND STRAWBERRIES

For the meringues
4 egg whites
225 g (8 oz) caster sugar

For the rose petal ice cream
2 fragrant red roses
450 g (1 lb) strawberries, hulled
juice of ½ lemon
150 g (5 oz) caster sugar
300 ml (½ pt) double cream

For the strawberry sauce
225 g (8 oz) strawberries, hulled
50 g (2 oz) caster sugar

For the decoration
300 ml (½ pt) double cream, whipped
225 g (8 oz) strawberries, sliced

To make the meringues, whip the egg whites stiffly, beat in half the sugar and beat until thick and glossy. Fold in the rest of the sugar. Pipe out as nests, shells or what you will. Dry out overnight in a cool oven, or cook at 120°C/250°F/Gas Mark ½ for about 2 hours.

To make the rose petal ice cream, purée the rose petals with the strawberries, lemon juice and sugar. Fold in the double cream and churn in an ice-cream machine or alternatively freeze in a rigid container until firm. Work in a food processor until smooth, then freeze again.

To make the strawberry sauce, purée the strawberries with the sugar in a food processor and then pass through a fine sieve.

To assemble, pour the strawberry sauce on to the plates, place a meringue nest on top of each and fill with the rose-petal ice cream. To decorate divide the whipped cream and strawberries between the meringues.
Serves 12

HOT PEACH BRIOCHE WITH PEACH LEAF ICE CREAM

4 slices of brioche
50 g (2 oz) unsalted butter
4 large or 8 small ripe peaches or nectarines
a dash of brandy
25 g (1 oz) vanilla sugar

For the peach leaf ice cream
3 egg yolks
100 g (4 oz) caster sugar
300 ml (½ pt) milk
3 peach leaves
300 ml (½ pt) double cream

To make the ice cream, put the yolks and sugar in a bowl and whisk until pale. Boil the milk with the peach leaves, remove and infuse for 10 minutes. Pour on to the egg mixture whisking well. Place in a double saucepan and cook gently without boiling until it coats the back of a spoon. Strain and cool then add the double cream. Freeze, preferably in an ice cream machine. Or, freeze in a container until firm then work in a food processor until smooth. Freeze again.

Preheat the oven to 220°C/425°F/Gas Mark 7.

Butter the brioche and lay on a baking tray, buttered side down. Pour boiling water over the peaches; refresh in iced water, drain, skin and slice thinly. Arrange on the brioche and sprinkle with a little brandy and vanilla sugar. Bake for 10 minutes in the oven, then finish under a preheated grill. Serve with the peach leaf ice cream.
Serves 4

DAVID WILSON

David Wilson is a merry Scotsman of the best sort. There is nothing he enjoys more than a good chuckle about life and he doesn't mind telling the odd story against himself – like the time he took his children to a panto in Dundee. The comic picked him out in the audience, set the spotlight on him and cracked, 'Ooh, boys and girls, look who we've got here tonight. It's Captain Birdseye!' His face says it all. The eyes crinkle, the mouth stretches into a boyish grin and the whiskers bristle with humour. At the Peat Inn, the menu is a serious celebration of Scotland's finest produce but the food is presented on exquisite white thirteen-inch plates which, on closer inspection, reveal something of a Euro-jeu d'esprit. The china is made in Stoke-on-Trent to a German design with a French label, 'Etoiles', while the salt and pepper pots are shaped like well-fed porkers and branded 'Elysée': 'Low-flying presidential pigs,' quips Wilson. 1992 and all that, I suppose.

The atmosphere at his wayside inn is, like the man, convivial and easygoing. There is no conscious effort to parade the formal trappings usually associated with the gastronomic gravitas of a restaurant of such quality. In the kitchen, culinary discipline is administered with a light touch and a song. David Wilson is forever humming and singing at his stoves from a repertoire that embraces anything and everything from Vivaldi to a television theme tune. M.A.S.H., a regular favourite, oddly enough seems to fit his personality to a T. Wilson is the Hawkeye Pearce of the British kitchen – a charismatic individual, brilliant at his work but seemingly incapable of taking life too seriously. This suggests a self-confidence and equanimity about his character which has worked to his advantage because, unlike the majority of the other chefs in this book, he has gained critical success compartively late in his career. He was 49 when he was awarded his first Michelin star.

However, it took Wilson all of 30 years to discover his métier and then it was largely as a result of the faith and encouragement of his wife, Patricia, who convinced him to grab the proverbial bull. He was born in 1938 just outside Glasgow, where his father ran a family business as a glass merchant and glazing contractor. Life was pretty cushy and at school he was a bit of a lad, stirring up mischief in class like some prankster out of the *Beano* and caring little for his textbooks. He left when he was 16 and a year later his father died, leaving him to care for his bereaved mother. The shock jolted a new sense of responsibility into him and he recognized the need to buckle down so he enrolled as a part-time student on a marketing course, meanwhile earning his keep selling nuts and bolts for a local engineering distributor.

National Service interrupted his studies but as a keen amateur musician he spent much of his time playing the clarinet for his RAF station's band. On his return to Glasgow he went professional, joining a jazz troupe as a saxophonist, but he soon found that his ability did not quite coincide with his enthusiasm. So he took up his old job again and resumed work on his diploma.

Throughout his life, Wilson's progress seems to have been touched by a succession of revelations and turning points. The first – and greatest – of these came at a party in 1963 when he met Patricia in a scenario worthy of Rodgers and Hammerstein. It really was love at first sight. And it really did happen across a crowded room.

Their courtship was conducted across the candle-lit dinner tables of central Scotland. Both shared a love of good food and wine, although neither had any practical knowledge of restaurant cooking.

'I remember sitting in a place one evening and saying to Patricia that the food in this country was generally pretty dreadful. We felt that we could do better,' Wilson recalls.

The seeds were sown but the gestation period was to last a good five years. Meanwhile, they were married, Wilson passed his diploma with honours (collecting with it the Saward-Baker Award as the top marketing graduate in Britain) and they moved to Sheffield where he was snapped up as a potential high-flyer by the manufacturing industry.

However, the corporate rhinoceros with its politics and pecking orders frustrated the promising executive and in 1968 Patricia lit the blue touch-paper by pointing out a tiny advertisement in the *Daily Telegraph* asking for a 'young person to train in all aspects of restaurant work'. Wilson telephoned his prospective employer, a Mr Somerset Moore of the Pheasant Inn at Keyston near Kettering, and received the reply he was expecting. Thirty was not Mr Moore's idea of young. Besides, he was only paying £16.00 a week which was hardly compatible with a marketing manager's salary of £2,700. Neither was he offering a company car.

Brave or mad or both, Wilson persisted and in the end Moore

relented. Meanwhile, Patricia presented her husband with a son – an event which might have had a bearing on their decision but didn't in spite of the family's forced separation which was relieved only by David's two-hour home run up the A1 on his day off.

Wilson allowed himself a year's apprenticeship at the Pheasant before returning to the Derbyshire nest to begin the search for his own restaurant. Eventually, love-of-country drew them back to Glasgow and another small advertisement – this time in the *Scotsman* – sent them posthaste to Fife where both the address and telephone exchange of their destination were the blunt syllables 'Peat Inn' repeated three times.

'It's got a great address if it hasn't got anything else,' noted Wilson at the time. And he was right. It was a damp-ridden, shambolic old pub which had been built in the 18th-century on the edge of a peat bog in the middle of nowhere. But they loved the place and anyway it was all they could afford.

In November 1972, they moved in and began the slow process of the inn's repair and renewal while continuing to trade as a pub. Wilson made a modest start in his kitchen pioneering 'bar food' which was almost unheard of in Scotland at the time, and his restaurant tables offered a simple menu based largely on what he had learned from Somerset Moore. But they were ambitious and in the

Below: *Fresh off the boats at Pittenweem. A box of langoustines up for sale at the early morning market.*

early years they used their time off visiting and revisiting the best restaurants in England – notably those closest to the Scottish border; Sharrow Bay, Miller Howe and the Box Tree at Ilkley.

However Wilson's culinary road to Damascus came in 1976 when he and Patricia undertook their first gastronomic tour of France: 'That was when we really saw what we had to do.' The highlight of their trip came when they stopped at Boyer in Reims. They arrived for lunch without a reservation and for five minutes they sat in their car with the rain pelting down outside, plucking up the courage to walk in. Somehow the prospect of eating at the table of one of the great masters of France mixed with the risk of being turned away filled Wilson with awe. Patricia practically had to drag him in and they were not disappointed. When they returned to Fife, Wilson knew he had to start all over again.

The Peat Inn as public house and popular eaterie was dismantled to make way for the Peat Inn, class restaurant, and when they abandoned their famous bar snacks the queues outside the door simply melted away. But with a prayer and a song the business survived and by the early Eighties Wilson was beginning to receive favourable notices in the guidebooks. Meanwhile, the pilgrimages to France continued and he often insinuated himself upon the likes of Guérard, Vergé, Troisgros *et al.*, who allowed him odd half-days inside their kitchens. Finally, his relentlessly nomadic education was rewarded when Egon Ronay published his 1985 guide in which he elevated the Peat Inn to two stars. Two years later Michelin added its own high-gloss stamp of approval.

As a self-confessed Francophile, David Wilson believes his cooking strikes a blow for the Auld Alliance: 'We do our own thing but the influence is French. The people excite me and I come back from France feeling refreshed and challenged. I do not get that same excitement in England.'

However, while style and technique owe much to *la cuisine moderne*, the joy of Wilson's food is his single-minded use of excellent Scottish supplies, most of which are to be found on his doorstep. The sole, halibut, turbot and monk for a fish stew are landed at Pittenweem, an ancient fishing village with a reputation in Scotland that is synonymous with quality. The lobsters come from Anstruther, a neighbouring port just a mile up the road, and only the scallops and mussels are bought from Oban on the West Coast.

Predictably, Wilson is also well looked after for game. His friend

Ian Duncan, who farms near St Andrews, is a fancy shot and keeps the Peat Inn supplied with pigeon, partridge, wild duck and even roe deer, woodcock and teal. Indeed, Wilson's network of friends is enviable. The rich soil of north-east Fife has spawned a canny flush of smallholders who have been marshalled into fulfilling most of his demands for fresh vegetables, salad leaves and soft fruits. But the ace in his pack is an academic gentleman with an unusual nose for truffles. East Lothian is, it seems, the Périgord of Scotland and Wilson gladly accepts these marvellously pungent edible coals in exchange for cash at the rate of £75 a lb.

The Gallic tone of Wilson's cuisine does, nevertheless, regularly spill over into inventions which are undeniably Scottish in origin. Arbroath Smokies – the eponymously cured haddock – are reworked into a mousse wrapped in smoked salmon which is presented on a bed of shredded cabbage and toasted pine nuts to provide a lively crunch in the eating. The lemony saucing points up the flavours of smoke and brine which linger on the palate and tickle the gills. In another creation, Wilson mixes his wit and patriotism with a praline ice cream which he displays in a lacy biscuit cup made from a paste of Scots porridge oats. But in the end, the heart of France guides the aspirations of the Peat Inn's kitchen. Game roasts may reflect the traditions of Scotland but these dishes are often enlivened with sauce preparations which might include crème fraîche or integral garnishes like pastry tartlets, forcemeats and vegetables to deliver the textural combinations and zest which raise the cooking to a higher plane.

Of all the French chefs who have spurred him on, Wilson feels a special affinity with Georges Blanc at Vonnas: 'Although his restaurant is grander, we feel closer to him than any other chef in France.' Certainly, there are unconscious echoes of Blanc in the high-backed chairs, tapestries and beams at the Peat Inn and the Wilson's admiration for the man is evident the moment you meet their white cat. He's called Georges, of course.

Now past his fiftieth year, David Wilson is still going strong. By this stage in life, the satisfaction of success and the physical strain of the kitchen tempt many chef-proprietors to wind down, leaving the daily slog to their ambitious surrogates while they play mine host, perhaps write a book or indulge in *le business* of a little self-exploitation. Wilson, on the contrary, is still charging ahead with the drive and exuberance of a lion cub. However, beneath the stamina and the passion lies a man of great courage. He may have been late to

Above: *Some of the natural spoils of Scotland left on David Wilson's back doorstep. Partridges from Fife and truffles from East Lothian.*

discover his culinary talents but, with the faith and support of his wife, he harnessed a dream fearlessly and succeeded. Even now there are no horizons in sight and no grand delusions about his ability; 'I'm still an apprentice,' he says. But David Wilson still has bags of confidence and plenty of time.

A FLAN OF ARBROATH SMOKIE AND SMOKED SALMON

For the flan
1 pair Arbroath Smokies to yield
275 g (10 oz)
3 eggs
6 tbls crème fraîche
juice of ½ lemon
freshly ground black pepper
75 g (3 oz) smoked salmon

For the sauce
1 lemon
120 ml (4 fl oz) green virgin olive oil
1 tsp caster sugar

For the garnish
175 g (6 oz) savoy or spring cabbage,
shredded
vegetable oil
1 small carrot, shredded
1 small courgette, shredded
1 small raw beetroot, shredded
1 tbls toasted pine kernels (optional)

Split the Smokies in half and remove all flesh from the skin. Put the fish in a food processor and work to a fine paste, then add the eggs. Blend in, and then add the crème fraîche, blending again. Pass this mixture through a conical sieve. Mix in the lemon juice and season with freshly ground black pepper. Cover and reserve in the refrigerator until required.

To make the sauce, peel the lemon and remove the membranes. Put the lemon segments in a liquidizer and blend, then slowly add the olive oil, then the sugar and blend until emulsified. This can be made in advance.

Take six moulds or ramekin dishes approximately 8 cm (3¼ inches) in diameter and 3.5 cm (1¼ inches) deep. Line with thin slices of smoked salmon then fill with the fish mixture. Place the moulds in a bain marie half filled with hot water, cover and simmer very gently on top of the stove until the mixture is set; this will take approximately 7–8 minutes.

To serve, stir the shredded cabbage in a little oil to warm through then spoon on to the centre of each plate. Sprinkle a few toasted pine kernels on top of the cabbage then turn the flans out on top. Put a little of the mixed shredded raw vegetables on top of each flan. Gently warm the sauce in a small pan (do not allow to boil) and pour over the top. Serve immediately.
Serves 6

Above: *A little 'stew' of fish and shellfish with young vegetables in a herb-flavoured stock with cream*
Far right: *Roast young partridges on a bed of cabbage with its juices*

A LITTLE 'STEW' OF FISH AND SHELLFISH WITH YOUNG VEGETABLES IN A HERB-FLAVOURED STOCK WITH CREAM

6 baby turnips, trimmed
salt
12 baby carrots, trimmed
6 baby leeks, trimmed
1 × 175 g (6 oz) fillet of sole
1 × 175 g (6 oz) fillet of monkfish
1 × 175 g (6 oz) fillet of turbot or halibut
6 shelled langoustine tails
3 scallops, sliced across in half
6 fresh mussels
1 tomato, skinned, deseeded and chopped
1 tbls chopped chervil

For the sauce
120 ml (4 fl oz) vegetable stock
1 tbls crème fraîche or double cream
50 g (2 oz) unsalted butter, cut in small pieces

Put the turnips in boiling salted water and cook for 2 minutes. Add the carrots, cook for a further 6 minutes then add the leeks and cook for a further 2 minutes. Drain, reserve and keep warm.

Cut each fillet of fish into 6 pieces. Place all the fish except the mussels in a steamer and steam for about 1–2 minutes until opaque and just firm to the touch.

To make the sauce, simply put the vegetable stock and crème fraîche in a saucepan, bring to the boil then whisk in the butter piece by piece. Simmer until the sauce has reached a good consistency. Cook the mussels in the sauce and remove when open, about 2–3 minutes. Remove the mussels and discard the shells.

To serve, spoon the sauce around the plates and arrange the fish and shellfish decoratively. Add the vegetables. Dot the diced tomato on the dish then sprinkle a little chopped chervil on to the sauce. Serve immediately.
Note: The fish can be varied to meet seasonal availability. The quantities given are for a starter portion but can be increased to make an attractive main dish.
Serves 6

ROAST YOUNG PARTRIDGES ON A BED OF CABBAGE WITH ITS JUICES

6 young partridges, plucked and drawn
salt and pepper
175 g (6 oz) streaky bacon
225 g (8 oz) green cabbage, shredded
approx 2 tbls dry white wine
150 ml (¼ pt) game stock
50 g (2 oz) unsalted butter

Preheat the oven to 230°C/450°F/Gas Mark 8. Season the partridges with salt and pepper and cover the breasts with the bacon.

Put the cabbage on the bottom of a roasting tin and pour on the dry white wine and the stock. Place the partridges on top of the cabbage and roast in the oven for approximately 10 minutes. The birds should be underdone (when the breasts are pressed between forefinger and thumb they should 'give' slightly).

Remove the birds from the roasting tin, strain the cooking liquid into a saucepan and place over heat. Reduce by fast boiling to half its volume. Finish off the sauce by whisking in the butter in small pieces. Check the seasoning and keep warm.

To serve, remove the breasts and legs from the birds, then remove the skin. Cut each breast into 3 thick slices. Spoon a little cabbage on to each plate, place the sliced breasts on top and the legs above each breast. Spoon the sauce around and serve immediately.
Serves 6

BREAST OF WOOD PIGEON ON A PASTRY CASE FILLED WITH WILD MUSHROOMS

6 wood pigeon breasts
50 g (2 oz) unsalted butter
175 g (6 oz) wild mushrooms (chanterelles
or cèpes), finely chopped, plus 18 whole
cèpes, sautéed, for garnish
225 g (8 oz) puff pastry
beaten egg, to glaze
salt and pepper
6 sprigs flat-leaf parsley

For the sauce
150 ml (¼ pt) pigeon stock
1 tbls crème fraîche or double cream
sprig of fresh rosemary
25 g (1 oz) unsalted butter
salt and pepper

To make the sauce, pour the pigeon stock into a saucepan and add the crème fraîche and rosemary. Bring to simmering point, whisking occasionally. Pass through a sieve then reheat, whisking in the butter in small pieces. Reduce to the required consistency. Check the seasoning and reserve until needed.

To cook the pigeon breasts, preheat the oven to 230°C/450°F/Gas Mark 8. Remove the small fillet from each breast, chop finely and set aside. Sauté the breasts (with the skin on) in 25 g (1 oz) butter, then place in a roasting tin and finish cooking in the centre of the oven for about 5–6 minutes. Remove and allow to rest in a warm place.

To cook the mushrooms, place in a pan with the remaining butter (use the same pan as for the breasts) and stir until juices start to run. Add the chopped fillet and cook for a further minute. Set aside and keep warm.

Roll out the puff pastry about 3–5mm (⅛–¼ inch) thick and cut out six large crescent shapes about 10 cm (4 inches) along the straight side and 7.5 cm (3 inches) wide. Brush with egg glaze, score and bake in the hot oven until golden brown, about 10 minutes. Cut the top off each and remove excess pastry dough in the centre. Keep warm until required.

To serve, place the pastries on plates and

fill with the finely chopped mushroom and pigeon fillet. Slice the pigeon breast across then place the slices on top of the pastry. Surround with the sauce and place the lid against the pastry case. Serve immediately garnished with whole cèpes and parsley.
Serves 6

SADDLE OF HARE ON A BASE OF FORCEMEAT AND WILD MUSHROOMS IN A RED WINE SAUCE FLAVOURED WITH ROSEMARY

3 saddles of hare, trimmed
a little oil and unsalted butter, for roasting

For the base
75 g (3 oz) hare meat (taken from saddle when filleting)
75 g (3 oz) wild mushrooms
1 egg
approx 1 tbls double cream
salt and pepper

For the sauce
150 ml (¼ pt) red wine
1 tbls sherry vinegar
2 tsp redcurrant jelly
300 ml (½ pt) game stock
sprig of fresh rosemary
50 g (2 oz) unsalted butter
salt and pepper

For the garnish
6 wild mushroom caps
25 g (1 oz) unsalted butter

To make the bases, finely chop the hare meat and mushrooms in a food processor, then add the egg and cream. Mix well and season (this can be done in advance and reserved).

To make the sauce, put the red wine, sherry vinegar and redcurrant jelly in a saucepan. Reduce until it is sticky and almost caramelizing then add the game stock and the sprig of rosemary. Bring back to a simmer and reduce again to the required consistency, whisking in the butter piece by piece at the last moment. Pass the sauce through a fine sieve, check the seasoning and keep warm

Above: Saddle of hare on a base of forcemeat and wild mushrooms in a red wine sauce flavoured with rosemary

Far left: Breast of wood pigeon on a pastry case filled with wild mushrooms

until required.

To cook the saddles, preheat the oven to 230°C/450°F/Gas Mark 8. Seal the saddles in a little oil and butter in a sauté pan then cook in a roasting tin in the oven for about 5 minutes, removing while the saddles are still pink. Leave to rest in a warm place.

To cook the base, put the hare and mushroom farce in 6 round baking dishes approximately 9 cm (3½ inches) in diameter and 1 cm (½ inch) deep. Cook in the bottom of the oven in a bain marie until set, about 3–4 minutes. Keep warm until required.

To serve, turn out a cooked farce on to each plate. Cut the saddles across into pieces of about 1 cm (½ inch) thick. Arrange like petals, on top of the farce. Place a mushroom cap cooked in a little butter in the centre. Surround with the sauce. Serve immediately.
Serves 6

WHOLE LOBSTER IN A LIGHTLY SPICED SAUCE WITH BARSAC

6 live lobsters each about 500 g (1¼ lb) in weight

For the sauce
300 ml (½ pt) fish stock
150 ml (¼ pt) double cream
85 ml (3 fl oz) Barsac
sliver of root ginger
sprig of coriander
a pinch of curry powder
50 g (2 oz) unsalted butter
salt and pepper

To make the sauce, pour the fish stock, cream and Barsac into a saucepan, add the root ginger, coriander and curry powder, bring to the boil and simmer for about 10 minutes. Pass the sauce through a fine sieve, bring back to a simmer and whisk in the butter in small pieces. Check the consistency; if too thin, reduce, or if a little thick, add some more fish stock. Check the seasoning and keep warm.

To cook the lobsters, bring a very large pan of salted water to the boil and plunge them in. As soon as the water returns to the boil the lobsters should be cooked. Allow to cool slightly in the water. When cool remove the shell by cutting down each side of the belly with scissors, detach the membrane and take out the tail meat in one piece. To remove the claw meat, crack them open using a rolling pin or the back of a heavy knife, then twist the small pincer with your fingers and thumb to remove the central cartilage and the meat should slip out in one piece. Repeat this with all the lobsters.

To serve, take each lobster tail and cut it into slices. Spoon the sauce on to each plate and lay out the lobsters, in their original shape on top of the sauce.

This dish can be served with lightly cooked vegetables. You could also make little pastry tartlets and fill them with avocado and apple balls and a little of the sauce.
Serves 6

Right: *Whole lobster in a lightly spiced sauce with Barsac*

PRALINE ICE CREAM IN A LACY BISCUIT CUP WITH A COFFEE BEAN SAUCE

For the praline powder
225 g (8 oz) whole blanched almonds
225 g (8 oz) granulated sugar
piece vanilla pod, split (or 1 tsp vanilla essence)

For the ice cream
6 egg yolks
1 tbls granulated sugar
150 ml (¼ pt) water
300 ml (½ pt) double cream
½ tsp instant coffee
a dash of boiling water

For the lacy biscuits
150 g (5 oz) soft margarine
100 g (4 oz) granulated sugar
100 g (4 oz) porridge oats
1 tsp vanilla essence

For the coffee bean sauce
300 ml (½ pt) milk
65 g (2½ oz) caster sugar
1 tsp freshly ground coffee
3 egg yolks

Above: *Praline ice cream in a lacy biscuit cup with a coffee bean sauce*

To make the praline powder, toast the almonds in a baking tin under a very hot grill until golden brown. Put the sugar in a saucepan with the vanilla and melt carefully, then pour over the toasted almonds. Leave to cool, then break into pieces, wrap in a kitchen towel and beat with a rolling pin to make powder. Store in an airtight container if making in advance.

To make the ice cream, beat the egg yolks in a food processor for 5–6 minutes. Meanwhile dissolve the sugar in the water and boil together to make a thin syrup. Pour this syrup slowly into the eggs with the food processor set at the lowest speed. Pour the mixture into a double saucepan and cook over low heat until it thickens enough to coat the back of a spoon. Remove from the heat and place the pan in a basin of cold water and ice to cool. When cool add the double cream. Dissolve the instant coffee in the boiling water and add to the mixture. Add

the praline powder to the mixture, reserving a little for decoration, and then pour into an ice-cream making machine. Alternatively pour into a rigid container and freeze until firm then work in a food processor until smooth. Freeze again until required.

To make the biscuit cups, preheat the oven to 180°C/350°F/Gas Mark 4. Cream the margarine and sugar together, add the porridge oats and vanilla essence, then roll into balls about the size of a golf ball. Place 4 balls – well spaced – on an oiled baking sheet, one at each corner, and place in the oven for 12–15 minutes until golden brown. Cool very slightly then remove from the tray with a slice and press gently into bowls about 10 cm (4 inches) in diameter to shape. Allow to cool and set then store in an airtight

container. Repeat until the mixture is used up (makes 7–8 cups set aside the 6 best).

To make the coffee bean sauce, boil the milk with half the sugar. Remove from the heat, add the coffee, cover and leave to infuse for approximately 5–10 minutes. In a bowl, whip the egg yolks with the remaining sugar until light and creamy. Add the milk and coffee mixture slowly, mixing at the same time. Pour into a double saucepan and heat gently to thicken, stirring frequently. Set aside to cool.

To serve, spoon the sauce over six cold plates and place a biscuit cup in the centre of each. Fill with scoops of praline ice cream then sprinkle a little praline powder over. Serve immediately.
Serves 6

RICHARD SHEPHERD

High up on the corner where Stratton Street meets Piccadilly, a red neon sign proclaims the way to Langan's Brasserie. It is a redundant gesture for a restaurant which has become a landmark on London's high-society carousel and an institution which, even after 13 years, seems to be impervious to the fickle pendulum of fashion.

Inside, ceiling fans hover low over closely packed, paper-draped tables like a fleet of helicopter gunships. Dragged paintwork in shades of camel and tobacco covers walls and ceilings, suggesting an aura of advanced but homely wear and tear. Wall lights hang like wilting amber bluebells, lilies and foxgloves. Nothing matches. The place is an interior designer's Armageddon and a picture gallery with no theme. Hockneys hang with posters of the Folies Bergères. Pastiche and montage compete with sepia prints and portraits of the three famous partners – Michael Caine, Richard Shepherd and the late Peter Langan. A crass advertising slogan, 'For your throat's sake smoke Craven A', shares space with a Keating self-portrait and two large paintings of Chelsea football ground and a boxing match at the Royal Albert Hall. There are wood carvings of swans and cockerels, a stuffed exotic bird behind a glass case and a chaotic jumble of lost titles is stacked on sagging book shelves.

Langan's makes no sense. In a world which has become accustomed to restaurant chic and designer food, Richard Shepherd continues to see off his rivals. Each day his basement kitchen feeds 650 of the faithful while upstairs his restaurant staff repeat the words, 'I'm sorry, we're full,' to those foolish or arrogant enough to expect a table without booking well ahead.

A clue to the brasserie's success lies in Shepherd's fundamental outlook, both as a chef and as a restaurateur. The great restaurants of the world – according to the laws and definitions laid down by the guide books – create dishes and decor which demand the attention and approbation of their customers. Shepherd makes no such demands. He cooks food that people want, not what he would like them to eat. His stars are his customers and not the miniature symbols prescribed by Michelin. At heart he is a man of simple tastes and he has no grandiose conceptions about himself as a chef. He is uninfluenced and unimpressed by the grand masters of cuisine today and it amuses him that most chefs rarely eat what they cook: 'I eat all the dishes on my menu because I enjoy them.'

So food at Langan's is not a religion and in this sense the experience is a comfortable reflection on the British character. Indeed, 'comfort' is a word to describe Shepherd's cooking. The dishes on the menu are old friends, instantly recognizable by name and immediately satisfying when they arrive at your table. There are the puds granny gave you when you came to stay in the school holidays – treacle tart, lemon meringue pie and bread and butter pudding; and there are mum and dad's old favourites when they travelled in France – *champignons farcis*, *coq au vin*, seafood salad and the rest.

The odd paradox about the menu is that it does little to reflect Shepherd's culinary pedigree, which is rooted firmly in the lofty traditions of French *haute cuisine*. In the hierarchy of the new breed of professionally trained British chefs he was the first to make his mark, and his path to the top has established him as the standard-bearer for a whole generation.

Richard Alan Shepherd was born in the spring of 1945 and grew up on a council estate in Weston-super-Mare. His father was an aero engineer who supplemented the family's income by working in a local pub at night and his mother also took a job as a home help. He talks nostalgically of evenings spent in front of the fire with his mother, helping to cream butter and sugar for sponge cakes. At school he came close to being branded a cissy as the only boy to ask to

do domestic science. His request was denied and, instead, he was told to take up woodwork or technical drawing. Undaunted, he pursued his early fascination for cooking by working in the resort's cafés and hotels during his holidays and by the time he was 15 his mind was made up. He left school and the cosy security of home to accept a three-year apprenticeship at a small hotel in Great Malvern. His youthful ambition and determination soon overcame his early homesickness and by his eighteenth birthday he had mapped out his whole future: 'One day I want to be head chef at the Savoy or the Dorchester.'

Shepherd wrote to the Savoy Company and was offered an interview at Simpsons in the Strand. His father borrowed a friend's motor car and on the drive up to London he told his anxious young passenger the story of how he got his first job. 'If you want it, you must go for it hard and you'll succeed.' It was a piece of advice which his son would never forget. He got the job.

And so from 1963 Shepherd embarked on a course which was

precise in its calculation and classical in its nature. There were to be no concessions to anything that might be considered remotely second-rate on his CV. He used Simpson's as a springboard into the kitchens of the Savoy Grill and in early 1967 he was rewarded with a season as a *stagiaire* at the Grand Hotel du Cap-Ferrat on the Côte d'Azur. He soon fell in love with Provence — an affair commemorated on his menus ever since — and, no doubt, destiny decreed that this could be the only setting for his match to Christine, his future wife.

He decided to stay and in the autumn of 1967 he was appointed *chef de partie* in the larder of La Réserve at Beaulieu-sur-Mer, a resort of quite a different hue to the muddy sands and modest guest houses of Shepherd's home town on the Bristol Channel.

By 1969 he was ready to return to London armed with a quality of experience which he knew few of his contemporaries could equal. He accepted a senior post at the Dorchester before becoming Head Chef at David Levin's new hotel, the Capital in Basil Street, when it opened in 1971. What he did not realize when he left the Dorchester was that he had been earmarked as a potential successor there to Eugene Kaufeler, *maître chef des cuisines*, who was approaching retirement. However, his boyhood dream was not to be realized.

Success came at the Capital and this is where Shepherd made his reputation. He was acclaimed in the press, notably by Quentin Crewe, and culinary honours followed in 1975 when Michelin published the second edition of their British guide and awarded the Capital a star.

Several of his dishes from those years still keep their place on the menu at Langan's today and, predictably, their provenance is the South of France. *Carré d'agneau rôti aux herbes de Provence, artichaut farci à la Nissarda* and *loup de mer farci* are all souvenirs of his happy summers in Beaulieu.

By 1976 David Levin's business interests were expanding and, sadly, the close relationship between proprietor and chef deteriorated. Shepherd quit without a job to go to. 'After a good five years, it broke my heart to leave the Capital. I remember driving home that day and breaking down in tears inside my car. I just could not believe it.'

The news of Shepherd's departure made instant gossip around the kitchens of London. In a matter of days, Peter Langan, who had opened his Brasserie three months previously and who had come to know the Capital's young star, appeared at Shepherd's house one evening and offered him a partnership. Recalling his father's words 13 years before, Shepherd went for it.

Peter Langan's brilliant concept of a big, bustling and laid-back eaterie set Shepherd off on a new course. He was no longer in the business of teasing intellectual palates; his task now was to appeal to the hearts and bellies of the city's children of fortune. Some of his distinguished colleagues were shocked by his move but, like every other major decision in his life, it was a well-calculated step and, moreover, an irresistible challenge: 'I'll show them that I can make it work and that it will be the best of its kind.'

Langan made a profound impression on his new partner by opening his eyes to a restaurant world beyond the kitchen stove. Shepherd's outlook changed and widened. He stopped just thinking as a cook and realized that people did not use restaurants exclusively for the pleasure of the cuisine. And so he aimed to provide an experience which reached beyond a reputation based solely on good food.

So what is Langan's Brasserie? Its success is based more on phenomenon than formula and it has happened through the medium of a volatile partnership which has created its own magnetic field.

Right: *The exterior of Langan's Brasserie and a window for London's paparazzi.*

Far right: *The famous Langan's* carte *topped by David Hockney's illustration of the three partners — the late Peter Langan, Michael Caine and Richard Shepherd.*

Peter Langan conceived the idea and paraded it before the gossip columns with his notorious appetite for consuming champagne and spilling insults – and more – on his customers. Michael Caine imported Hollywood to Stratton Street and spread its aura for all to enjoy. And Richard Shepherd provided mortar for the fabric and oil to drive the turbine. The result falls somewhere between a reinvention of café society and a works canteen for London's glitterati.

However, beneath the glitzy veneer lies a restaurant with a broader appeal. There is none of the charade of restaurant protocol and there is no sense of customer intimidation. Suits and evening dress blend harmoniously with jeans and open-neck shirts – unthinkable in the Savoy Grill. Power lunchers may plot at one table while their secretaries chatter at another. Tables are not set with baffling ranks of knives, forks and glasses. There is just one of each. The wine list does not induce fits of panic or embarrassment because it is short and the names on the labels are familiar. In the final analysis, Langan's Brasserie is a roaring success because it is populist, not fashion conscious. Peter Langan's idea and the lustre of Michael Caine's patronage have provided the seeds for what is today Richard Shepherd's achievement – a commercial success which he is quick to share with his elder brother, Michael, who acts as the partnership's administrator and accountant: 'My brother has been the backbone of the business.

But populism is not always an attribute that endears itself to an acerbic fraternity of food critics in this country and it niggles Shepherd's professional pride that sometimes he has not been given proper credit for the quality of food he serves. His cooking owes little to the stylized presentations of the modern idiom. His menu lists about 90 dishes, the themes drawn as much from the English nursery and public school as they are from the classical French repertoire. If you want bubble and squeak and mashed swedes with your *moules farcies florentine*, you can have them. All his produce is fresh and delivered daily. This is gutsy, no-frills food for regular eating. 'You could not dine at Raymond Blanc's or Nico's restaurant every night,' he says. 'but you can at Langan's. I have the balance and I have the variety on the menu.' His customers love it and they keep coming back for more.

Richard Shepherd has been a chef for 30 years. His parents taught him the virtues of hard work. At school he confronted prejudice and

the stigma associated with work in a commercial kitchen. His early training taught him the joys and honour of a craft to which he has dedicated his life. In 1984 his peers voted him Restaurateur of the Year and three years later the Académie Culinaire de France invited him to become chairman of its Filiale de Grande Bretagne, thus making him the first Briton to assume high office of this staunchly chauvinistic association embracing the élite of the trade. Like every Boy's Own hero, he has proved that grit and graft can conquer the world and his only concession to the affectation of success is his cigarette holder and packet of Gauloises.

SALAD OF OYSTER MUSHROOMS

1 head frisée lettuce
a few radicchio leaves
150 ml (¼ pt) vinaigrette made with
English mustard and white wine vinegar
50 g (2 oz) unsalted butter
450 g (1 lb) oyster mushrooms
50 g (2 oz) shallots, chopped and cooked in
a little white wine
salt and pepper
50 g (2 oz) radishes, chopped
50 g (2 oz) fresh parsley, chopped

Wash the lettuce and radicchio and divide it between four plates. Dress the salad with the vinaigrette.

Heat a frying pan over a high flame. Add the butter and continue to heat until it is just starting to brown. Add the mushrooms and toss until evenly cooked. Add the shallots and season to taste.

Divide between the plates and then sprinkle with the chopped radish and parsley.
Serves 4

SEAFOOD SALAD

100 g (4 oz) squid, cooked
6 Mediterranean prawns
100 g (4 oz) mussels (or cockles), cooked
100 g (4 oz) Norwegian prawns
100 g (4 oz) scallops with coral, cooked
50 g (2 oz) cucumber
50 g (2 oz) celery
50 g (2 oz) artichoke hearts, cooked
50 g (2 oz) spring onion
100 g (4 oz) peppers (any colours available)
15 g (½ oz) fresh basil

For the dressing
65 ml (2½ fl oz) raspberry vinegar
300 ml (½ pt) olive oil
salt and pepper

For the garnish
100 g (4 oz) mushrooms, sliced
75 g (3 oz) French beans, cooked

Cut the fish into even-sized pieces, leaving the mussels and Norwegian prawns whole.

Above left: *Seafood salad;* Above right: *Salad of oyster mushrooms*

Peel the cucumber and cut into batons. Chop the celery, artichoke hearts and spring onions into even pieces. Slice the peppers and finely chop the basil. Mix all the ingredients thoroughly.

Mix the dressing and then pour over and mix through the salad. Divide the salad on to plates and garnish with sliced mushrooms and chopped French beans.
Serves 6

COLD CUCUMBER AND MINT SOUP

1 cucumber
1 bunch fresh mint
300 ml (½ pt) plain yoghurt
150 ml (¼ pt) double cream
150 ml (¼ pt) single cream
salt and pepper

Peel the cucumber, pick over the mint (reserving a few leaves for garnishing) and liquidize together. Add the yoghurt and cream and blend again. Season and chill.

Before serving, adjust the consistency if necessary by adding more single cream and garnish with the reserved mint leaves.
Serves 4

SPINACH SOUFFLE WITH ANCHOVY SAUCE

75 g (3 oz) unsalted butter
75 g (3 oz) plain flour
600 ml (1 pt) milk, heated and infused
with onion, bay leaf and clove
100 g (4 oz) spinach leaves, stalks removed
salt
4 eggs, separated
a pinch of cayenne pepper
a pinch of ground nutmeg

For the anchovy sauce
1 tbls water
3 egg yolks
225 g (8 oz) clarified butter, melted
a pinch of cayenne pepper
salt
lemon juice to taste
1 × 50 g (2 oz) can anchovy fillets,
squeezed free from oil

Preheat the oven to 180°C/350°F/Gas Mark 4.

Make a roux by melting the butter and adding the flour. Cook slowly; do not allow it to colour. Add the strained infused milk to the roux gradually, stirring constantly, making sure there are no lumps. When all the milk has been added, simmer very gently for 5–10 minutes.

Cook the spinach in a little boiling salted water and refresh in cold water. Squeeze to remove excess water and chop finely.

Add a pinch of salt to the egg whites and beat until very stiff.

Off the heat, season the sauce with cayenne, nutmeg and salt. Add the egg yolks and mix. Add the spinach, continue to mix, and fold in the beaten egg whites.

Fill six well-buttered individual soufflé moulds and cook in the oven for about 20 minutes.

Make the anchovy sauce by adding the water to the egg yolks. In a double saucepan cook over a gentle heat, whisking continuously to a pale, creamy foam. Allow to cool slightly and slowly add the warm clarified butter. When combined, add the cayenne, salt and a squeeze of lemon juice.

Blend the anchovy fillets with a drop of water to a smooth paste. Put into a bowl and add the sauce, whisking continuously until thoroughly mixed. Pass through a fine sieve and serve with the soufflés.
Serves 6

NICOISE STUFFED ARTICHOKES

300 ml (½ pt) dry white wine
a few coriander seeds
a few peppercorns
2 tbls lemon juice
sprig of fresh thyme
1 bay leaf
salt and pepper
6 globe artichoke hearts, rubbed with
lemon juice
500 g (1¼ lb), mushrooms, chopped
double cream, to taste (optional)
50 g (2 oz) shallots, chopped
75 g (3 oz) cooked ham, diced
300 ml (½ pt) hollandaise sauce
chopped chives, to garnish

Reserve 4 tbls of the white wine to cook the shallots. Put the remaining wine in a pan and make a court bouillon of one part white wine to three parts of water. Add a few coriander seeds and peppercorns with the lemon juice, thyme, the bay leaf and salt. Cook the artichoke hearts in the bouillon until tender (test with the point of a small knife).

Cook the mushrooms until all the moisture has evaporated. (If the mushrooms are a little bitter, add a drop of cream.) Simmer the shallots in the reserved wine, then reduce to a glaze by fast boiling. Add the shallots and ham to the mushrooms and season with salt and pepper.

Arrange the artichokes on a serving dish and fill with the mushroom mixture. Cover with hollandaise sauce, sprinkle with chives and serve hot.
Serves 6

Below: *Spinach soufflé with anchovy sauce*

STUFFED MUSSELS

24 green lipped mussels
1 large glass dry white wine
50 g (2 oz) shallots, chopped
100g (4 oz) leaf spinach, cooked
a little unsalted butter
salt and pepper
50 g (2 oz) Parmesan cheese
fresh parsley, to garnish

For the mornay sauce
2 tsp water
2 egg yolks
200 ml (7 fl oz) béchamel sauce
50 g (2 oz) Cheddar cheese

Steam the mussels with the white wine and shallots until opened. Discard any which do not open. Remove the flesh from the shells, reserving 28 half shells.

Make the mornay sauce by adding the water to the egg yolks. In a double saucepan cook over a gentle heat, whisking to a foam. Combine with the remaining ingredients.

Toss the spinach with butter and seasoning and divide between 24 shells. Reheat the mussels in the cooking liquor and place one in each shell.

Cover each mussel with sauce, sprinkle with Parmesan and glaze under a hot grill. Garnish each with half a shell and parsley.
Serves 4

Below: *Stuffed mussels*

CRUSTED SEA BASS

1.5 kg (3½ lb) whole sea bass
salt and pepper

For the farce
225 g (8 oz) unsalted butter
225 g (8 oz) fresh white breadcrumbs
1 hard-boiled egg, sieved
100 g (4 oz) mushrooms, chopped
25 g (1 oz) shallots, chopped
1 tbls chopped chives
1 tbls chopped fresh parsley
salt and pepper

For the cooking liquor
600 ml (1 pt) fish stock
1 bay leaf
a pinch of thyme
2 shallots, chopped
½ glass dry white wine
salt

For the sauce
225 g (8 oz) unsalted butter
salt
a pinch of cayenne pepper
juice of ½ lemon

To make the farce, allow the butter to go soft and then thoroughly mix all the ingredients.

Preheat the oven to 190°C/375°F/Gas Mark 5.

Fillet the fish by cutting down either side of the backbone, removing it but leaving the head and tail on. (This can always be done by a local fishmonger.) Then season the cavity and fill with the farce.

Place in a large ovenproof dish with all the ingredients for the cooking liquor, cover and cook in the oven for 15–20 minutes. When cooked, take the fish out of the liquor and put under a preheated grill until golden brown.

To make the sauce, strain the cooking liquor into a pan and reduce to three-quaters its volume by fast boiling. Remove to the side of the stove and whisk in the butter a little at a time until just melted. Do not reheat the sauce or it will separate. Season with salt, cayenne pepper and lemon juice. Serve the sauce separately.
Serves 4

BUBBLE AND SQUEAK

1.5 kg (3½ lb) large potatoes
100 g (4 oz) white cabbage, shredded
100 g (4 oz) green cabbage, shredded
salt and pepper
a little vegetable oil
50 g (2 oz) onion, finely chopped
100 g (4 oz) clarified butter

Boil the potatoes in their jackets until half-cooked. Allow to cool. Blanch the cabbage then drain and cool.

Peel and grate the potatoes. Mix three-quarters with the cabbage and season well.

In a pan heat the oil and gently cook the onion until soft. Remove from the heat and add to the cabbage and potato mixture.

Preheat the oven to 200°C/400°F/Gas Mark 6. Heat a non-stick pan until very hot. Add half the clarified butter and the unmixed potato and cook over a fairly strong heat until the potato slides like a pancake in the pan.

Away from the heat, add the potato and cabbage mixture to the pan. Press down to form a cake. Then pour over the rest of the clarified butter. Place in the oven for 35–40 minutes, shaking occasionally.

Remove from the oven and turn out of the pan. Leave to rest before serving.
Serves 6

Above: *Roast lamb with provençal herbs*
Below left: *Bubble and squeak*

ROAST LAMB WITH PROVENCAL HERBS

2 best ends of lamb, chined and trimmed
for roasting
salt and pepper
bunch of fresh rosemary
a little oil for roasting
Dijon mustard
a little meat stock

For the persillage
100 g (4 oz) butter
50 g (2 oz) shallots, chopped and cooked in
a little white wine
50 g (2 oz) fresh parsley, chopped
225 g (8 oz) fresh white breadcrumbs

Preheat the oven to 200–220°C/400–425°F/Gas Mark 6–7.

Prepare the persillage by melting the butter and adding the other ingredients. Mix well; persillage should be soft, not sloppy.

Heat a roasting tray in the oven. Season the racks of lamb with salt, pepper and rosemary. Add a little oil to the roasting tray, place the lamb in the tray fat side down and cook in the oven for 4–5 minutes.

Turn the lamb on to the bones and cook for a further 4–5 minutes, or until pink. Remove the lamb from the tray and leave to rest for 5 minutes in a warm place.

Brush the back of the lamb with Dijon mustard. Spread the persillage as thinly as possible over the lamb, pressing firmly to make it stick.

Glaze under a hot grill until the persillage is evenly browned, then carve into cutlets and serve. To make a gravy, skim the excess fat from the pan juices, add a little meat stock and bring to the boil; reduce to half its volume. Pour through a fine sieve and serve with the lamb.
Serves 4

GRATIN DE JABRON

4 potatoes, approx 1.25 kg (2½ lb)
75 g (3 oz) unsalted butter
2 cloves garlic, crushed
salt and pepper
150 ml (¼ pt) double cream
150 ml (¼ pt) single cream
150 ml (¼ pt) milk
75 g (3 oz) Cheddar cheese, grated

Preheat the oven to 200°C/400°F/Gas Mark 6.

Half cook the potatoes, allow to cool for about 10 minutes. Peel and cut each one into about 5 or 6 slices.

Place the butter in a frying pan and allow to melt, add the garlic and mix well. Add the sliced potatoes and toss together, then season and place into an ovenproof dish. Mix the creams and milk together and pour over the potatoes, then sprinkle with cheese. Place in the oven for about 15–20 minutes until cooked.
Serves 4

Above: *Treacle tart*

CREME BRULEE

600 ml (1 pt) double cream
1 vanilla pod
3 egg yolks
100 g (4 oz) caster sugar
100 g (4 oz) demerara sugar

Put three-quarters of the double cream in a heavy saucepan or double boiler with the vanilla pod and bring to the boil. Mix the remaining cream well with the egg yolks and caster sugar and pour into the boiling cream. Stir constantly over a gentle heat until the mixture thickens, but do not allow it to boil or it will curdle. Remove from the heat and allow to cool.

Discard the vanilla pod, then pour into individual heatproof dishes and chill in the refrigerator until set. Sprinkle an even layer of demerara sugar over the top of each dish and flash under a really hot grill so that the sugar caramelizes quickly. Chill again in the refrigerator before serving.
Serves 6

TREACLE TART

120 g (4½ oz) fresh white breadcrumbs
365 g (12½ oz) golden syrup
zest of ½ lemon, finely grated
juice of 1 lemon
250 g (9 oz) pâte sucrée or rich shortcrust pastry

Preheat the oven to 190°C/375°F/Gas Mark 5.

Mix together the breadcrumbs, golden syrup, lemon zest and juice. Line a 25 cm (10 inch) flan ring with most of the pâte sucrèe and pour in the mixed ingredients. Using the leftover pastry, make a lattice pattern across the top. Then place in the oven for 20–25 minutes.
Serves 8

BREAD AND BUTTER PUDDING

100 g (4 oz) sultanas
8 slices white bread
100 g (4 oz) butter, melted
1 tbls honey, melted

For the custard mix
1 litre (1¾ pt) milk
100 g (4 oz) caster sugar
4 eggs
a pinch of mixed spice

Preheat the oven to 180°C/350°F/Gas Mark 4. Thoroughly mix all the custard ingredients together.

Place four individual dishes in a deep oven tray and evenly sprinkle the bottom of each dish with sultanas. Then, after trimming the crusts off the bread and cutting each piece into quarters, dip into the melted butter. Layer the bread neatly into the dishes, allowing 2 slices per dish.

Fill the dishes with the custard mix and pour 1 cm (½ inch) of hot water into the oven tray to surround the dishes. Place in the oven for 20–25 minutes until just set and golden brown. Brush the top of each pudding with melted honey and serve.
Serves 4

Below: *Gratin de Jabron*

Above clockwise from top left: *Bread and butter pudding, Lemon meringue pie, Crème brulée*

LEMON MERINGUE PIE

225 g (8 oz) shortcrust pastry

For the filling
100 g (4 oz) butter
5 eggs
juice of 4 lemons
100 g (4 oz) caster sugar

For the meringue topping
3 egg whites
70 g (2¾ oz) caster sugar

Preheat the oven to 180°C/350°F/Gas Mark 4.

Line a 25 cm (10 inch) flan ring with the shortcrust pastry and place greaseproof paper inside. Then fill it with dried beans and bake it blind for 15–20 minutes. Remove from the oven, remove the ring and allow the pastry to cool.

To make the filling, melt the butter in a double boiler. In a separate bowl, mix together the eggs, lemon juice and sugar.

Once the butter is boiling, whisk in the other ingredients and keep whisking until the mixture is smooth and thick (do not allow it to boil again). Then pour the lemon filling into the pastry case, set aside and leave to cool.

Raise the oven temperature to 220°C/425°F/Gas Mark 7. To make the topping, whisk the egg whites until they form stiff peaks, then gently mix in the sugar. Pipe the meringue generously on to the lemon filling and brown in the oven for 3 minutes.
Serves 4

BRIAN TURNER

Cross the threshold of Turner's and the first impression is not that of the self-conscious formality of a classy Chelsea restaurant. Instead you are met by a bevy of rouged gazelles whose smiles are a merciful relief from the starched sang-froid of the traditional major-domo. But there is no mistaking the *patron*, who comes bounding up behind his hostesses like a cocky labrador eager to welcome you to his pad. Brian Turner is not just in the business of feeding, he wants you to be entertained as well. He revels in his work and enjoys his status as a leading light on the London restaurant circuit with a place of his own neatly encamped within that fashionable enclave bounded by Walton Street and Sloane Avenue which includes the likes of Bibendum, Zen, Fifty-One Fifty-One, Le Suquet and many more.

Behind the glitter and *joie de vivre*, the scene is altogether more Orwellian. The kitchen at Turner's is as tiny and windowless as a submarine galley and seven cooks ranged shoulder to shoulder work sandwiched between hot stoves and stainless steel preparation tables like proverbial sardines in their can. Given the conditions, the atmosphere promises as much calm as a short fuse in a bundle of gelignite. But the charm and lively humour which Turner weaves upon his guests are applied equally on his staff, who busy themselves happily to the sounds of Capital Radio from a transistor perched between bottles on a shelf. 'It keeps us in touch with the outside world,' he says. Certainly, Turner has a way with people which is rare amongst chefs, who are often autocratic in their demands or too preoccupied to look to the left or the right of their copper pans. If sparks fly in his kitchen, they come from his tongue alone and he does not stand for any silliness. Yet his style is more subtle in that he has the uncanny gift of mixing as one of the boys while leaving them under no illusion as to who is the leader of the pack. The result is a motivated brigade who enjoy an *esprit de corps* essential in a cramped

kitchen playing for high culinary stakes in a very competitive field.

However, Turner's attitude to people extends beyond his own restaurant. Through his work with the Académie Culinaire de France and as chief adjudicator for the City and Guild's Advance Cookery Examination, he is deeply committed to the education of the young. There has always been a strong streak of the teacher inside him and this has endowed him with a natural talent for bringing up those under his command. He knows how to delegate and during each service the burden of supervision at the hotplate falls principally to Mark Clayton, whom Turner calls 'Chef' – the traditional form of address normally reserved for the boss. Brian Turner is less the craftsman-cook and more the chef-impresario who has achieved the top grade by shrewd direction and the careful training of an enthusiastic team.

The path that led to the Gucci-trodden environs of SW3 began in a transport café on a trunk road south of Leeds – a convenient stop-off for escaped cons from Wakefield Prison who regularly raided the place for cigarettes and cash on fog-bound nights. On Saturdays and school holidays, Brian helped his dad dish up hearty plates of fried staples for the hungry truck drivers who passed by and even now he enjoys making bacon sandwiches for himself and his friends before their summer pilgrimages to Lords – although the ritual today is more likely to be accompanied by a bottle of Bollinger than a mug of tea.

The buzz of the café and the smell of bacon fat set the seal on the young Yorkshireman's future. In 1959, when he was just thirteen, Brian took up cookery at his local grammar school in Morley. By now he was also an active member of the Salvation Army and in time he became an accomplished tuba player in the band. Inevitably, the presence of an adolescent Bible-thumping cook provided the boys at

Morley Grammar with some rich bait for a little sport in the playground. But they did not get very far. Their prey may have had an artistic and spiritual soul but it was cloaked in a stubbornly ambitious six-foot persona with muscles to prove it. 'If I slap you one on the nose, you'll know I'm not a sissy,' he would tell them.

In his cookery classes, he was something of a star and undoubtedly teacher's pet. Elsie Bibby – a bespectacled spinster who had once taught the late Michael Smith, the distinguished food writer and TV cook – took Brian under her wing and pointed the way forward. When he left school he went to Leeds Technical College where he took a general catering diploma and emerged as one of the leading movers and shakers of his year – although his tutor concluded that he would never make a great chef but might do well in management.

In 1964 Turner travelled to London and took up residence in the Caledonian Home for Christian Gentlemen – a sombre institution of grey walls and grey blankets in Kings Cross – before starting work at Simpsons in the Strand on the modest wage of £9 a week. The first

person he met in the kitchen was Richard Shepherd, one year his senior, and, by a strange conspiracy of fate, from that point on Turner's career shadowed Shepherd's route through the Savoy Grill to a spell in Europe before returning to London and ultimately joining forces at the Capital Hotel. They have been like blood brothers ever since.

It was after his transfer to the Savoy at the end of 1965 that Turner really came to grips with the rudiments of classical cuisine. But the knowledge he acquired in the different departments of the kitchen did not satisfy a young man bent on advancing his education and he put himself through college again – this time to qualify professionally in hotel and catering management.

The determined process of self-improvement did not end there. His next step was to learn French, which he did as a *commis chef* at the Beau Rivage Palace in Lausanne. Outside work he studiously avoided mixing with a clique of expatriate staff and, instead, made friends with the local division of the Salvation Army where he was hailed as a bit of a hero for exercising his broken French at meetings and, not least, for playing his tuba.

By 1970 Turner was back in England and shooting for the top. He had spent seventeen months in the kitchens of Claridges when Richard Shepherd invited him to be his *sous-chef* at the Capital, which opened in May the following year.

Turner came to rest at the Capital for the next fifteen years. There was one short break in 1973 when he became a tutor at South East London Technical College – a moment, perhaps, to test his innate gifts as a teacher. But he missed the adrenalin of the hotplate and Shepherd missed him.

When Richard Shepherd resigned in 1976 some of his key staff followed him to Langan's Brasserie, leaving Turner, who had taken over as head chef at the Capital, somewhat bereft in a kitchen with a Michelin star to foster. The pressures on both men put a strain on their longstanding friendship – an unhappy circumstance which was repaired in time and has since strengthened the bond between them.

In the ten years of his stewardship over the Capital's kitchen, Turner kept the sacred culinary star although it meant that he had to sacrifice the Salvation Army to the gastronomic altar – a matter of choice between the temperance of one movement and the professional intemperance of another. At first he clung to Shepherd's menu, a tried and tested formula which had become as much his own as his predecessor's. Then, with the encouragement of David Levin, the Capital's proprietor, he travelled to France and ate his way round the great tables of Paris, Burgundy and Bordeaux. He absorbed the styles of the contemporary masters, returned home and gradually applied what he had learned. His classical grounding evolved and Turner today is a chef moulded firmly on the modern French kitchen. But, given the necessary currency of critical approbation for his food, he also used the Capital as a rehearsal room for his personality as a restaurateur. He is a man with a substantial ego and the prestige of his Knightsbridge setting was the perfect backdrop for polishing his self-esteem as a high-profile London host to the rich and famous. 'I was building a reputation and I became known around the world. People would ask for Brian Turner,' he says blithely.

Right: *Demure Chelsea chic. A perfect backdrop for the lively wit and welcome of Brian Turner.*

Far right: *The tiny kitchen at Turner's. Patron and head chef, Mark Clayton, sauce the dishes moments before they are carried out to the tables.*

The name now hangs proudly above the door in Walton Street and the image is discreetly promoted by elegantly styled 'T'-shaped monograms etched on glass screens, china and even the occasional pudding – like the *roulé au chocolat blanc*, an 'orgasmic' confection of white and dark chocolate. However, Turner's flights of self-publicity in no way obscure the cast of his cooking or the atmosphere he has created in his restaurant. He deliberately eschews any attempt to make his place a shrine of gastronomic worship because he wants people to have fun as much as to eat well: 'I like to be compared with the best in town but I want my guests to say that they are *enjoying* this more.'

Turner's menus, therefore, make no pretence at innovation. His themes are derivative and based squarely on the honest tenets of *la nouvelle cuisine* with none of the excesses and fanciful tendencies which seem to have characterized the style to its detriment in recent years. All his dishes are executed with restraint. They are pretty, colourful and thoughtfully presented, but nothing interferes with the true flavours of the raw ingredients. Turner is a prime advocate of the old adage of *faites simple* and he insists that all his fresh produce is treated with reverence: 'When God created lettuce leaves,' he declares, 'he did it with love and care. So when we present those leaves on a plate, we should do the same.' A simple plate of vegetables demonstrates that love and care – a colourful, harmonious medley of cauliflower and broccoli florets, batons of carrots, French beans, mangetout and baby turnips crowned with a small potato gratin.

Turner has also mastered another of the great pleasures of this culinary idiom. With beauty and simplicity of presentation, his cooking succeeds in mixing finesse with real guts. The *brandade de sole*, innocent enough on the plate, packs a punch on the palate and is set off perfectly by its niçoise dressing. Similarly, a delicious contrast of taste and texture is achieved in a *tartare de St Jacques* with the sweetness of the raw scallops counterpointed by the sharpness of the gherkin.

Turner's professional development has been heavily influenced by his environment and a sophisticated metropolitan clientele which have steered his way as a chef. The route he chose was well-calculated and it has secured his place as a prominent figure in London's culinary establishment. His food, therefore, is an affair of the mind rather than of the heart. The one billet-doux contained on the recipe pages which does not feature in the repertoire of his kitchen is his remarkable

offering of Yorkshire pudding with fresh foie gras. Turner aptly describes the dish, saying, 'It is from where I started to where I have come.' The synthesis of the two classic components, each drawn from wildly different cultures, neatly expresses the spirit of a man who is equally proud of both his humble roots and his present standing. It is a raw pride which today embraces his pastoral commitment to the craft at large as much as it does to his own restaurant. About the youth entering the trade, Brian Turner – the apostolic chef – says, 'They are the future generation. Therein lies our salvation.' Of his own establishment, he says simply, 'The name's outside. It's Turner's. I want it to become an institution.'

RAW WEST COAST SCALLOPS SPIKED WITH PICKLED GHERKINS AND SHALLOTS

12 miniature gherkins
16 scallops, roe removed
2 tsp chopped shallots
1 tsp lemon juice
olive oil
salt and pepper
a selection of salad leaves – frisée, rocket,
lamb's lettuce, baby spinach leaves
vinaigrette, made with 3 parts oil to 1 part
vinegar and mustard to taste

Cut the gherkins into julienne. Chop up the white flesh of the scallops into fine dice. Place in a bowl with the shallots and gherkins. Add the lemon juice, olive oil, salt and pepper.

Shape the mixture on to the centre of four plates as for a steak tartare. Make up the vinaigrette by thoroughly whisking all the ingredients together. Toss the salad leaves in the vinaigrette – the salad leaves can vary but this mixture works very well. Place the leaves around the tartare to enhance the presentation. Serve immediately.
Serves 4

Above: *A light creamy purée of Dover sole on a bed of green beans*

Left: *Raw west coast scallops spiked with pickled gherkins and shallots*

A LIGHT CREAMY PUREE OF DOVER SOLE ON A BED OF GREEN BEANS

100 g (4 oz) potato
4 fillets Dover sole
150 ml (¼ pt) milk
bunch of spring onions, chopped
2 cloves garlic, cut into slivers
2 leaves gelatine, soaked
salt and pepper
a pinch of grated nutmeg
3 tbls olive oil
150 ml (¼ pt) double cream, lightly
whipped
225 g (8 oz) green beans, lightly cooked
25 g (1 oz) chopped shallots
4 tomatoes, diced
50 g (2 oz) green or black olives, chopped

Preheat the oven to 220°C/425°F/Gas Mark 7.

Boil the potato in its skin until just cooked. Place the Dover sole in a dish with the milk, spring onions and garlic. Cover and cook in the oven for about 5–7 minutes. Strain off the milk into a small pan and add the gelatine leaves; heat until they are dissolved. Set aside to cool slightly.

When the potato is cool enough to handle scoop out all the flesh into a mixing bowl and add the Dover sole and garlic; discard the spring onions. Beat until smooth and sieve if necessary. Fold in the cool gelatine mixture. Season to taste with salt, pepper, nutmeg and 1 tsp olive oil. Let the mixture cool, but not set. Then fold in the whipped cream and check the seasoning.

Mix the beans and shallots and season. Lay the beans on a plate in a circular shape. Form the fish mixture into a 'quenelle' shape with two dessertspoons and place on top of the beans. Place little piles of seasoned, diced tomato round the plate. Mix the remaining olive oil with the olives, pour around the fish purée and serve.
Serves 4

PAN-FRIED CORNISH SEA BASS ON A BED OF CARAMELIZED RED CABBAGE

4 × 175–200 g (6–7 oz) thick, meaty
portions sea bass, with skin left on
1 medium-sized red cabbage, shredded
75 g (3 oz) unsalted butter
300 ml (½ pt) red wine
85 ml (3 fl oz) crème de cassis
150 ml (¼ pt) veal stock
salt and pepper

For the sauce
300 ml (½ pt) fish stock
150 ml (¼ pt) dry white wine
150 ml (¼ pt) Noilly Prat
150 ml (¼ pt) veal stock
1 clove garlic, crushed
1 tsp chopped shallots
300 ml (½ pt) double cream

Make three incisions on the skin of each portion of fish with a sharp knife.

Place the cabbage in a saucepan with 25 g (1 oz) of the butter. Add the wine, cassis and veal stock. Bring to the boil and simmer gently on a low heat for approximately 45

Above: *Pan-fried Cornish sea bass on a bed of caramelized red cabbage*

minutes until the liquid has reduced and the cabbage has caramelized. Stir occasionally. Check for seasoning and keep warm.

To make the sauce, place all the ingredients except the cream in a pan and reduce by two-thirds by fast boiling. Add the cream and reduce again until the sauce is thick enough to coat the back of a spoon generously. Remove from the heat and pass through a fine sieve.

Heat the remaining butter in a pan until hot and seal the sea bass on the flesh side, then turn over on to the skin. Cook over medium heat until crisp, about 10 minutes.

To serve, divide the cabbage on to four plates. Lay the sea bass skin side up on top and pour the sauce around.
Serves 4

BREAST OF MAIZE-FED CHICKEN FILLED WITH CALVES' SWEETBREADS AND PEARL BARLEY

2 × 1.25 kg (2½ lb) maize-fed chickens
splash of egg white
salt and pepper
150 ml (¼ pt) double cream
450 g (1 lb) calves' sweetbreads, soaked in
cold water for at least 6 hours
1 tbls pearl barley, cooked in water for 1
hour
bunch of chives, chopped
a little vegetable oil

For the stock
dash of white wine vinegar
a few peppercorns
1 bay leaf
salt

For the sauce
600 ml (1 pt) veal stock
dash of red wine
dash of ruby port
1 tbls chopped shallots
25 g (1 oz) unsalted butter

Remove the breasts from the chickens, keeping the skin intact, and lightly beat out to flatten slightly. Bone one of the legs and remove the skin. Mince the flesh twice or liquidize in a blender and then pass through a fine sieve. Place in a metal bowl over ice with the egg white and a good pinch of salt. Mix well and gradually add the double cream. Check for seasoning and then rest in the refrigerator for 1 hour.

Rinse the sweetbreads thoroughly and place in a saucepan. Cover with water and add all the stock ingredients. Bring to the boil, then simmer for approximately 10 minutes. Drain and leave to cool. When cool, separate and remove all skin and sinew. Add the sweetbreads and drained, cooked pearl barley to the mousse mixture, add the chives and check for seasoning.

Preheat the oven to 220°C/425°F/Gas Mark 7. Lay one of the chicken breasts on a square of buttered foil, skin side down, season and spread over a thin layer of the

Above: *Breast of maize-fed chicken filled with calves' sweetbreads and pearl barley*

mousse. Roll the chicken breast up tightly, then twist the foil like a cracker. Repeat with the other breasts and rest in the refrigerator for 1 hour.

Place in a roasting tin with a little oil and cook for approximately 10–15 minutes.

To make the sauce, reduce the veal stock with the wine, port, shallots and butter until it reaches coating consistency.

Remove the chicken breasts from the foil and cut into slices. Arrange decoratively on the plates and spoon the sauce over and around. Serve immediately.

Serves 4

SADDLE OF ENGLISH LAMB WITH A VEAL AND WILD MUSHROOM STUFFING

1 × 1.75 kg (4 lb) short saddle of lamb, unboned
100 g (4 oz) lean veal
1 egg, lightly beaten
4 tbls double cream
salt and pepper
450 g (1 lb) wild mushrooms (trompettes, morilles, cèpes), cleaned, trimmed and chopped
25 g (1 oz) herbs in season, chopped
4 thin slices pork back fat
225 g (8 oz) white part of leek, thinly sliced
25 g (1 oz) unsalted butter
1 tbls vegetable oil

For the sauce
1 shallot, chopped
40 g (1½ oz) unsalted butter
85 ml (3 fl oz) Madeira
85 ml (3 fl oz) dry white wine
600 ml (1 pt) lamb stock reduced from 1.2 litres (2 pt)

Preheat the oven to 220–230°C/425–450°F/Gas Mark 7–8.

Remove the paper-thin skin from the outside of the saddle and bone out the saddle completely. (This can be done by your local butcher.) Keep the fillets separately and remove excess fat from the belly flaps, being careful not to make any holes. Tap the flaps out as thinly as possible and trim neatly.

Mince the veal finely, mix in the egg and 2 tbls of double cream. Season the mixture and add 100 g (4 oz) of the wild mushrooms and the herbs. Stuff the saddle with the mixture, using the flaps to hold in the stuffing. Reshape the saddle. Use the pork back fat to hold in the stuffing at each of the open ends and then tie with string to hold the saddle in its original shape.

Roast the meat for approximately 35–45 minutes, depending on the thickness, and test with a skewer if you are unsure. The meat should be fairly pink. Remove from the oven and allow to rest before carving.

While the meat is cooking make the sauce by sweating the shallot in 15 g (½ oz) butter until a light golden brown, add the Madeira and the white wine and reduce almost to a syrupy consistency. Add the lamb stock and reduce by two-thirds. Add the remaining butter and stir well. Pass the sauce through a fine sieve and check seasoning and consistency. Keep warm.

Toss the sliced leek in the butter until cooked, add the remaining double cream and boil until the cream thickens. Season and put to one side. Pan fry the remaining mushrooms in the oil; drain, season and put to one side.

To serve, put a tablespoon of the hot creamed leeks on to the middle of a plate. Spoon some mushrooms over them and finally lay a slice of the lamb on top. Spoon the sauce around and serve.
Serves 6

Below: *Saddle of English lamb with a veal and wild mushroom stuffing*

YORKSHIRE PUDDING WITH FRESH FOIE GRAS AND ONION GRAVY

5 eggs
300 ml (½ pt) milk
300 ml (½ pt) water
275–350 g (10–12 oz) plain flour
2 tsp salt
dash of malt vinegar
18 × 25 g (1 oz) pieces of foie gras
50 g (2 oz) duck or goose fat

For the sauce
225 g (8 oz) onions, thinly sliced
25 g (1 oz) duck or goose fat
85 ml (3 fl oz) Madeira
85 ml (3 fl oz) ruby port
600 ml (1 pt) veal stock
salt and pepper

Make the batter by breaking the eggs and beating lightly. Add the milk and water and mix. Sieve the flour and salt, add to the liquid and beat until the mixture is smooth, with the consistency of double cream. Allow to rest for an hour, then add the malt vinegar.

Make the sauce by slowly frying the onions in the duck or goose fat until golden brown. Drain off the fat from the onions, then add the Madeira and port to the pan. Reduce by two-thirds, then add the veal stock. Reduce the stock to a gravy rather than sauce consistency, then check the seasoning.

Preheat the oven to 220°C/425°F/Gas Mark 7. Put a little duck or goose fat into the bottom of 18 individual bun tins and place in the oven until the fat smokes. Remove from the oven and pour in the batter mixture to the top of each bun tin. Replace in the oven.

Cook for about 10 minutes – do not open the oven door during this time, or the puddings will not rise. Then remove the puddings quickly and pop a piece of foie gras into each one. Replace and cook for a further 3–5 minutes until the foie gras heats up. Do not overcook.

Allow three puddings per serving, pouring a little hot sauce around them. A quick grind of black pepper adds a touch of spice to the dish. Serve immediately.

Serves 6

Above: *Yorkshire pudding with fresh foie gras and onion gravy*

A CONFECTION OF WHITE AND DARK CHOCOLATE WITH A COFFEE SAUCE

For the sponge
2 eggs
40 g (1½ oz) sugar
10 g (¼ oz) cocoa powder
25 g (1 oz) plain flour
2–3 tsp kirsch

For the mousse
1½ leaves gelatine
50 ml (2 fl oz) water
a pinch of salt
50 g (2 oz) liquid glucose
350 g (12 oz) best white chocolate, broken
into small pieces
3 egg yolks
300 ml (½ pt) double cream, whipped

For the coffee sauce
600 ml (1 pt) milk
1 vanilla pod or 1 tsp vanilla essence
6 egg yolks
100 g (4 oz) caster sugar
1 tbls strong coffee or 2 tsp coffee essence

Preheat the oven to 190°C/375°F/Gas Mark 5.

To make the chocolate sponge, place the eggs and sugar in a heatproof bowl over a pan of hot water and whisk until the mixture has reached the ribbon stage and is pale in colour. Sift the cocoa and flour into the mixture and carefully fold in, taking care to lose as little air as possible. Pour the mixture into a greased and lined baking tray 20 × 20 cm (8 × 8 inches) and place in the preheated oven. Cook for 10 minutes.

To make the mousse, soak the gelatine in a little extra water. In a double saucepan, bring the measured water, salt and glucose to the boil over a gentle heat. Remove from the heat, add the soaked gelatine and stir until dissolved then pour over the chocolate. Stir to melt the chocolate and allow to cool. When cool, beat in the egg yolks and fold in the whipped cream very carefully so as not to dispel any air. Set aside.

Sprinkle the chocolate sponge with the kirsch and then cut into strips. Line a semi-

Above: *A confection of white and dark chocolate with a coffee sauce*

circular tube mould carefully and tightly with the strips of sponge and then fill to the top with the chocolate mousse. Cover and place in the refrigerator for 24 hours to set.

To make the coffee sauce, bring the milk to the boil, add the vanilla pod or essence and infuse for 10 minutes. Whisk the egg yolks with the sugar until pale and creamy. Pour the hot milk on to the mixture, whisking continuously. Place in a clean saucepan over gentle heat and, stirring all the time, gradually bring up to just below boiling point – do not allow to boil. Pass through a fine sieve, then add coffee or essence to flavour. Cool.

To serve, turn out the pudding and, using a warm knife, cut two thin slices per portion and serve with the cold coffee sauce.
Serves 6

RICHARD SMITH

Like a game of village cricket on a lazy summer's evening, Yattendon celebrates a singularly English state of mind. Pleasantly somnolent, comfortingly familiar, neat but not pristine and oh, so conservative, Yattendon finds the twentieth century eminently resistible. The houses are of weathered brick or white-washed and Tudor-timbered, and the tiny square wears its discreet emblems of local pride with a whisper of self-satisfaction. A modest woodcarving notes that Yattendon was voted Berkshire's best-kept village in 1978 and the old oak – long since deceased – was replaced by a sapling to mark the Queen's Silver Jubilee.

Across the square from the village stores and post office is the Royal Oak. A hostelry of yore, it too extols the values of the shire counties. Inside, the smell is all wood smoke and polish. There is a bar and a restaurant but both fuse harmoniously as one. In the bar the tables are decked with pinks and gypsophila and an antique high chair bids welcome to young children. Outside one window a wisteria hangs curiously and uncontrollably, casting a confetti of sunlight on the tiled floor, while the top of the bar glitters with a tinsel-chain of silver tankards – the christening mugs and inscribed trophies of a faithful patronage.

The window seats of the lounge are piled with books, newspapers and back numbers of the *Field* and *Country Life*. Sofas and armchairs are of the sink-into variety, there is a bowl of pot-pourri on an escritoire and the fireplace is embellished with eighteenth- and nineteenth-century Coalport. The dining room beyond sparkles with keenly polished mahogany and silver, softened by table arrangements of miniature orchids and giant glass goblets spilling over with fruits and nuts.

Like the village, the Royal Oak is snug, protective, friendly and reassuringly Old England. But, unlike in most English country inns,

the cooking is exceptional. Richard Smith is perhaps less famous than some of his contemporaries but he is, nonetheless, a top-ranking chef and a member of that élite crew, the Académie Culinaire de France, who has set his sights on capturing the middle-ground of British eating-out by the simple device of luring the people to their natural watering hole and then seducing them with good food of an order more commonly associated with a serious restaurant. Rooted as much in the fabric and heritage of our culture as the oak sapling in the square, Smith is breathing new life into the tired limbs and blocked arteries of the country pub.

Richard Smith was born at a most inconvenient time. His mother was making marmalade in the kitchen of her Clapham home when she went into labour one January afternoon in 1948 while his father, a police sergeant, was busy keeping crime off the streets of south London. Mother was fearsomely houseproud and a brilliant cook. The family ate royally on tripe and onions, lamb's tongues with parsley sauce, braised oxtails, Irish stews, herrings and haddock. The scent of cut flowers filled the house and there was always a large bowl of fruit on the dining room table.

In 1969 they moved to North Devon, where mother and father took on the Old Vicarage at West Down, near Ilfracombe, as a guest house. Richard meanwhile abandoned a career in retail management, which he had started four years previously, to pursue a more carefree life beside the sea and to reassemble his great love – an old TR2 sports model. She was an expensive mistress and to pay for her upkeep he took a job at the Candar, a holiday hotel in Ilfracombe. For the next three years he also attended North Devon Technical College on a block release course where he discovered that he shared his mother's aptitude for food. The drop-head playboy gradually began to see cooking and life in a more serious light. Loaded with credit listings

on his diploma, he took off to France for a final fling in his beloved TR and a summer at an hotel in the Dordogne where he was dubbed 'Coeur de Lion' for his ability to endure the intense heat of a cramped and unventilated kitchen. When the chef was struck by a nervous collapse, Smith found himself in charge and coped. He returned to Devon two stone the lighter but the experience filled him with new confidence for the future.

A year later he married Kate, an olive-eyed textile graduate from Leeds University who gave up a Ph.D to follow her husband to the Hôtel de la Paix in Lausanne, where she worked as a waitress. Within a week of her arrival, the happy sacrifice turned to drama when she was arrested by the immigration police for entering Switzerland without a work permit. However, the hotel came to an unspoken accommodation with the authorities and she was released. Shortly afterwards, the annual police ball was held at the de la Paix and Kate suddenly found herself serving her erstwhile gaolers – an exercise in charm and restraint which she has never forgotten.

The middle Seventies saw the Smiths as seasonal commuters chasing jobs between Lausanne, London and North Devon. The plan was for them eventually to take over the Old Vicarage but the ideas of the senior and junior branches of the family did not coincide and by 1976 Richard and Kate had decided to make their own way. She accepted a post as a tutor in the catering department of the Technical College and he enrolled on an advanced cookery course before taking up a position as head chef at the Watersmeet Hotel in Woolacombe. The inevitable happened – when Smith arrived for a lecture in wine service, he found his wife on the dais at the head of the room.

When the Watersmeet closed for the winter, it was time to think again. By now Smith was a well-qualified and highly professional cook who had inherited his mother's obsession with perfection. In all his jobs he had proved himself a determined worker and dedicated craftsman – qualities which also seemed to blend easily with his happy-go-lucky nature. But he was now approaching thirty and his career had yet to strike a rhythm or show any clear signs of a goal.

His major break came in 1977, when Kate was interviewed by Richard Shepherd at Langan's Brasserie for a job running the front-of-house. Kate left Shepherd with such a strong impression of the attributes of her husband that he ended up hiring him and not her. Smith spent the next five years as Shepherd's *sous-chef* and the two have been firm friends ever since, in spite of one calamitous occasion when Smith set a chip pan alight and devastated the whole of Langan's basement kitchen.

By 1982 Smith was well primed to command his own kitchen and he moved to the Greenhouse, David Levin's Mayfair offshoot of the Capital Hotel Restaurant. It was the final stepping-stone in a prolonged apprenticeship towards the couple's proprietorial dreams which, until then, appear to have lain dormant. Smith spent two good years at the Greenhouse while Kate led the search for a suitable property – a thankless effort which came to nothing. Eventually, as they were on the point of taking up the management of an hotel in Wiltshire, David Levin intervened with details about the Royal Oak. This, he said, was what they should go for and it was only after they had seen the old inn – once owned by Levin himself – that they believed him. They put the proposition to their bank, sold their house and by January 1984 were installed. Twelve months later Egon Ronay made the Royal Oak his 'Pub of the Year'.

Unlike David Wilson at the Peat Inn, who gave up his successful bar food trade, Smith has believed from the start that it would be wrong to concentrate exclusively on his restaurant. 'Pubs are the right setting for food in this country,' he says. 'To some extent, restaurants are alien to the English countryside and alien to our culture while pubs are part of our heritage.' It irritates him that pubs are too readily associated with a cheap, microwave mentality, and one senses a hint of a quiet but almost messianic passion in his desire to restore gastronomic self-esteem to a faded institution.

'It's much easier to sell food in a pub than in a restaurant,' he says. 'The only negative in customers' minds is price, because they have been conditioned to expect food for £2.00 or less. Good bar food must always offer value but it can never be that cheap. However, all the other factors in a pub are favourable. There is no obligation to buy. With a restaurant you have to make the commitment to book a table, walk through the door and eat. It's a much bigger step for someone who is not accustomed to doing that.'

The Smiths are in the business of removing any such steps and

Above: *The Royal Oak at Yattendon. The homely promise of its leafy exterior is fulfilled by the deliciousness of the food inside.*

building bridges in their place. Pub and restaurant coexist like a marriage made in heaven. One kitchen and the same chef produce the food for both and the two menus have no qualms about dishes overlapping into the other's province, although setting and price have a bearing on the materials and style deployed in each area. Grilled sardines and calves' kidneys with black pudding suit comfortably in the bar while red mullet and John Dory are more likely to grace the restaurant. The important point is that quality, integrity and conviction are common to both departments.

Smith's upbringing and culinary background have given him a very shrewd understanding of the psychology of appetite in an English rural setting. He does not pander to what might be the predictable tastes of his local clientele because that would be patronizing to them and unworthy of him. In form and content, his food is deceptively sophisticated but it succeeds in striking a clever balance between pleasing the eye and satisfying the belly. 'My food must invite people to eat rather than to admire. It must look appetizing rather than pretty,' he says.

Homemade noodles, lubricated with a lemon juice and fish stock reduction to which he adds unpasteurized Jersey cream, are dressed with langoustines, Cornish scallops and spears of asparagus. The appeal of the dish lies as much in its colour and arrangement as in the sight of the fat, juicy scallops which have been grilled whole with the corals hanging cheekily off their sides. The plate looks scrumptious and begs to be eaten instantly.

Part of the trick is to allow the raw ingredients to speak for themselves and never to put up dishes which look tortured to death. A loin of fallow deer is presented simply with its accompaniment of chestnuts and fresh figs. And this hearty, generous approach to the food applies equally to Smith's style in saucing which, like good wine, tends to be full-bodied, well-balanced and unctuous without any traces of bitterness or stickiness.

As befits a country inn of this class, cheeses and puddings rise to a gastronomic crescendo. The bar offers a patrician's version of the ploughman's lunch with a French and English mix of up to fifteen cheeses from Patrick Rance's store at Streatley, near Reading. The puddings properly lean towards England and even French-inspired confections like the *beignets soufflés* are Anglo-Saxon in spirit — whopping great big cloud balls of deep-fried choux buns rolled in cinnamon sugar. Similarly, a hot pancake is mercilessly generous with its stuffing of blackcurrants — the indulgence magnified outrageously with rich dollops of vanilla ice and piped cream. The whole is a magnificent exercise in contrasting colours, textures and temperatures.

While Smith's cooking is uncompromising in the standards he sets himself, in the end his only concern is the pleasure he brings to a large and faithful local following. He shies away from any attempt to impress in the manner of grand restaurants, which he holds up as the playgrounds of cynical palates and American tourists bent on doing the rounds of the multi-starred trougheries because it is the thing to

Above: *Richard and Kate Smith with some offerings from their bar menu. The 'Ploughman's' features up to 15 cheeses supplied by Patrick Rance.*

do. Many of his restaurant clients are regulars in the bar who have made an easy transition from one to the other because the familiar atmosphere and friendliness of the Royal Oak with its genuine sense of hospitality encourages them to cross that bridge.

Smith sees pubs as the natural bistros of Britain where good food will never intimidate but where people can learn to respect and enjoy eating out as an important element in their lives. As an accepted medium in our social culture, the pub should be well placed to universalize the habit. However, for the moment Richard Smith cuts a lonely figure.

CRAB AND AVOCADO SALAD

1 × 1 kg (2 lb) live cock crab
2–3 tbls mayonnaise
1 tsp chopped chives
1 tbls chopped parsley
dash of Worcestershire sauce
pepper
assorted salad leaves such as white and
yellow curly endive, Belgian endive,
batavia, oakleaf, radicchio, blanched
dandelion, lamb's lettuce and edible
flowers such as nasturtium and borage
2 avocados
corn-oil based vinaigrette made with 6 tbls
oil, 2 tbls wine vinegar and 1 tsp Dijon
mustard
300 ml (½ pt) mayonnaise flavoured with
Dijon mustard, to serve

Plunge the live crab into boiling, salted water and cook for 15 minutes. Remove from the pan and place the crab on its back. Twist off the claws and legs, crack the shell of each one carefully and extract all the flesh. Open up the crab by first pulling off the tail from the underside and throwing away. Slide the point of a knife between the shell and body, loosen and ease it out, set aside. Scrape out the flesh from the inside but discard the abdominal sac just behind the mouth. Remove the soft gills from around the body, cut in half down the middle and extract all the flesh from the cavities and leg sockets. Discard all the shell and unusable flesh.

Mix the brown meat with the mayonnaise, chives and parsley. Season with a little Worcestershire sauce and pepper to taste.

Arrange the salad leaves on the plates. Divide the brown crabmeat between the plates and surround with small piles of white crabmeat.

Stone and peel the avocados and fan by slicing very thinly from top to bottom. Arrange on the plates then dress the salads with a thin thread of vinaigrette. Serve with a sauceboat of mayonnaise flavoured with Dijon mustard.
Serves 4

Right: *Crab and avocado salad*

HOMEMADE NOODLES WITH LANGOUSTINE, SCALLOPS, ASPARAGUS AND LEMON SAUCE

12 live langoustines
12 asparagus spears
8 scallops, rinsed and drained
15 g (½ oz) unsalted butter
sea salt and black pepper
a little fish stock

For the noodles
150 g (5 oz) plain flour
a pinch of salt
a drop of olive oil
1 egg
2 egg yolks

For the lemon sauce
juice of ½ lemon
85 ml (3 fl oz) good fish stock
150 ml (¼ pt) Channel Island double
cream
salt and pepper

To make the noodles, combine all the ingredients together to form a smooth paste and rest for 1 hour. Roll out *very* thinly and cut into fine strips. Put into boiling salted water and bring back to the boil. Take off the heat and drain immediately, then leave in cold water for 20 minutes.

Drop the langoustines into boiling salted water, bring the water back to the boil and remove them almost immediately. Remove the shells, keeping the heads on four langoustine for garnish.

Trim 4 cm (1½ inch) tips from the asparagus spears and blanch in boiling salted water. Refresh in iced water and set aside.

To make the lemon sauce, place the lemon juice and fish stock in a saucepan and reduce by seven-eighths. Then add the cream, season and put aside.

Grill the scallops on a charcoal grill or sauté them in a very hot frying pan for about 30 seconds to 1 minute each side. They should be succulent inside.

Drain the noodles, then toss in the butter in a warmed frying pan. Do not let the butter burn. Season with salt and pepper and toss several times until hot.

Above: *Homemade noodles with langoustine, scallops, asparagus and lemon sauce*

Reheat the asparagus tips in boiling salted water for a few seconds. Reheat the peeled langoustines in a little fish stock, but do not boil.

Place the noodles on individual plates or a serving dish and put the scallops, langoustines and asparagus tips on top. Pour a thread of sauce over the noodles, leaving the fish uncovered.

Serves 4

LOIN OF VENISON WITH CHESTNUTS AND FRESH FIGS

8 well-hung medallions of venison,
approximately 7 mm (⅓ inch) thick
24 chestnuts, blanched and peeled
4 figs

For the sauce
1 tbls vegetable oil
1 knuckle of veal
2.25 kg (5 lb) venison bones and trimmings
3 large onions, roughly chopped
225 g (8 oz) carrots, roughly chopped
½ head celery, chopped
1 leek
water, to cover
a sprig of fresh thyme
a few parsley stalks
3 bay leaves
50 g (2 oz) chopped shallots
1 tbls clarified butter
black pepper
200 ml (7 fl oz) ruby port
salt

To make the sauce, heat the oil in a large saucepan. Fry the bones and vegetables until golden then cover with water, add the herbs and bring slowly to the boil, skimming regularly. Simmer for 4–5 hours, ensuring that the stock is kept clear of fat and scum; by the end of the cooking time it should have attained a pale golden colour. Strain and reduce on a high heat, removing any scum, until the sauce almost coats a spoon.

Fry the shallots in 1 teaspoon clarified butter with a little black pepper in a heavy-based saucepan. Add the port to the pan and reduce. Add 300 ml (½ pt) venison stock to the pan and simmer for 10 minutes. Strain out the shallots and reduce the sauce until it coats the back of a spoon. Adjust the seasoning.

Add the remaining butter to a frying pan and heat until very hot, almost smoking. Add the medallions and cook for 30 seconds–1 minute, depending on thickness, on each side. They should be sealed on the outside but still pink and juicy inside.

Simmer the chestnuts in the sauce until cooked. Slice the figs on to a buttered tray and place under a grill to cook through.

To serve, place 2 medallions of venison on each plate and arrange the chestnuts in the centre, and the figs to one side. Spoon a little sauce on to each portion.
Serves 4

SUPREME OF CHICKEN WITH SCALLOPS, WILD MUSHROOMS AND CREAMY CURRY SAUCE

2 tbls clarified butter
4 chicken supremes, skinned and trimmed of fat
salt and pepper
8 scallops, rinsed and drained
225 g (8 oz) wild mushrooms (cèpes, chanterelles, mousserons, morilles, girolles etc), cleaned, trimmed and stalks scraped as necessary
1 tbls chopped chives, to garnish

For the curry sauce
50 g (2 oz) finely chopped shallots
½ bay leaf
1–2 tsp clarified butter
½ tsp good quality curry powder or paste
50 ml (2 fl oz) chicken stock
150 ml (¼ pt) double cream

To make the curry sauce, fry the shallot and bay leaf in the butter until golden brown. Add the curry powder or paste and dilute with the chicken stock. Simmer for 10 minutes to reduce by about one-third until the consistency is that of a paste. Add the cream and simmer; if it is too thick, add more chicken stock, if too thin reduce again. Pass through a fine sieve and keep warm.

Preheat the oven to 230°C/450°F/Gas Mark 8.

Heat an ovenproof frying pan, add 1 tbls clarified butter and, when moderately hot, add the seasoned supremes, outer side down. Agitate the pan to prevent them sticking. When they begin to colour on the underside, put the pan in the oven, checking that they are not sticking.

Grill the scallops for about 30 seconds to 1 minute on each side, making sure that they are cooked right through but still juicy.

Above: *Supreme of chicken with scallops, wild mushrooms and creamy curry sauce*
Far left: *Loin of venison with chestnuts and fresh figs*

Sauté the mushrooms in the remaining butter and season. Drain on kitchen paper and keep warm.

After about 5 minutes remove the supremes from the oven; they should be cooked through but juicy. Place on a serving dish, golden side up, with the sautéed mushrooms. Run a thread of sauce over the mushrooms and on the plate, avoiding the chicken. Add the scallops and sprinkle with chopped chives.
Serves 4

GREAT BRITISH CHEFS

RED MULLET, JOHN DORY AND MUSSELS WITH CHIVE SAUCE

300 ml (½ pt) mixed fish stock and dry
white wine
600 ml (1 pt) mussels, cleaned and
scrubbed
120 ml (4 fl oz) double cream
salt and pepper
2 × 350 g (12 oz) John Dory fillets, skinned
and trimmed
2 × 275 g (10 oz) red mullets, filleted
2 tbls chopped chives

Put the fish stock and white wine into a
heavy-based pan and bring rapidly to the boil.
Add the mussels, cover with a tight-fitting lid
and cook until the mussels open. This should
only take a few seconds. Remove the mussels
and set aside. Discard the shells and any
mussels which don't open.

Strain 200 ml (7 fl oz) of the liquor into a
measuring jug and set aside. Reduce the
remaining liquor with the double cream and
adjust the seasoning as well as the consistency, if necessary adding more fish stock to
make a light coating sauce. Set aside.

Put the fish fillets in a pan and cover with
the reserved strained liquor, adding more
fish stock and white wine if necessary. Cover
the pan with tinfoil or a tight-fitting lid and
bring to the boil. Turn off the heat and allow
the fish to sit in the liquor for a minute or
two. Add the mussels to warm through. Take
all the fish out and drain quickly. Add the
chives to the sauce and reheat.

Pour the sauce on to a serving dish or
plates and place the fish on top. Serve
immediately.
Serves 4

Above: *Hot blackcurrant and sloe gin pancakes*

Below: *Red mullet, John Dory and mussels with chive sauce*

HOT BLACKCURRANT AND SLOE GIN PANCAKES

For the pancakes
100 g (4 oz) plain flour
a pinch of salt
2 eggs
300 ml (½ pt) milk
2 tbls melted butter

For the sauce
750 g (1½ lb) blackcurrants
150 ml (¼ pt) sloe gin
caster sugar to taste
1 tbls arrowroot, to thicken

To serve
scoops of homemade vanilla ice cream and
Guernsey double cream, whipped to
decorate

Mix and cook the pancakes in the normal way
and place on a serving dish. Set aside and keep
warm.

To make the sauce, cook the blackcurrants

and sloe gin together until the currants are tender, about 15–20 minutes. Add sugar to taste and thicken with arrowroot.

To assemble, lay out each pancake and spoon on plenty of the sauce. Fold the pancakes in half and let the filling spill out.

Serve hot with homemade vanilla ice cream and whipped cream.

Serves 8

BEIGNETS SOUFFLES WITH LEMON SAUCE

For the choux paste
150 ml (¼ pt) water
150 ml (¼ pt) milk
100 g (4 oz) unsalted butter
a pinch of sugar
a pinch of salt
150 g (5 oz) plain flour
4–5 eggs, beaten
a little caster sugar mixed with powdered cinnamon

For the lemon sauce
100 g (4 oz) unsalted butter
100 g (4 oz) caster sugar
grated zest and juice of 4 lemons
3 egg yolks

To make the choux paste, bring the water, milk, butter, sugar and salt to the boil. Add the flour and beat until it leaves the sides of the pan. Add the eggs and beat well.

Heat the oil in a deep fryer to medium and drop in the choux paste in 2.5 cm (1 inch) balls. Allow to puff up, turning occasionally. Remove after approximately 8 minutes, drain and roll in cinnamon sugar.

To make the lemon sauce, melt the butter, sugar, lemon zest and juice in a double boiler. Add the egg yolks and stir frequently until thickened. This will take about 30 minutes. Remove from the heat and pass through a fine sieve. Check the flavour and adjust the sugar if necessary. Serve in a sauceboat with the beignets.

Serves 6–8

Right: *Beignets soufflés with lemon sauce*

STEPHEN ROSS

The white Rolls Royce looked uncomfortably out of place as it pitched over the cattle grid past the flock of Jacob sheep and Tom, Dick and Harry, three disagreeable West African pigmy goats, grazing in their paddock. The car drew to a halt outside the front door and from its white-upholstered, lace-cushioned interior emerged a short, stout, Havana-drooling man who blanched visibly at the absence of any uniformed staff. Nevertheless, he asked the jolly-faced young assistant who welcomed him to arrange for his car to be valet parked. Disguising her anxiety, she referred the request to the proprietor of the house who willingly performed the task. On his return to the front hall, the new arrival confronted his host – whom he took to be the head gardener from the informality of his dress – and enquired tetchily if all were well.

'There are an awful lot of trees growing in that car park,' he snapped.

'Goodness me,' replied Stephen Ross, 'the trees are far too valuable to risk damaging them.'

This exchange does more than just demonstrate Ross's wry humour which he delivers in a smooth bass monotone that is almost Clement Freudian in its pitch. He is particular about where his priorities lie and the philosophy behind Homewood Park, his *restaurant avec chambres*, is shared enthusiastically by both staff and clients alike. His brand of hospitality shows little patience for the chic paraphernalia, gloss and pretension which have become standard fare on the English country house hotel scene. As far as he is concerned, the best environment for people to unwind in is an informal one. Good quality staff in his vocabulary have less to do with professional dexterity and more to do with friendliness and person-ality. He is not gulled by food fashion because he knows that intellectual appreciation is not necessarily a prerequisite of culinary

excellence: 'To create a feeling of *home*, the cooking must be very good, but it must never dictate.' Ross is one of the few chef-proprietors who have studiously avoided the pitfalls of confusing quality with technical indulgence in the kitchen because, as he sees it, his first duty is to give people a good time. Instinctively, he knows that hype and grandeur are not the honest answers to restoring the stressed spirits of human beings. Better than most, he understands people and what pleases them.

The first 17 years of Stephen Ross's home life were spent in Grimsby, at the mouth of the Humber estuary – 'as far from any centre of gastronomy as you could get'. He was born into the Ross Fish dynasty, a powerful family business founded by his grandfather which at its zenith owned a fleet of 200 trawlers. As a child he saw little of his busy father and his mother, a formidably talented lady, ran a precisely ordered household which at table enjoyed the perks of their privileged status. Lobster and Dover sole were part of the regular diet and Stephen still recalls the wonder of his mother's steamed halibut with egg sauce.

Ross was educated at Dover College in Kent, and his schooldays were made of the stuff of boy-heroes: head of school, captain of cricket, the 1st XV and a comfortable academic record which took him on to read politics and economics at Bristol University.

However, at home his father had grown tired of the cut and thrust of the fish industry. In 1965 he sold up and moved the family to Worcestershire, where he bought the Cottage in the Wood in Malvern Wells for his eldest son Michael who had cut his teeth as a hotel manager with Trusthouse Forte. With Michael and his wife running the kitchen and restaurant, mother hosting the bar 'with great panache' and father fussing over the accounts, young Stephen soon became seduced by the buzz of their new life and a grand

scenario was hatched to bring him into the business with a view to establishing a new Ross dynasty of hotelkeepers.

At Bristol, Ross abandoned the graduate mill and the promise of a blue-chip job in international marketing. He also fell in love with a bright young linguist and went on to score a double coup by attaching an extraordinary business proposition to his proposal of marriage. She accepted both and it was agreed that, after a suitable period of training, the future Mrs Penny Ross would join the family firm as a full-time employee.

So in the summer of 1970, the happily betrothed collected their degrees and postponed the wedding for a year to apprentice themselves to two of the grandees of the British restaurant stage. Penny went to the Hole in the Wall in Bath under George Perry-Smith and, after some persuasion, Kenneth Bell agreed to take Stephen on at Thornbury Castle – Egon Ronay's first 'Restaurant of the Year' in 1969 and, along with the Hole in the Wall, one of the most illustrious places outside London.

Ross accepted a beggar's wage of £10 a week which barely paid for his digs in a 'converted pigsty' nearby. It was a brief but worthwhile sacrifice which soon led Bell to adopt him as his most favoured graduate. However, in the early days, this was hard work on the sink-or-swim principle: 'You had to learn fast or not at all.' On one occasion, Bell simply handed him Elizabeth David's *French Country Cooking* and instructed him to make a *coq au vin*. Ross had never heard of Elizabeth David, let alone her *coq au vin*, but he was quick to master the recipe and the rest of Thornbury's catholic repertoire of dishes, many of which were inspired by Bell's own travels to France, Spain, Portugal and Greece.

In September 1971, having exchanged their vows at the altar, Stephen and his bride went home to the Malvern Hills where they were set to fulfil their secular promise with the family. However, within six months the professional marriage of the two brothers hit the rocks and it became clear that the original plan would have to be scuttled.

The family schism was a traumatic period in the young couple's life but when Kenneth Bell visited the Cottage in the Wood for lunch one day in early 1972, Ross's problems evaporated into joy; his mentor offered him a partnership in a new restaurant he was thinking of opening in Bristol. By the spring of that year, Stephen was back at Thornbury where he and Penny were installed, more agreeably this time, in one of the Castle's staff flats.

The search for premises in Bristol drew a blank. Eventually, on Bell's security, they bought the lease on a handsome Georgian house in Bath which was once the residence of the famous 18th century dandy Beau Nash. The new restaurant opened in July 1973 and they called it Popjoys — a name which was greeted with sombre disapproval by the licensing justices who considered it promoted 'connotations of popular music and revelry'. Ross enlightened the bench by explaining that Beau Nash's mistress was a certain Juliana

Popjoy who had been caused such anguish after her lover's death that she had lived the last days of her life in a hollow tree to avoid the temptation of sleeping with another man. Suitably humoured, the magistrates granted the licence and just two months off his twenty-fifth birthday Stephen Ross found himself at the head of his first kitchen with Penny supervising the restaurant's two dining rooms.

Inside 18 months, Michelin, Egon Ronay and the *Good Food Guide* had all invested Popjoys with their respective decorations and Ross took his place in the gallery of the good and the great. Wisely, Kenneth Bell never interfered with the work of his junior partner and although the new restaurant's parentage cast it in the hue of 'son of Thornbury', Ross went his own way and in many respects Popjoys was ahead of its time. Even the china was a trendy chocolate brown — an aberration which now fills him with disgust — and his menu struck a mix of orthodoxy and invention. Traditional braises and stews were contrasted with fanciful confections like scallop-sculpted pastry shells filled with creamed and herbed seafood.

The Rosses had little trouble attracting customers to their tables but in spite of this success and the opening of a food shop as an additional source of revenue for the restaurant, the business rewarded their pride more than their pockets. In 1980 they decided that it was time to move on, having concluded that the economics of running a small country house hotel looked like offering a more secure prospect for the future. Kenneth Bell sold them his share of the company they had set up eight years previously and, against all advice, Ross bought Homewood Park, a large Victorian house in 10 acres of land just five miles south of Bath, before he had found a buyer for Popjoys. Worse still, as Homewood was a private house, there was no planning consent and no licence to run it as an hotel and restaurant.

But the confidence of youth conquered sound judgement and in December 1980 Popjoys was reincarnated as Homewood Park — a restaurant with eight bedrooms. Flying the colours of goodwill and good reputation, the business was an instant success and, after breaking even in their first year, the Rosses have since expanded their retreat to a complement of 15 rooms.

The fascination and joy of Stephen Ross's cooking lies in its wilful exploitation of the gustatory preferences of the British. He likes to describe his style as 'contemporary English' because of his use of local, and often home-grown, materials which he cooks and assembles in a particularly English way. However, while presentation and technique may often appear 'contemporary' – to hint at the French origins of *nouvelle cuisine* – the substance is essentially patriotic in execution. There are, of course, many modern British chefs who are vaguely pursuing this line but none is doing it with quite the philosophical application of Ross. Whereas some cooks may go to the markets for their inspiration, his approach to planning dishes is academic. He is at his most creative sitting at a desk working on food with pen and paper before testing his ideas in the kitchen.

Ross has a well-developed sense of geography, climate and culture which underpins his grasp of what satisfies the British appetite. Crispy coatings and spiciness, pies and tarts, fillings and stuffings – all adored by this nation – are signals of his approach. His spiced sweetbreads, which are sautéed in flour seasoned with cumin, cardamom and coriander, even smack of 'fish and chips' applied to offal. Saucing adopts a similar strategy, appealing to the Englishman's partiality for thicker and more textural liquids.

However, Ross is neither chauvinist nor xenophobe. Much of his cooking is squarely French provincial in its derivation: cassoulet is echoed in his stuffed duckling with lentils, bacon and garlic, and his braised shoulder of lamb is rooted in an old Elizabeth David recipe for *daube à l'avignonnaise*. The writings of Vergé and Guérard have also provided a stimulus for his creative gifts and culinary wit. He loves to amuse and entertain his guests with flashes of novelty like his stuffed breast of guinea fowl which he wraps in a coil of puffed pastry – an invention tempered by the technical advantage of a casing with no edges.

In spite of the intense competition induced by the proliferation of country house hotels in the 1980s, Homewood Park has carried off more prizes than most, including the *Good Hotel Guide*'s César award for best of the genre in 1986 and Egon Ronay's 'Hotel of the Year' in 1987. The record of success is one which Ross insists on sharing with his staff and he prefers to talk of the 'Homewood style' as the result of his team's effort rather than the consequence of any personal achievement. Nevertheless, behind his deceptively modest and easy-going exterior lie an astute mind and a generosity of spirit which rely firmly on the principle that people, not extravagant furnishings and designer food, are the true ingredient of good hospitality.

Left: *Built in the 18th-century and enlarged in the 19th, Homewood Park is set in 10 acres of garden and woodland just south of Bath.*

Right: *Stephen and Penny Ross in the walled garden where they grow a wide variety of fruits, vegetables and herbs for the kitchen.*

Above: *Salad of spiced sweetbreads and girolle mushrooms*

SALAD OF SPICED SWEETBREADS AND GIROLLE MUSHROOMS

225 g (8 oz) calves' sweetbreads
1 stick celery, chopped
1 carrot, chopped
a few black peppercorns
75 g (3 oz) plain flour
salt and pepper
a large pinch of ground cumin
a large pinch of ground cardamom
a large pinch of ground coriander
selection of decorative lettuces,
endive and cucumber
3 tbls olive oil
1 tbls hazelnut oil
1 tbls white wine vinegar
75 g (3 oz) clarified butter
50 g (2 oz) fresh girolles

Clean the sweetbreads and place in a pan of boiling salted water with the celery, carrot and peppercorns and blanch for approximately 15 minutes. Remove from the pan and carefully trim the sweetbreads of any membrane. Carefully press under a weight to remove excess blood. When cool cut into 5 mm (¼ inch) thick slices.

Prepare a highly seasoned flour by adding the salt, pepper, cumin, cardamom and coriander.

Shortly prior to serving, dress the salad materials in a vinaigrette made with olive oil, hazelnut oil and vinegar and arrange decoratively on large plates.

Roll the sliced sweetbreads in the seasoned flour then sauté in hot clarified butter until golden. Season and sauté the girolles in the same way. Arrange around the salad.

Serves 4

WATERCRESS PANCAKES FILLED WITH SAFFRON CRAB

1 small onion, chopped
a little unsalted butter
150 ml (¼ pt) single cream
150 ml (¼ pt) milk
8–10 bunches watercress, leaves only

For the pancakes
4 eggs
50 g (2 oz) unsalted butter, melted
4 tbls plain flour
oil for cooking

For the filling
1 large crab, cooked
salt and pepper
a pinch of saffron powder
4 tbls double cream
fresh parsley, chopped

Sweat the onion in the butter. When soft, add the cream and milk and bring to the boil. Add the watercress and cook for a further 2 minutes. Blend in a liquidizer and then pass through a sieve.

Make the pancake batter by working all the ingredients in a liquidizer for a few minutes until well blended. Combine the pancake mixture with the watercress purée, put to one side and rest the batter. In a pan, heat some oil until very hot and make 8 × 20 cm (8 inch) wafer-thin pancakes and keep warm.

For the filling, mix together the brown and white meat of the crab. Place in a pan, season with salt and pepper, and add the saffron, cream and fresh parsley. Heat gently until the mixture is hot. Spoon this mixture into the pancakes, fold decoratively and serve immediately.

A beurre blanc is an excellent accompaniment, or just serve extra filling lightened with additional cream.

Serves 4

HOT SCALLOP TARTS WITH CHICORY AND LIMES

225 g (8 oz) puff pastry
beaten egg to glaze
20 fresh scallops with roe
150 ml (¼ pt) concentrated fish stock
150 ml (¼ pt) dry white wine
grated zest and juice of 2 fresh limes
150 ml (¼ pt) double cream
1 large head Belgian chicory, finely sliced

Preheat the oven to 220–230°C/425–450°F/ Gas Mark 7–8.

Trim and wash the scallops then slice them in half horizontally.

Roll out the puff pastry to 5 mm (¼ inch) thickness and cut out 4 circles 13 cm (5 inches) diameter. Using a 7.5 cm (3 inch) plain cutter make an indentation in the centre of each round. Lay on an oiled baking tray and brush with beaten egg to glaze. Cook in the oven for 15 minutes until golden brown, remove and allow to cool.

Carefully lift off the lid of each pastry case and set aside. Discard any uncooked pastry from the middle.

Poach the scallops for 30 seconds in the stock, then remove with a slotted spoon and set aside.

Add the wine, zest and juice of the limes to the stock and reduce by fast boiling. Add the cream and check the consistency of the sauce. Add the chicory and scallops at the last minute. Fill the tart cases and replace the pastry lids.

Serve any additional sauce around the tarts.
Serves 4

POT AU FEU OF CRAYFISH AND RED MULLET

24 live crayfish
1 onion, chopped
1 carrot, chopped
1 stick celery, chopped
1 clove garlic, chopped
1 tomato, peeled and chopped
a little olive oil
1 tbls tomato purée
¼ bottle good dry white wine
1 medium-sized red mullet, scaled and filleted
a selection of baby vegetables such as 8 carrots, 24 mangetout, 8 spring onions
2 shallots, chopped
150 ml (¼ pt) double cream
salt and pepper
a pinch of saffron powder
fresh parsley, chopped

Cook the live crayfish in boiling salted water for 5 minutes. Cool. Keep at least four whole for decoration; shell the remainder carefully. Keep all the shells.

Sauté the onion, carrot, celery, garlic and tomato in a little olive oil until just colouring. Add the tomato purée, then the crushed shells. Cover with water and white wine and simmer for 3–4 hours. Pass the liquid through a fine sieve and reduce the crayfish stock to about 600 ml (1 pint).

Cut the mullet into decorative strips. Prepare the baby vegetables decoratively, blanch in boiling salted water and refresh.

Poach the red mullet for 1 minute only in the crayfish stock with the shallots. Remove the mullet, then add the cream, seasoning and saffron and reduce to a thick soup.

At the last minute add the shelled tails, mullet, vegetables and parsley and serve garnished with whole crayfish.
Serves 4

Below: *Pot au feu of crayfish and red mullet*

STUFFED DUCKLING WITH LENTILS, BACON AND GARLIC

2 small, top quality ducklings

For the stuffing
2 onions, finely chopped
100 g (4 oz) mushrooms, finely chopped
finely grated zest and juice of 1 orange
salt and pepper
1 tsp fresh thyme, chopped
1 tsp fresh basil, chopped
1 egg
100 g (4 oz) fresh brown breadcrumbs

For the sauce
225 g (8 oz) mixed coloured lentils, soaked
overnight
25 g (1 oz) clarified butter
1 rasher bacon, chopped
1 onion, finely chopped
1 clove garlic, finely chopped
300 ml (½ pt) good jellied duck or
chicken stock
150 ml (¼ pt) double cream

Preheat the oven to 190°C/375°F/Gas Mark 5. Remove the legs and breast flesh from the duck. Remove the bones from the legs and beat out flat. Only the legs are to be stuffed.

Make the stuffing by cooking the onions, mushrooms, orange zest and juice, seasoning and herbs together in a covered saucepan until completely soft. Add the egg and breadcrumbs to bind. Stuff the legs then tie them up. Roast the legs slowly for approximately 40 minutes, to cook right through. Keep the breasts separate and roast in a hotter oven at 220°C/425°F/Gas Mark 7 until 'pink', about 15 minutes. Do this just before serving.

To make the sauce, thoroughly rinse the lentils. In a pan, melt the clarified butter and colour the bacon with the onion and garlic, add the stock and the lentils and cook for 15–20 minutes. Finish by stirring in the double cream.

Arrange the sliced pink duck breasts on top of the lentil sauce, along with the whole legs.
Serves 4

Below: *Stuffed duckling with lentils, bacon and garlic*

SADDLE OF SOMERSET ROE DEER WITH TWO SAUCES AND MOUSSE OF LIVER

about 150 g (5 oz) boned saddle of roe
deer per person, trimmed
75 g (3 oz) clarified butter
salt and pepper

For the garlic cream sauce
12 cloves garlic, skinned
300 ml (½ pt) concentrated chicken stock
100 g (4 oz) button mushrooms
salt and pepper
150 ml (¼ pt) double cream

For the redcurrant and port sauce
300 ml (½ pt) jellied veal stock
150 ml (¼ pt) ruby port
salt and pepper
1 tbls raspberry vinegar
100 g (4 oz) redcurrants
1 tsp redcurrant jelly

For the liver mousse
100 g (4 oz) roe deer liver (if not available
use calves' liver)
salt and pepper
a little grated nutmeg
1 egg white
1 egg
150 ml (¼ pt) double cream

To make the garlic cream sauce, blanch the garlic in fresh water three times, for 3 minutes each time. Add the garlic to the chicken stock with the mushrooms and seasoning. Simmer for a further 15–20 minutes. In a liquidizer blend to a smooth purée and add the cream.

To make the redcurrant and port sauce, reduce the veal stock with the port, seasoning and vinegar to a rich, dark consistency. Add the redcurrants and redcurrant jelly just before serving.

To make the liver mousse, preheat the oven to 110°C/225°F/Gas Mark ¼. Carefully trim the liver, place in a liquidizer and blend with the seasoning, egg white and whole egg. Pass through a fine sieve, then beat in the cream to form a light mixture. Spoon into 6 buttered dariole moulds and cook in a bain-

STUFFED BREAST OF GUINEA FOWL IN PASTRY WITH PIQUANT LIME SAUCE

4 breasts of guinea fowl, skinned and boned
225 g (8 oz) puff pastry
beaten egg to glaze

For the stuffing
1 carrot, finely diced
1 leek, finely diced
1 stick celery, finely diced
2 shallots, finely diced
a little hazelnut oil
a large pinch of fresh thyme
2–3 tbls chicken stock
2–3 tbls double cream
salt and pepper

For the sauce
150 ml (¼ pt) reduced chicken stock
juice and zest, cut into julienne, of 3 limes
1 tbls lime vinegar
50 g (2 oz) butter
salt and pepper

To make the stuffing, sweat the carrot, leek, celery and shallots in a little hazelnut oil with the thyme. Add the chicken stock and cream.

Reduce to a thick, rich texture. Season well and allow to cool.

Preheat the oven to 150°C/300°F/Gas Mark 2.

Make a slit in the pointed end of each breast and work the knife from side to side to form a pocket (not cutting down through the side). Spoon or pipe the stuffing into the breast and fold the pointed end over the pocket. Wrap the breasts in foil or cooking film, and roast for 15–20 minutes. Remove and allow to cool completely.

Turn the oven up to 200°C/400°F/Gas Mark 6. Roll out four squares of puff pastry 3 mm (⅛ inch) thick. Cut into strips 5 mm (¼ inch) wide. Wrap the strips around the breasts from the pointed end upwards, overlapping each strip to form a 'ribbed' cornet. Glaze with beaten egg and place in the refrigerator to chill. Cook until a golden colour, about 15 minutes.

To make the sauce, reduce the stock, lime juice and vinegar by half and finish by whisking in knobs of butter to make the sauce shine. Season.

Serve the stuffed breasts on the sauce, garnished with the blanched julienne of lime zest.
Serves 4

Above: *Saddle of Somerset roe deer with two sauces and mousse of liver*

Right: *Stuffed breast of guinea fowl in pastry with piquant lime sauce*

marie for 15–20 minutes in the oven until set. Allow to rest for 15 minutes before turning out.

Sauté the roe deer saddle in hot clarified butter and season well. Cook until just set – about 10 minutes, depending on the size of the saddle. It must be very pink. Allow to rest.

To serve, arrange the two sauces on each half of the plate. Place the roe deer slices on the sauces with the liver mousse.
Serves 6

Above: *Shoulder of English lamb braised with red wine, oranges and rosemary*

SUMMER PUDDING

The idea of a summer pudding recipe must be to use the fruit growing in the garden, so there can be no fixed recipe.

Prepare your assembled fruits – raspberries, strawberries, blackcurrants and redcurrants may all be ready at the same time.

Bring the fruit to the boil with 25 g (1 oz) sugar per 450 g (1 lb) fruit. *Do not add water.* Allow 100 g (4 oz) fruit per person. When boiled remove from the heat and strain the liquid from the fruit – perhaps several times. Allow to cool.

Using *stale* white bread with crusts removed, cut the slices into wedges suitable for lining your pudding basin – either for individual puddings or a large pudding. Soak the bread slices in the fruit juice until soggy. Line the basin.

Spoon in the fruit, pressing down well, and put more bread slices over the top. Weight, not too heavily, and chill for at least 3 days.

Turn out the pudding and serve the remaining juices separately or poured over the top.

Below: *Summer pudding*

SHOULDER OF ENGLISH LAMB BRAISED WITH RED WINE, ORANGES AND ROSEMARY

1.5 kg (3 lb) shoulder of lamb, boned
salt and pepper
4 cloves garlic, chopped
1 tsp fresh thyme
1 tsp fresh rosemary
1 bottle full-flavoured red wine
grated zest and juice of 3 oranges
75 g (3 oz) unsalted butter
2 onions, chopped
2 rashers streaky bacon, chopped
4 tbls plain flour

Take the boned lamb, open it out and lay it as flat as possible, then season on the inside with salt, pepper, 1 clove garlic, and ½ tsp each of thyme and rosemary. Roll and tie up. Marinate in the red wine with the orange zest and juice, and the remaining thyme and rosemary. It is best left for a minimum of 12 hours and a maximum of 48 hours.

To cook, wipe the lamb dry, retaining the marinade. Sauté in the butter in a large pot until coloured on all sides. Remove and set aside. Add the onion, bacon, remaining garlic and seasoning and cook until well browned. Stir in the flour, replace the lamb, cover with marinade and simmer for at least 2 hours, depending on the size of the shoulder.
Serves 6

PRUNE AND ARMAGNAC TART

350 g (12 oz) sweet shortcrust pastry
225 g (8 oz) Agen or Californian prunes
which have been macerated in armagnac
for at least 48 hours

For the filling
100 g (4 oz) unsalted butter
100 g (4 oz) icing sugar
100 g (4 oz) ground almonds
50 g (2 oz) plain flour
3 eggs
25 ml (1 fl oz) dark rum

To serve
300 ml (½ pt) double cream whipped with
a little sugar and armagnac to taste from
macerating the prunes

To make the filling, beat the butter until soft.
Mix the sugar and almonds together well,
then work into the butter. Work in the flour.
Add the eggs one by one, beating until light.
Finally, add the rum.

Preheat the oven to 180°C/350°F/Gas
Mark 4.

Roll out the pastry as thinly as possible.
Line a 25 cm (10 inch) flan ring with a
removable base or 6 × 10 cm (4 inch) individual rings. Spread half the filling over the
base of the tart, add a layer of well drained
macerated prunes (save the juice for adding
to the cream), then cover with the remainder of the filling.

Bake in the oven for 30 minutes. If
cooking individual tarts only cook for 15–20
minutes. After 10 minutes lower the oven
temperature to 150°C/300°F/Gas Mark 2
and cover if the centre of the tart is not
completely set. Cool slightly then turn out of
the flan case and serve warm with the
flavoured double cream.

Makes a large tart for 8 or individual tarts
for 6

Right: *Prune and armagnac tart*

THE McCOY BROTHERS

The British feel perfectly at home in the company of a little gentle eccentricity. It is an endearing quality which we like to admire and slightly envy. The *Good Hotel Guide* even awards laurel wreaths for it. But when a taste for the unconventional is mixed with conventional wisdom, when flamboyance is matched by modesty and when the tenets of a Christian faith mingle with the subculture of alternative society, you have a very curious conundrum. It's all a bit Irish – like the brothers McCoy, who are Yorkshire born and bred but whose grandparents nevertheless came from Ireland.

Take the Tontine Inn, for instance, sandwiched between two thunderous arterial roads just south of Teesside: The forbidding exterior looks like a seminary for novices and the scene within moved Quentin Crewe to liken it to 'a run-down Welsh brothel' while *Punch* suggested 'a Chinese opium den'. Gastronomically serious but decoratively bizarre, McCoys is to eating what a cross between Eton and St Trinian's might be to education.

Before the smell of good food, the first sensation is the scent of rose-perfumed oil of pot-pourri smoking from a table lamp in the hall. Incense before the high table. The bar and restaurant are a violent collision of time, kitsch and culture – a cornucopia of art deco, chinoiserie and Victoriana set amidst a jungle of palmiers and hanging ferns. The rich plum ceiling of the bar turns to racing green on walls patterned with extravagant flowers in pinks and yellows. Chinese lanterns and octagonal bamboo side tables perch beside lumpy sofas in flocked velour and wicker chairs of the type my granny used to put out for tea in her Sussex garden. In the restaurant, the tables are dressed in a conventional shade of powdery-pink but the walls come in tawny port or silver and the room is dominated by two enormous Japanese parasols echoed by two others stuck in the necks of a pair of stately Chinese vases standing on a magnificent mahogany

sideboard. It is all comfortably and deliciously the worse for wear and looks as if it might have been brilliantly cobbled together from the props department of a bankrupt repertory company.

Everything about the McCoys – the cooking as well – is slightly offbeat but done with a great sense of style. Often zany but always precise, their talent is for flair and surprise combined with technical discipline.

They took their cue from their parents, who for 25 years ran a pub-cum-eating place in Middlesbrough called the Masham Hotel – although this hotel was different from most in that it had no bedrooms to let. During the Fifties and Sixties the brothers, Peter, Tom and Eugene, spent much of their childhood and teens helping out between their Catholic education at St Mary's Grammar School. The business prospered. Mrs McCoy insisted on setting an immaculate table and earned a wide reputation for her roasts and hot chicken sandwiches while Mr McCoy set the tone with his own racy style. On occasions, the boys would have to suffer the gibes of their classmates when their father drove them to school wearing his pyjamas, a smart cravat and a large fedora. But Mr McCoy was a singular individual.

For a short time after their father's death in 1967, Peter and Tom continued to run the Masham while Eugene sought stardom as a rock 'n' roll singer with a group he founded, called 'The Elastic Band'. It lasted little more than a year but his modest successes included a gig with Tom Jones. Meanwhile, his two older brothers started a boutique over an ice cream parlour and they were the first to introduce Jean Muir, Ossie Clarke and Gina Fratini to the better-heeled swingers of Middlesbrough. When the big chains caught on and undercut them they moved across the road and took over the Purple Onion, a run-down coffee bar owned by their eldest brother

John who was moving to Kirklevington to open a country club.

The Purple Onion operated on a time-share principle with much of their irredeemable equipment cast on roller skates. Scene changes took place during the course of the day depending on who was coming in or from which hole in the roof the rain was leaking through. Curtain-up was at 7.45 am with tea, toast and scones served on bone china to the shop ladies on their way to work. By 9.00, the china was locked up and replaced with large mugs for the service of coffee to the local student and hippy community. The lunchtime office trade was made welcome with permutations of sausage, beans and eggs where the only common denominators were chips and the McCoys' best china. Afternoons reverted to the beatnik routine.

Edwina Currie would have denounced the menu but Mrs Thatcher would have applauded the unusual enterprise of the place which was staffed by a rum collection of faithfuls. There was Lily – a four-foot-ten-inch *wunderkind* with 39 years' service with the McCoy family – who baked the scones. There was Flory who managed the Purple Onion's precarious cash flow: as fast as Tom took the money, Flory zipped down the road to buy more provisions. And there was the mad Oxford don – a regular customer who, uninvited, chanted orders and assisted at table in his Bermuda shorts when he had tired of his poetry.

It was not until the early Seventies that the McCoys began to take a serious interest in cooking. Now in their mid-twenties and joined by Eugene, Peter and Tom moved to the Kirklevington Country Club where their brother John put them in charge of the catering. They started a dining club, a hit-and-miss affair which at least served as a culinary test-site based on the recipes of Elizabeth David and Robert Carrier and the helpful encouragement of their friend Mara Berni at San Lorenzo, the brothers' favourite restaurant in London. Peter experimented with fancy soups like cucumber, Tom bought his first truffle and tried his hand at a *dodine de canard*, and Eugene humoured the club members with his garrulous charm.

It was all a huge success, so in April 1973 the trio opened their own restaurant – the first McCoys – on the same premises and then nearly

move to the Tontine Inn at Staddlebridge – a great Yorkshire landmark which they had always coveted. Two years later, in November 1978, Ronay endowed a second star and awarded the McCoys his Gold Plate for 'Restaurant of the Year'. It was a supreme double-accolade which, in the north of England, they now shared only with the fabled Box Tree at Ilkley. Unwittingly, Egon Ronay was heralding the phenomenon of the 1980s – the arrival of a new breed of young, highly gifted British chef.

In the early years at the Tontine, Eugene continued to oversee the restaurant while Peter and Tom ran the kitchen. Later they opened six bedrooms upstairs and converted their basement into a bistro where Eugene presides as both cook and lively host. Peter now fronts the show amongst the palms and parasols although he still superintends the puddings. This leaves Tom as the principal force at the stoves.

His cooking is cast in the modern mould, tinged by the brush of some of the great European chefs. He prefers to describe it as eclectic – a bit like the decor – but as with everything the McCoys do, Tom's mark is the dash and wit of his dishes which he tempers with a keen sympathy for the tastes and appetites of his Teesside clientele. 'In the end,' he says, 'they are looking for a sizeable piece of protein.' He delivers the goods with, for example, slabs of Scotch beef counterpointed with two feather-light supporting acts – the one a girolle mousse parcelled in a thin pancake, the other a puff pastry tartlet filled with puréed parsley.

Peter's approach in the pudding department displays similar zeal. He doesn't mess about. Choc-o-Block Stanley – a rich chocolate fondant framed with Tia Maria-drenched sponge biscuit fingers and soothed with a coffee bean sauce – is the most decadently delicious dessert I have ever confronted. Stanley, incidentally, was an old boy who used to deliver the McCoy's evening paper. On cue, every night, he would ask, 'Are you busy?'

'Oh yes, Stanley, we're chockablock,' was the standard retort, irrespective of the state of play.

However, at the heart of the McCoys' cooking lies a devotion to their raw materials. Tom talks with a passion about 'the purity of the ingredients' and it shows in his light touch, subtlety and clean execution. He has eaten his way round many of the three-star chefs of France, but his idol is Frédy Girardet: 'Purity is what Girardet's food is all about.'

closed it 24 hours later. Their first night was an unmitigated disaster. The ventilation system went into reverse, spraying the entire kitchen with a thick layer of black soot. Vital items of equipment went AWOL – Lily was observed kneeling on a stool rolling out pastry with a milk bottle. And because all the bookings were made up of friends of friends, everyone arrived at once and insisted on eating together. At the end of the evening, Eugene found his desolated head waiter weeping over the bonnet of his Mini repeating the immortal words: 'Fucking San Lorenzo was never like this.'

They persevered, taking uncommon care in the choice of their suppliers. Until they bought a second-hand Alpha-Romeo to make their weekly journeys to London, all their meat came up by train – from Harrods. Finally, they were discovered by Egon Ronay and rewarded with a star in the 1976 edition of his guide just before their

In 1985, Tom went to Crissier and ate three meals in two days at Girardet's restaurant – one as the master's guest in his own kitchen. It was a very rare honour, made the more so by Girardet's insistence on cooking personally for the stranger from the north of England. With a glint of mischief in his eyes, and in the spirit of his *cuisine spontanée*, Girardet decided to parody fish 'n' chips. Tom's main course was sea bass roofed by a layer of wafer-thin potato flakes and then grilled. By the time the potatoes were golden crisp, the fish was perfectly cooked.

It is not surprising, therefore, that there are glimpses of Girardet in some of Tom's cooking – like in his use of pasta. Ravioli may come filled with a langoustine mousse and sauced with lemon, truffle and lobster. But there is nothing stereotypical or thematic about the menu. 'There are no barriers for me,' says Tom. 'I'll cook anything that appeals to me.' The result is a breathless array of wares which mixes a serious and often liberal deployment of expensive ingredients like foie gras with lamb or *pigeon de Bresse* and the McCoys' wonderful sense of whimsy. Toasted coconut chippings crown the tops of fat scallops bathing on a curried sabayon or, most ticklish of all, there is

Tom's amazing, but completely over-the-top, mono-cum-mushroomgrammed puff-pastry case filled with a variety of French fungi and moistened with a perfectly balanced and delicately herbed Muscadet sauce made from vegetable stock.

Like Richard Shepherd in London and Stephen Ross in Bath who also rose to prominence in the mid-Seventies, the McCoys were forerunners of the British *nouvelle vague* which was to sweep the Eighties. However, while Shepherd and Ross were pioneers in their time, the manner of the McCoys' coming was more in the style of a band of buccaneers upturning the feeding troughs of the barren north. They were products of the age of student protest and the Rolling Stones and, epitomizing the spirit of the day, they inspired an enthusiastic following. At the same time, their upbringing anchored them to the values of self-discipline and the Catholic Church which have formed the foundation of their lives. Their Irish charm – urbane in Peter, quiet but articulate in Tom and thoroughly extrovert in Eugene – combined with their unique mix of talents have brought the McCoys immense success and a special place in the folklore of the British kitchen.

Far left: *The garden entrance to the Tontine Inn. First built in 1804 as a post house, it is now a lonely curiosity beside the A19 trunk road near Northallerton. An unlikely setting for such a distinguished table.*

Left: *The restaurant. Victoriana, art deco and the Orient collide merrily to create a deliciously eccentric interior designer's salmagundi.*

SCALLOPS WITH COCONUT

10 scallops, cleaned and halved and 4 roes
reserved
25 g (1 oz) clarified butter
¼ fresh coconut, grated
4 sprigs flat-leaf parsley, to garnish

For the sauce
1 egg yolk
120 ml (4 fl oz) vegetable stock
1 tbls double cream
1–2 drops curry essence or a pinch of
curry powder
25 g (1 oz) unsalted butter, softened
salt
fresh lime juice

Make a small slit in the scallop roes. In a pan fry the roes and scallops in the clarified butter for about 30 seconds to one minute, turning once. Toast the coconut lightly under the grill.

To make the sauce, whisk the egg yolk with the stock over gentle heat until it is foaming. Beat in the cream and curry essence or curry powder and then the softened butter. Season with salt and a little fresh lime juice.

Arrange five scallop halves and one roe on each plate and pour a little sauce over each portion. Sprinkle with coconut and flash under a hot grill to glaze. Garnish with sprigs of parsley.
Serves 4

Above: *Wild mushroom and walnut mousse
wrapped in cabbage with sauce riesling*

Below: *Scallops with coconut*

WILD MUSHROOM AND WALNUT MOUSSE WRAPPED IN CABBAGE WITH SAUCE RIESLING

50 g (2 oz) pork fillet
50 g (2 oz) chicken breast
175 ml (6 fl oz) double cream, chilled
salt and pepper
4 tbls chopped girolles
2 tbls chopped shallot
15 g (½ oz) unsalted butter
1 tbls blanched walnuts, chopped
4 large savoy cabbage leaves
chicken stock and water in equal
quantities, for poaching

For the sauce
120 ml (4 fl oz) Tokay riesling wine
120 ml (4 fl oz) chicken stock
25 g (1 oz) unsalted butter
black pepper

Blend the pork and chicken together in a food processor. Work in the cream and season generously. Sweat the girolles and shallot in the butter until soft and add to the meat mixture when cold. Add the walnuts.

Blanch the cabbage leaves in boiling water for 1–2 minutes until bright green, and refresh in cold water. Drain, remove the stems and place a quarter of the mixture on each leaf and wrap into a neat shape. Place the cabbage parcels in a saucepan, cover with chicken stock and water and poach for 5–7 minutes until firm. Drain and keep warm.

To make the sauce, reduce the riesling to half its volume by fast boiling. Add the chicken stock and reduce to a light syrup. Whisk in the butter piece by piece and season with pepper.

Cut the cabbage-wrapped mousses into thick slices and arrange a portion on each plate. Pour a little sauce around each plate and serve immediately.
Serves 4

WILD MUSHROOM PASTRY

225 g (8 oz) assorted wild mushrooms, trimmed and washed
175 g (6 oz) puff pastry
egg yolk to glaze

For the sauce
120 ml (4 fl oz) double cream
120 ml (4 fl oz) vegetable stock
2 tsp finely chopped shallot
1 clove garlic, crushed
25 g (1 oz) unsalted butter
salt and white pepper
2 tsp chopped fresh chives
2 tsp chopped fresh chervil
2 tsp chopped fresh parsley

Preheat the oven to 200°C/400°F/Gas Mark 6. Grill the wild mushrooms until they are just soft.

Roll out the pastry thinly and cut out four large mushroom shapes about 13 cm (5 inches) in diameter. Using a small sharp knife, mark out a lid about 1 cm (½ inch) in from the edge of the 'mushroom cap' and score the top in a lattice pattern. Place the pastry cases on a baking sheet, brush with egg yolk and bake for 7–8 minutes until all the cases are crisp and golden.

Above: *Wild mushroom pastry*

To make the sauce, reduce the cream, stock, shallot and garlic to a light cream consistency. Whisk in the butter piece by piece, season to taste and add the herbs. Stir in the mushrooms.

Remove the lids and centres from the pastry cases and fill with the mushroom mixture. Transfer to individual plates, replace the lids and serve at once.
Serves 4

and cook in the oven for 3–4 minutes.

To make the sauce, reduce the veal and chicken stocks together to a light syrup. Add the juices from the lamb and whisk in the butter piece by piece. Stir in the diced tomato, the truffle if using, and parsley leaves, and season to taste.

Cut the lamb into slices and arrange in a fan on each plate. Pour a little sauce around each portion and garnish with a red capsicum tart – a puff pastry tartlet filled with a mousse of skinned red pepper, chives, double cream and egg and baked – and a cooked artichoke heart filled with a mixture of lightly grilled wild mushrooms in a foie gras and port cream.
Serves 4

Above: *Boned lamb with a light sauce*

BONED LAMB WITH A LIGHT SAUCE

4 × best ends of lamb, with six bones only, boned and trimmed
50 g (2 oz) clarified butter

For the sauce
250 ml (8 fl oz) veal stock
250 ml (8 fl oz) chicken stock
25 g (1 oz) unsalted butter
1 tomato, skinned, deseeded and diced
a little julienne of fresh truffle (optional)
a few flat parsley leaves
salt and pepper

For the garnish
red capsicum tarts
artichoke hearts with mushroom and foie gras cream

Preheat the oven to 230°C/450°F/Gas Mark 8. Seal the best ends of lamb on all sides in the clarified butter then place in a roasting tin

FILLET OF BEEF

4 × 100 g (4 oz) portions fillet of beef
50 g (2 oz) unsalted butter

For the sauce
300 ml (½ pt) Beaujolais
600 ml (1 pt) veal stock
¼ onion, finely chopped
1 carrot, finely chopped
3 shallots, finely chopped
1 stick celery, finely chopped
25 g (1 oz) unsalted butter
black pepper

For the garnish
wild girolle crêpes
parsley purée tarts

Below: *Fillet of beef*

Preheat the oven to 230°C/450°F/Gas Mark 8. Seal the fillets of beef on all sides in the butter then place in a roasting tin and cook in the oven for 4–6 minutes.

To make the sauce, simmer the wine, stock and vegetables together for 15 minutes then strain and reduce to a syrupy consistency. Whisk in the butter piece by piece and season with black pepper.

Cut each beef portion into two thick slices, arrange on plates and pour a little sauce around. Garnish with a wild girolle crêpe – a small herb pancake filled with a mousse of girolles and double cream, folded over, brushed with melted butter and cooked in a very hot oven for 3 minutes – and a tiny puff pastry tartlet filled with parsley purée, sautéed shallots and double cream.
Serves 4

FILLET OF TURBOT WITH SAUCE SOUBISE

4 × 175 g (6 oz) turbot fillets, skinned
salt and pepper
vegetable stock and dry white wine in
equal quantities, for poaching

For the sauce soubise
1 onion, thinly sliced
25 g (1 oz) unsalted butter
120 ml (4 fl oz) vegetable stock
50 ml (2 fl oz) double cream
salt and pepper

For the mushroom essence
450 g (1 lb) flat mushrooms, chopped
3 shallots, finely chopped
1 fat clove garlic, crushed
150 ml (¼ pt) water
25 g (1 oz) unsalted butter

For the garnish
julienne of basil
chopped parsley
8 spring onions, poached until tender

To make the sauce soubise, sweat the onion in half the butter for 5 minutes. Add the vegetable stock and cook until tender. When soft, purée in a blender with the cream.

Above: *Fillet of turbot with sauce soubise*

Season to taste and pass through a fine sieve. Reheat and whisk in the remaining butter piece by piece. Keep warm.

To make the mushroom essence, place the mushrooms, shallots, garlic and water in a saucepan and sweat down until a strong juice is obtained. Pass through a sieve, return to the pan, reduce by half and whisk in the butter piece by piece. Keep warm.

Place the turbot fillets in a saucepan, season and cover with the vegetable stock and dry white wine. Poach until just opaque. Drain well and arrange a portion on each plate. Pour a little sauce soubise around. Glaze the turbot with some mushrooms essence and garnish with the fresh herbs and spring onions.
Serves 4

HOMEMADE RAVIOLI FILLED WITH A MOUSSE OF LANGOUSTINE, BASIL AND TRUFFLE

For the pasta
8 egg yolks
2 eggs
4 tbls olive oil
2 tsp salt
8 tbls cold water
500 g (18 oz) plain flour

For the filling
225 g (8 oz) raw shelled langoustines
250 ml (8 fl oz) double cream
2 small slices fresh truffle, cut in brunoise
1 tsp salt
2 small basil leaves, chopped
a pinch of cayenne
1 tsp truffle juice

For the lobster sauce
1.25 kg (2½ lb) lobster shells
65 ml (2½ fl oz) olive oil
300 g (11 oz) carrot, finely chopped
425 g (15 oz) shallot, finely chopped
200 g (7 oz) celery, finely chopped
sprig of thyme
450 g (1 lb) tomatoes, chopped
½ bottle dry white wine
double cream
25 g (1 oz) unsalted butter
cayenne
lemon juice
salt and pepper

For the garnish
3 raw langoustine tails per person, sautéed
in a little olive oil until just cooked
brunoise of fresh truffle
sprigs of chervil

To make the lobster sauce, sweat the lobster shells in the olive oil with the carrot, shallot and celery. Add the thyme, tomatoes, dry white wine and sufficient water just to cover. Simmer for 1½ hours, strain into a clean pan and reduce to a well-flavoured stock. Measure the amount of stock and then add half that amount in double cream. Reduce to a sauce consistency, whisk in the butter piece by piece and season the sauce to taste

with cayenne, lemon juice and salt and pepper. Keep warm.

To make the pasta dough, blend the egg yolks, eggs, oil, salt and water with the flour until a dough is formed. Cover and rest for 30 minutes.

To make the filling, blend the langoustines with the cream in a food processor then fold in the remaining ingredients.

Roll out the pasta as thinly as possible and stamp out 9 cm (3½ inch) rounds. Spoon a little of the langoustine filling into the centre of a pasta round and top with another, sealing the edges well. Repeat until all the pasta and filling is used up.

Cook the ravioli in boiling salted water for 3 minutes, drain well and serve three per portion with lobster sauce, garnished with langoustine tails, truffle and chervil.
Serves 10

CHOC-O-BLOCK STANLEY

4 egg yolks
150 g (5 oz) caster sugar
65 g (2½ oz) cocoa powder, sieved
165 g (5½ oz) unsalted butter
65 g (2½ oz) plain chocolate
300 ml (½ pt) double cream
25 g (1 oz) icing sugar, sieved
8 sponge fingers
sponge fingers soaked in Tia Maria, to decorate

For the coffee bean sauce
6 egg yolks
150 g (5 oz) caster sugar
600 ml (1 pt) milk
25 g (1 oz) coffee beans, freshly ground

Above: *Choc-o-block Stanley*
Far left: *Homemade ravioli filled with a mousse of langoustine, basil and truffle*

Whisk the egg yolks and sugar together until pale and frothy. Beat the cocoa powder and butter together. Melt the chocolate and add it to the egg mixture.

With a balloon whisk, whip the cream and icing sugar together, then stir in the egg mixture and the cocoa butter until evenly combined.

Spread one third of the mixture over the base of an oiled 1 kg (2 lb) loaf tin. Lay half the sponge fingers in two rows down the length of the tin. Repeat the layering until all the mixture is used up. Chill until set then unmould on to a serving plate – warm the tin very gently if necessary.

To make the sauce, whisk the egg yolks and sugar together until pale and frothy. Meanwhile gently warm the milk. Gradually add the warmed milk to the egg mixture and stir. Place in a double boiler over a low heat and cook, stirring constantly, until the mixture is thick enough to coat the back of a spoon. Do not allow to boil. Remove from the heat and stir in the ground coffee. Chill.

Cover the top and sides of the chocolate loaf with sponge fingers soaked in Tia Maria. Cut in thin slices and serve with the coffee bean sauce.
Serves 10

SHAUN HILL

Chagford in Devon is the quintessential English village. Even the local bank is a thatched cottage and in summer the shops, tea rooms and rose-fronted guest houses plant out their hanging baskets which line the streets like coronation bunting. In the village square, cloth-capped pensioners sit side by side on a parish bench clutching their sticks — motionless, silent and staring. If a stranger disturbed their midday reveries to ask the way to Gidleigh Park they might just know it, but it would require a few moments' thought and anyway the significance of their inquisitor's impatience would be lost on them.

If I were asked directions to heaven on earth, I'd point the way to Gidleigh Park — Paul and Kay Henderson's Garden of Eden hidden on the fringes of Dartmoor at the end of one-and-a-half miles of absent-mindedly tarmacked track.

Spring or autumn, summer or winter, there is a natural poetry and peace about the place. In season, a vast blanket of pale purple rhododendron wraps itself around the back of the house while vast tubs of geraniums stand guard on the long terrace with its striking views of the moor's hilltops. Mature oaks, beech trees and evergreen woodland fill the middle distance and in the foreground lawns, rockeries and beds of azalea, delphinium and heather tumble steeply down to the North Teign River.

Inside all is quiet, serene, immaculate but cosy. A fire glows in the hearth all year round. The staff are handsome, young and caring. Ask and it shall be given.

It took Shaun Hill almost 20 years to arrive at his country idyll and with it has come a peace of mind which is unusual among the chefs of the new generation who are more commonly fuelled by angst and ambition. However, while his experience is rich in the variety of culinary influences that have touched and shaped him, his career has also been punctuated by frustrations and mismatches which, inevit-ably, affected his cooking. Gidleigh Park and his relationship with the Hendersons, in particular, demonstrate vividly the impact that environment and proprietor can have on the success of a chef.

Born in 1947, Hill was a child of the Sixties and his looks still echo the age of the Beatles, flower-power and Katmandu. His Irish parents had settled in London and he, along with his three brothers, lived in a large, rambling house within earshot of the lions in Regents Park. His father wrote books and was news editor of the *Daily Mail*. He also loved eating and would take his son off to the markets in Soho, Camden and Islington to buy the provisions for the household, although it was mother who always did the cooking. Young Shaun's curiosity was aroused by the ingredients they found such as fresh snails and exotic fruits. He remembers using his pocket money to buy a Chinese gooseberry — better known today as the modern cook's cliché, the kiwi fruit — when they first appeared on the streets of North London. He ate it skin and all and thought it was horrible.

However, although he was fascinated by his edible discoveries, there was no great desire to cook for a living until, in his late teens, he started to read Robert Carrier and Elizabeth David, who matched visions of wonderful raw materials with images of French farmhouses and Greek olive groves. Ever since, he has seen cooking as an extension of the land from where the ingredients come rather than a first step in the catering process.

Hill left school with 'A' levels in Latin, Greek and ancient history. In spite of the pressures of the prevailing culture and the low esteem of cooking as a proper career for a bright young thing, he raised two fingers at conventional wisdom and turned down his place at Queen's University, Belfast. Instead, in 1966, he went to work at Carrier's in Camden Passage.

Seduced by the atmosphere and excitement of the place, Hill

learned quickly and was exposed to many of the culinary traditions of the world which have formed his outlook and ideas today. He learned that there were good dishes from Indonesia, Spain and Greece as well as from France. He learned about satays and filo pastry and the way to fashion flavours with spices and herbs. Because the brigade was small, he also learned to do everything and he suffered none of the restrictions of apprentices in the big conventional kitchens. He blesses Carrier for what he gave him. Certainly, Hill is sure that if he had gone to the Savoy, he would have been fired: 'Anyway, those kind of places had more in common with what went down with the *Titanic*.'

He enjoyed playing the maverick and four years later, in 1970, he moved on – to the Gay Hussar, Soho's fabled Hungarian eaterie where he was a good match for Victor Sassie, the restaurant's eccentric and pugnacious proprietor. At his interview, after asking him how often he got drunk, Sassie accused Hill of being a namby-pamby with a posh accent who ought to find a proper job elsewhere.

But by the end of their meeting, Sassie agreed to take him on and doubled his salary.

Hill spent three happy years at the Gay Hussar, learning about the cooking of central Europe, helping his boss with the accounts and enjoying the political irony of a place which was famous for a left-wing establishment clientele who dined obliviously on dishes prepared by Austrian veterans of the Wehrmacht and refugees of the '56 Uprising.

But from 1973, Hill was ready to take his career through a series of gear changes to bring him up to speed. He joined the London Intercontinental, where Peter Kromberg impressed on him the disciplines of managing a large kitchen without losing sight of the excellence of the food. Then, in 1976, after a spell as head chef at the Montcalm which established his credentials as a serious cook but frustrated him by its imposition of big-company bureaucracy, he went to the Capital as working head chef under Brian Turner, who had just assumed the executive role vacated by Richard Shepherd.

However, by this time Hill was going on 30 and his confidence as a cook sought greater freedom to express his own eclectic ideas. With a menu originated by Shepherd and still classically anchored, he felt that the Capital was a 'prisoner of its past', reluctant to change a formula which had earned the restaurant its Michelin star.

It was hardly surprising, therefore, that he jumped at the opportunity to be Anouska Hempel's first chef when she opened Blakes, her arty hotel in a leafy tributary of South Kensington. This suited Hill right down to his white clogs and it was here that Paul Henderson first came to admire his culinary range and talent. He used tahini to make dips for his crudités, and teriyaki, vegetable cannelloni and samosas figured alongside racks of lamb and grilled sweetbreads on watercress.

In 1980 Hill moved out of London. For some years he had watched the growing significance of cooking in the English country house hotel and he wanted to be part of an exciting movement which would also bring him closer to the source and inspiration of his cooking – his raw ingredients. For three years he was chef at the Lygon Arms at Broadway, Britain's most famous country inn but an hotel rooted in the traditional values of English hospitality. It was an experiment which failed. Management and chef had different priorities and he confesses that he must have been difficult to work with there. More seriously, he damaged his credibility as a cook.

So in 1983, he borrowed £65,000 and opened shop eponymously in a 16th-century farm building in Stratford-upon-Avon. As a chef he was now a happy man but as a *patron* it was a struggle. He loved to work his fish soups, pasta, game and offal dishes but he hated coping with VAT inspectors and cashflow forecasts for the bank. Although he broke even in his second year he needed money to spend on repairs and when the lavatories packed in he decided to call it a day.

The timing was perfect. Hill needed a white knight who would allow him a free rein in the kitchen but who would release him from the tiresome bureaucracy. Paul Henderson needed a head chef who had the ability to protect a Michelin star which his wife Kay had first earned in 1981. The heart of Gidleigh Park was its restaurant and, moreover, the size, location and atmosphere of the place were precisely what Hill had been searching for since his decision to leave London. With his wife Anja and their three children, he settled in Chagford in November 1985.

The early days were not all roses and honeysuckle. Hill was inheriting a kitchen which had already established a highly acclaimed pedigree but at the same time Kay Henderson had to learn to let go.

Right: *Half-a-mile from the hotel, a sign at the edge of the narrow, twisting lane reads 'Keep heart, you are still en-route for Gidleigh Park'. At the end of the trail Dartmoor's hidden jewel is dramatically revealed.*

Far right: *The boardroom at Gidleigh Park ... a leafy glade on the banks of the North Teign River. Kay and Paul Henderson celebrate a good year's trading with Shaun Hill*

However, it is the intellectual rigour of Hill's cooking which makes him so impressive and different. Despite his catholic approach, he has refused to be trapped by any temptation of gastronomic gimmickry. There is no conflict between style and ingredients because the former is cast firmly as servant of the latter. His dishes are a celebration of his raw materials and it is his suppliers who have dictated his outlook more than the grand arbiters of kitchen fashion: 'You can't put a piece of fish or meat into a straitjacket of preconceived notions or recipes. The characteristics of your ingredients must be looked at individually and then you can bring your ideas and knowledge into play.'

That knowledge includes his grasp of the nature of spices and herbs which began at Carrier's. It gives his food a subtlety and complexity without betraying the substance of the dish. His scallops with lentil and coriander sauce is remarkable for the layers of flavour which touch the palate. The lentils are a perfect foil for the strong aromatic flavours of the fried garlic, ginger and crushed cardamom seeds. The coriander leaves go in late which gives the dish its freshness and immediate appeal, leaving trace elements of all the other flavours lingering on the palate.

Hill's other great theme is his use of vegetables whose status he wants to elevate. This is not only a move to reflect a more vegetarian culture but, clearly, another index of his respect for Asian cooking where vegetables are very important. Hence his steamed sea bass and calves' sweetbreads share the honours with, respectively, baby vegetables and wild mushrooms rather than billing these accompaniments as thoughtless appendages to a main dish.

Although the spirit of the *chef-patron* may still lurk silently somewhere beneath the surface, Shaun Hill is at last a contented man. He has made Chagford his home and Gidleigh Park has been his making. He takes great pride in his craft without being obsessive about it but his self-mocking air belies the substance of his achievement. His experience, driven by an innate curiosity, has given him a depth of knowledge and a culinary range which very few other chefs have dared, or been able, to apply.

Nevertheless, he sees himself still with plenty of room to develop, although he is hesitant about the fulfilment of that promise: 'I don't want to be a wise old man having been a promising person for a long time in between. The danger is that I shall end up as Nestor before I have ever been Achilles.'

Occasionally they fought, and after one famous row she turned on Hill, saying 'You're the rudest man I've ever met.'

'That's impossible,' Hill retorted. 'You're married to him.'

Paul Henderson's bark has indeed won some notoriety within the trade but, as with his earlier relationship with Victor Sassie, Hill has staked out his ground at Gidleigh Park and there is a great deal of visible trust, respect and affection between the proprietors and their chef.

Like the character of the man himself, there is no conformity about Hill's cooking today and there is no allegiance to any particular culinary school. Instead he revels in making menus which suggest a promiscuity of style or technique but which do not offer reworkings of dishes that are obviously ethnic in origin. His bresaola, which he likes to offer with baby leeks or English asparagus, is a lonely exception.

HOME-CURED BEEF (BRESAOLA) WITH BABY LEEKS

1.75 kg (4 lb) topside of beef
1.5 kg (3 lb) baby leeks

For the brine
½ bottle red wine
450 g (1 lb) coarse salt
10 g (¼ oz) saltpetre
100 g (4 oz) brown sugar
1 tbls peppercorns, crushed
1 tbls crushed juniper berries
sprig of fresh thyme
225 g (8 oz) sliced carrots
6 chillis
1 stick cinnamon

For the dressing
150 ml (¼ pt) good quality olive oil
2 tbls sherry vinegar
1 tbls Dijon mustard
1 egg yolk
salt and pepper

Bring all the brine ingredients to the boil then allow to cool completely. Marinate the beef in the brine for 4 days, turning every day, then hang in a warm, dry place for 2–3 weeks, or until hard.

Carefully cut away the dried outside and slice thinly on to plates. Poach the baby leeks until just tender. Set aside until cold. Mix the dressing ingredients together and spoon over the leeks.
Serves 12

Above right: *Terrine of duck foie gras*
Below: *Home-cured beef (Bresaola) with baby leeks*

TERRINE OF DUCK FOIE GRAS

3 duck foie gras (livers), about 1.75 kg (4 lb) in weight
salt and pepper
½ nutmeg, grated
1 glass tawny port
½ glass armagnac
300 ml (½ pt) chicken consommé

Slice each liver horizontally into three or four pieces. Cover and allow to warm slowly to room temperature. Carefully pick out all the nerves and veins, not forgetting the outer membrane. Season each slice liberally with salt, pepper and nutmeg, then arrange in layers in a 30 × 7.5 cm (12 × 3 inch) terrine with the port and armagnac. Refrigerate for 6–8 hours.

Preheat the oven to 150°C/300°F/Gas Mark 2.

Place the terrine in a roasting dish half-filled with cold water and cook in the oven for 20 minutes (it should look very pink). Lay a plastic card along the top and then press it with three 50 g (2 oz) weights. When the terrine is cold and set remove the weights. Pour off any juices and add to the consommé.

Reduce the consommé by fast boiling to half its volume. Cool then pour over the terrine and chill until set. Serve thinly sliced with brioche or toast.
Serves 12

SHAUN HILL

Above: *Scallops with lentil and coriander sauce*

SCALLOPS WITH LENTIL AND CORIANDER SAUCE

16 large, very fresh scallops
salt and pepper
3 tbls groundnut oil
50 g (2 oz) brown lentils
1 large clove garlic, crushed
½ onion, chopped
2.5 cm (1 inch) piece root ginger, crushed
and then chopped
1 tsp cardamom seeds, crushed
2 large ripe tomatoes or 2 tbls passato
300 ml (½ pt) chicken stock
50 g (2 oz) unsalted butter
1 tbls crème fraîche or soured cream
juice of ½ lemon
small bunch of coriander leaves, chopped

Clean the scallops thoroughly and discard the roe. Slice them horizontally into three or four pieces. Season well and brush with groundnut oil.

Soak the lentils overnight or for a minimum of 4 hours. Drain and rinse in cold water, place in a saucepan of fresh water and parboil them until tender. Fry the garlic, onion and ginger in groundnut oil until golden. Add the cardamom seeds and allow to cook for a few seconds. Peel, deseed and finely chop the tomatoes and add to the pan; alternatively use the passato.

Add the stock and half the drained lentils. Boil for 10 minutes then liquidize. In a clean pan, reheat the lentil purée, whisking in the butter, cream and lemon juice. Add the coriander leaves and the remaining whole lentils to the sauce. Spoon the sauce on to the plates.

In a very hot, dry frying pan, cook the lightly oiled scallop slices for just a few seconds on each side, then place them on the sauce and serve immediately.
Serves 4–6

Above: *Salad of lettuces with warm lobster and sesame dressing*

SALAD OF LETTUCES WITH WARM LOBSTER AND SESAME DRESSING

4 miniature artichokes
1 tsp lemon juice
4 asparagus spears
1 lobster weighing 450–500 g (1–1¼ lb)
salt and pepper
1 tsp fennel seeds
1 tbls wine vinegar
selection of leaves such as lollo rosso,
feuilles de chêne (oak leaf), corn salad, cos
lettuce, Belgian endive
2 tomatoes, peeled, deseeded
and diced

For the sesame dressing
1 tbls sesame oil
1 tbls groundnut oil
½ tsp rice vinegar
½ tsp Japanese soy sauce

For the garnish
carrots, finely diced
chives
sesame seeds

To prepare the artichokes, remove the stalk and using a sharp knife cut the base flat and remove the leaves. Neatly trim the outside of the heart, then remove the choke. Rub with lemon juice. Peel and blanch the asparagus.

To cook the lobster, fill a large pan with water, add salt, pepper, fennel seeds and wine vinegar and bring to the boil. Drop the lobster into the boiling water and boil for 10 minutes. Remove and refresh under cold, running water

To extract the flesh from the lobster, remove the meat from the eight hind claws, and from the 2 front claws. Cut lengthwise down each side of the belly and take out the tail meat, making sure you scrape out every

morsel of meat left in the body shell. Slice the meat and divide into four portions.

Whisk the sesame dressing ingredients together. Wash and dry the lettuce leaves and mix in the artichokes, asparagus, tomatoes and warm lobster pieces. Dress with sesame dressing.

To finish, garnish with carrot, chives and sesame seeds.
Serves 4

CALVES' SWEETBREADS WITH WILD MUSHROOMS

225 g (8 oz) calves' sweetbreads
1 small onion, sliced
1 carrot, roughly chopped
salt and pepper
sprig of fresh thyme
1 tbls wine vinegar
100 g (4 oz) each chanterelles, black
trumpets, amethyst deceivers, and oyster
mushrooms
25 g (1 oz) morels
600 ml (1 pt) chicken consommé
300 ml (½ pt) veal stock
a little olive oil
50 g (2 oz) shallots
1 potato, peeled

Soak the sweetbreads in cold water overnight. Remove and carefully cut away most of the outer membrane. Place in a saucepan, cover with water, add the onion, carrot, salt and pepper, thyme and vinegar. Bring to the boil. Once boiled remove from the heat and leave to cool in the cooking liquid. Remove and cut into slices.

Carefully clean and trim the mushrooms. Add the morels to the consommé and veal stock and reduce by two-thirds by fast boiling. In a little olive oil, shallow fry the shallots and mixed mushrooms.

Brush olive oil on the slices of sweetbread and quickly colour on each side in a red-hot frying pan.

Grate the potato, season with salt and pepper, shape into flat ronds then fry in a little olive oil in a frying pan.

To serve, place the sweetbreads and potato rounds on top of the sauce and scatter the fried shallots and mushrooms on top. Young spring vegetables make a lovely accompaniment.

Serves 4

Right: *Calves' sweetbreads with wild mushrooms*

STEAMED SEA BASS WITH BABY VEGETABLES

Buy as large a quantity of baby vegetables as you can eat!

4 × 100 g (4 oz) fillets of sea bass
600 ml (1 pt) good fish stock
150 ml (¼ pt) double cream
1 tsp fresh chives, chopped
1 tsp fresh dill, chopped
juice of ½ lemon

Baby vegetables
baby bunched carrots
baby fennel
baby sweetcorn
broad beans
mangetout
asparagus tips
oyster mushrooms

Fill a saucepan a quarter full of water and bring to the boil. Place the sea bass fillets in a steamer or other perforated container over the saucepan, cover and steam for about 10 minutes until cooked.

Bring the fish stock to the boil and cook the baby vegetables. Make sure you put the ones which take longer to cook in first. Drain, reserving the stock in the saucepan, and set aside to keep warm.

Stir the cream, herbs and lemon juice into the stock. To serve place the sea bass on a plate, surround with the vegetables and spoon over the sauce.
Serves 4

Below: *Steamed sea bass with baby vegetables*

NECTARINE AND CARAMEL TART

4 ripe nectarines, halved and stoned
175 g (6 oz) unsalted butter
250 g (9 oz) demerara sugar
25 ml (1 fl oz) armagnac

For the sweet pastry
225 g (8 oz) plain flour
75 g (3 oz) ground almonds
100 g (4 oz) caster sugar
175 g (6 oz) unsalted butter – softened
2 egg yolks
½ tsp vanilla essence

For the caramel ice cream
225 g (8 oz) granulated sugar
300 ml (½ pt) double cream
300 ml (½ pt) milk
8 egg yolks

To make the ice cream, dissolve the sugar in a little water over a low heat. When dissolved, boil hard until it caramelizes. Take the pan off the heat and let it cool. When cool, gently pour on the cream and milk.

Whisk the caramel mixture on to the egg yolks. Put in a double saucepan and stir over a low heat until it begins to thicken. Cool, then freeze in an ice cream machine. Or, freeze in a rigid container until firm then work in a food processor until smooth.

To make the pastry, sift all the dry ingredients together. Rub in the butter, egg yolks and vanilla essence. Rest the pastry for at least an hour in the refrigerator.

Preheat the oven to 180°C/350°F/Gas Mark 4.

Roll out the pastry on to floured cling film 3 mm (⅛ inch) thick. Turn into four 10 cm (4 inch) tart cases, and remove the cling film.

Rest the tart cases for another hour then bake blind for 10 minutes. Should the cases bubble, gently pat them down. Remove and cool. Purée half the nectarines, then spoon into the pastry cases.

Put the butter, sugar and armagnac into a small saucepan and cook until it caramelizes.

Slice the remaining nectarines and arrange them across the purée. Coat with the warm sauce. Serve the tarts with the ice cream.
Serves 4

WARM BRIOCHE WITH POACHED RED FRUIT AND CINNAMON ICE CREAM

225 g (8 oz) mixed red fruits – such as
raspberries, cherries, plums, strawberries,
rhubarb
150 ml (¼ pt) sugar syrup, made from
150 ml (¼ pt) water and 100 g (4 oz)
granulated sugar
4 small brioche buns

For the cinnamon ice cream
300 ml (½ pt) milk
300 ml (½ pt) double cream
4 sticks cinnamon
8 egg yolks
175 g (6 oz) caster sugar
10 g (¼ oz) ground cinnamon
dash of rum

To make the ice cream, bring the milk, cream and cinnamon sticks to the boil, remove from the heat and leave to infuse for 10 minutes. Whisk the egg yolks and sugar together until pale and creamy. Strain the milk and cream mix on to the egg, whisking all the time. Stir over a low heat until the mixture thickens slightly. Alternatively place the mixture in a double boiler and stir gently until thick.

Add the ground cinnamon and a dash of rum. Freeze, preferably in an ice cream-making machine. Alternatively, freeze in a rigid container until firm then work in a food processor until smooth. Freeze until required.

To cook the fruit, place in the sugar syrup and bring to the boil. Remove from the heat and set aside.

To assemble, slice off the top third of each brioche to make a lid and remove a little of the brioche dough to form a container. Place some of the cooked fruit inside each brioche and arrange the remainder around the plate with the juice. Place two or three scoops of ice cream around the plate and serve.
Serves 4

Right: *Warm brioche with poached red fruit and cinnamon ice cream*

IAN McANDREW

Ian McAndrew was one of the first of the new British *wunderkinder* – that breed of under-30s who startled the culinary scene at the beginning of the 1980s. However, unlike several of his promising contemporaries at the turn of the decade – chefs who either fell as casualties of the revolution or simply drifted into obscurity – McAndrew, still well short of his fortieth birthday, has lasted the course and looks primed to hit top billing in the 1990s.

Nevertheless, in spite of his hard-earned celebrity over the past ten years, he is an enigmatic individual; a bit of a loner who appears to maintain a safe distance from the mainstream of his trade but who is, in fact, riding hard on the inside track. Most of the chefs in this book offer some semblance of logic to their progression, no matter how eccentric. In McAndrew, there is no such logic. His position today was born out of an early life which was strangely empty and lacking in direction. After he left school, it took eight years for his aimlessness to work itself out and only when he went to the Dorchester – an experience which swept over him like a religious conversion – did the blindfold come down and his career take off.

While his cooking is unapologetically self-centred to the point of self-indulgence, he feels a passionately altruistic responsibility for his craft, fearing that it is in danger of sacrificing basic skills to the pressures of convenience and profit. Although he grudgingly acknow-ledges a debt to the culinary heritage of Europe, he refuses to be part of the principal establishment of the profession – the UK branch of the Académie Culinaire de France – 'because it is French and I don't want to be a second-class French citizen'. Instead, he is chairman of the British Culinary Institute – an organization with similar aims – and he likes to refer to the institute's work as 'our struggle'. It is a posture which has put him out in the cold in some circles but, in his quest to declare UDI for the British profession, it has made him a leader of Britain's culinary revival and a crusader for a craft which is trying to stand on its own two feet.

McAndrew is an almost literal reincarnation of the famous Kitchener recruiting poster but his British bulldog spirit of the 'your country needs YOU' variety also hides a talent with the artistic sensitivity of a 19th-century Impressionist. To prove the point, his first book *Feast of Fish*, which was published in 1987, has been translated into French and is being exported across the Channel this year. 'Coals to Newcastle,' he says wryly. 'Our next target is Italy.' It is a poignant demonstration of the impact young Brits are making in the higher reaches of international gastronomy.

McAndrew's curt north-country vowels brand him a Geordie, although technically he is a Wearsider. Born in Seaham, a small mining and fishing town south of Sunderland, in 1952, he grew up in a community which offered its youth few alternatives aside from a life down the pit. At school he felt trapped and frustrated. He was neither academic nor sportive and his only refuge was the art room, where he displayed an unconscious gift with paints and pastels. Eventually, the futility and drudgery of his metalwork option drove him to his headmaster who allowed him to join the girls in the domestic science class where the appeal lay in the company rather than the work. 'I saw no practical use in cookery and I did not even know restaurants existed,' he says.

At 16, when he had to face the big wide world as a school-leaver, the only suggestion of any novelty came from his form master, who pointed him towards a catering course in either Sunderland or Durham. The prospect of escaping from his home town filled the young lad with a mild sense of adventure, so he chose the college at Durham because, of the two, it was further away.

Unlike school, college life was fun because it spelt freedom, the

pub and an opportunity to earn 1s 3d an hour doing nights at a local hotel. Course work was incidental and on one occasion Ian played truant for four days to join a catering crew on the *Atlantic Conveyor*, a new container ship undergoing sea trials out of Newcastle. Twelve years later the boat sank off the Falklands, the tragic victim of an Exocet missile.

In 1970 student life came to an abrupt end and again McAndrew had to ask himself the question 'What now?' His answer was to find a job rather than to start a career and for the next couple of years he attached himself to some of British Transport Hotels' more forgettable properties. He enjoyed life – 'I used to be a bit of a drunk in those days' – but it never occurred to him that he might do better and, besides, he had no reason to entertain any great expectations of himself.

In 1972 money lured McAndrew south, where a busy trade in buffets at the Cavendish at Eastbourne led him to experiment in fat carvings from the lamb suet he saved in the larder. His Santa Clauses

and angels won modest approbation until he learned that butter was a more pliant medium. The therapy not only rekindled his own artistic abilities, it also begat a less ambivalent interest in cooking.

Life began to look brighter. He married and, two years later, he and his wife Jane followed a chum to the Intercontinental in Hamburg where, for the first time, McAndrew was struck by the professional buzz of a super-grade kitchen. At last the clouds which had hung over his own aspirations broke and he began to see his purpose.

On his return to England in 1976 and after a brief spell at the Park Tower in Knightsbridge, Ian McAndrew joined the brigade of the Dorchester as the junior *chef de partie* in the larder on the same Monday that Anton Mosimann picked up the reins from Eugene Kaufeler as *maître chef des cuisines*.

The Dorchester changed McAndrew's life. Mosimann seemed to cast a spell over him and when he describes the experience, the measured monotone of the Geordie suddenly becomes animated: 'After a few weeks at work, it was as if I had always been there, that

Right: *Final touches to the dish seconds before it leaves the kitchen. Roasted cloves of garlic are arranged around the fish.*

Far right: *Alchemist and artist, McAndrew lovingly ladles fish stock into the pan — part of the preparation of his red wine sauce for the roast fillet of monkfish.*

I had always been the person that I then was — which was very different to the person I had been six months previously.'

Mosimann, who led the modern movement in Britain in the late Seventies, furnished McAndrew with the culinary disciplines and stylistic understanding which he had been searching for. 'All of a sudden, everything became clear,' he says. 'This is what I was here to do. There was more to food than just cooking it. It could be good to look at as well as good to eat.'

Within six months, Mosimann's ardent disciple was promoted to senior larder chef and he earned notoriety as a bully. One colleague who knew him at the time recalls that 'Ian was the biggest bastard to walk this earth'. McAndrew does not quarrel with the description. In him there was an innate desire to achieve the best results at any cost and, in so doing, to please his master who, by contrast, he saw as 'the kindest, most genuine man I have ever met'.

However, although McAndrew's devotion to Mosimann was as that to a cult leader, the will to succeed in his own right became a

more powerful emotion and in 1978 he went to Bernard Gaume at the Carlton Tower before accepting the job of head chef at Eastwell Manor, near Ashford in Kent, a country house hotel of Hollywood-esque magnificence which opened in February 1980.

Eastwell's proprietors gave McAndrew carte blanche in the kitchen and two years later Michelin acknowledged his young talent with a star. When the hotel was sold in 1983, his culinary liberty was too precious to risk the imposition of compromise in another's employment, so he and Jane sold up and moved the dozen-odd miles to Canterbury where, in December the same year, they opened shop as Restaurant Seventy Four in a panelled and inglenooked 16th-century house in Wincheap. By January 1985, the Michelin men had repeated their earlier compliment. Yet, as McAndrew was to discover, the admiration of the guides was not an automatic key to the hearts and appetites of his Kentish customers. His refusal to brook the dictates of an employer applies equally to the fancies of his diners. In the end he found no alternative but to move closer to an audience which might better appreciate the nuances and charms of his cuisine – which is why he returned to London in 1989 to open at 116 Knightsbridge.

McAndrew's work is an extraordinary mixture of art, instinct and meticulous cooking practice. 'I never need to taste a new dish to know whether or not it will go on the menu,' he says. 'If I do everything correctly and if it feels good as I am doing it, the dish will work and will taste wonderful.' Apparently arrogant statements like this are not uncommon among chefs of a paler hue, but in McAndrew there is only one real priority, to satisfy his own culinary integrity. Any deviation in his outlook, any compromise in his ways would make him feel as if he were selling his gifts like a prostitute her body.

While Mosimann may have provided the springboard for McAndrew's ascendancy in 1976, the stimuli for his inspiration today are anyone's guess. He writes books, but he does not read much. He rarely eats out and has travelled less: 'I have never worked or eaten in France and I have no great desire to do so.' But, ironically, the immediate impression of his cooking suggests that it is in the manner of the great French masters of the modern era and what is striking is the immense care in the preparation of all the constituents of each dish. Indeed, the one chef McAndrew does admire greatly and regards as a kindred soul is Nico Ladenis, whose cooking has been deeply influenced by Roger Vergé. 'I love the intensity of colours and flavours in Nico's food,' he says. McAndrew's cooking equally bears these trademarks – notwithstanding both men's considerable share-holdings in gastronomic bloodymindedness.

However, unlike Ladenis's brief sojourn in the sleepy Berkshire countryside which drove him screaming joyfully back to London in 1986, McAndrew's flight to the capital was made reluctantly. In truth he hates the place, but if he had to make a sacrifice it was bound to be his location, not his style of food. 'Although things are looking up in Britain, out there in the country it is still a bloody struggle,' he says.

At heart McAndrew is a country lad and if there is any obvious source of his creativity, it is his love of the land. He is fanatical about seeking out good-quality raw materials and in Canterbury he used to spend every afternoon in his wellies at some farm or smallholding picking fruits and vegetables. The idea of relying on the London and Paris markets irritated him and so he determined to dig for Kent, mobilizing a handful of local producers to grow specifically for his kitchen and to his merciless standards.

It was this experience which led the British Culinary Institute to introduce its suppliers' logo – a kind of BCI tried and tested badge of excellence which recipients could attach to their products. The scheme immediately attracted plaudits from such luminaries as Jane Grigson and Jeremy Round, and when the *Independent* conducted its own blind tasting, pitching BCI approved products against those recommended by its readers, the Institute came out smelling of roses. McAndrew had struck another blow for Britain.

Whatever the paradoxes of McAndrew's persona – culinary philanthropist or gastronomic egotist, introvert artist or public standard bearer, outsider or patriot – he is one of the most striking and enduringly impressive examples of the British kitchen's youth movement. At the end of the day he is a very private man who enjoys his own company and that of his two cocker spaniels, Truffle and Beluga. But in spite of their names, he remains unaffected and unimpressed by his success: 'When I go home,' he says, 'I still like to eat a Chinese take-away.'

CARROT MOUSSE WITH A CLAM SAUCE

225 g (8 oz) Venus clams
a little oil
75 g (3 oz) mirepoix (celery, leek and
onion), roughly chopped
150 ml (¼ pt) fish stock
50 ml (2 fl oz) dry white wine
1 parsley stalk
450 g (1 lb) carrots, roughly chopped
pared zest and juice of ½ orange
250 ml (8 fl oz) double cream
2 eggs, beaten
salt and pepper
1 tsp chopped parsley
cooked baby carrots, to garnish

Place the clams in a bowl of cold fresh water for at least 15 minutes to clear out most of their salt and a lot of sand. Replace with fresh clean water twice to rinse them thoroughly.

Heat the oil in a saucepan, add the mirepoix and sweat until soft. Add the fish stock, white wine and parsley stalk and bring to the boil. Add the clams, cover and cook over a high heat until they open – this will only take 4 or 5 minutes. Stir occasionally. When cooked, drain the clams in a colander until cold, reserving the cooking liquor. When cold remove the flesh from the shells, strain the cooking liquor through a muslin and reserve. Cook the carrots in the orange juice, a little water to cover and the orange zest until soft. Drain and work in a food processor or blender until a smooth purée is formed. This will probably be quite wet; if so place it in a heavy-based saucepan over a low heat until some of the moisture has evaporated, stirring occasionally. Cool.

Preheat the oven to 200°C/400°F/Gas Mark 6. Add the cold carrot purée and 50 ml (2 fl oz) of the cream to the beaten eggs; season to taste. Butter four round or oval moulds 6 cm (2½ inches) in diameter and 4 cm (1½ inches) deep and fill each with the carrot mixture. Cover each mould with buttered aluminium foil, place in a *bain marie* and cook in the oven for 20 minutes.

While the carrot mousses are cooking set the clam liquor in a saucepan over a high heat and reduce until it has almost all gone. Add

the remaining cream, return to the boil and reduce until it starts to thicken.

Once the carrot mousses are cooked, tip them out of their moulds on to the centre of each plate. Add the clams to the sauce and allow to soak for 1 minute over a very low heat. At the last minute add the chopped parsley to the sauce, pour over the mousses and serve garnished with baby carrots.
Serves 4

SLICES OF TURBOT MARINATED IN TOMATO AND WALNUT OIL

8 medium tomatoes
50 ml (2 fl oz) sherry vinegar
85 ml (3 fl oz) walnut oil
salt and white pepper
1.75 kg (4 lb) turbot, filleted, skinned and rinsed
2 handfuls assorted salad leaves tossed in a little walnut oil and lightly seasoned
30 fresh basil leaves

Roughly cut up six of the tomatoes and place them in a food processor or blender along with the sherry vinegar, walnut oil, a good pinch of salt and a few turns of the pepper mill. Process this until smooth. Pass through a muslin or fine sieve to remove all skin and seeds. Check the seasoning – it needs to be quite highly seasoned or the fish will taste a little bland.

Slice each fillet of turbot into thin slivers and lay them in the marinade. Cover and allow this to sit in the refrigerator for at least 6 hours. Blanch the remaining tomatoes and skin them. Cut into quarters and remove the seeds, then cut each quarter into thin strips.

To serve, place a few assorted salad leaves in the centre of each plate. Lay the slices of turbot on the plates, whisk the marinade if it has started to separate then pour a little of this over the fish. Scatter the strips of tomato and basil leaves over the top.
Serves 6

Left: *Carrot mousse with a clam sauce*
Right: *Slices of turbot marinated in tomato and walnut oil*

QUARTET OF LAMB WITH BASIL AND TOMATO

2 lamb's brains
450 ml (¾ pt) court bouillon
a little white wine vinegar
a few fresh herbs such as bay leaf, thyme,
parsley and rosemary
1 best end of lamb
salt and white pepper
2 lamb's kidneys
100 g (4 oz) lamb's liver, cut in 4 slices
2 tomatoes
a little oil for frying
25 g (1 oz) unsalted butter
85 ml (3 fl oz) dry white wine
450 ml (¾ pt) veal or lamb stock
16–20 basil leaves, shredded

Soak the lamb's brains in salted water overnight to draw out any blood. Bring the court bouillon to the boil, add a little vinegar and a few fresh herbs, plunge in the brains and barely simmer for about 5 minutes. Remove from the heat and allow to cool in the stock. Once cold, break the brains into two lobes and cut each lobe into two.

Remove the eye of meat from the best end of lamb – this should give you a fillet about 15 × 4.5 cm (6 × 1¾ inches). Season. Skin each kidney and cut into four slices. Cut each slice of liver into two. Blanch, peel and deseed the tomatoes then cut their flesh into strips. Set aside.

Heat the oil and half the butter in a frying pan and gently cook the fillet of lamb, leaving the centre pink. Remove from the pan and keep warm. Put the brains in the same pan and lightly brown on both sides; keep these warm with the fillet. Pour off the fat and, over a high heat, add the white wine and reduce until it has almost all gone, then add the veal or lamb stock and reduce until it starts to thicken.

At the last minute heat a little oil in a separate frying pan along with the remaining butter and quickly cook the slices of liver and kidney. Add the tomatoes and basil to the sauce. Pour the sauce on to the plates and arrange the liver, brains and kidney on this. Cut the fillet of lamb into 16 slices and arrange these on the plates. Serve immediately.
Serves 4

Above: *Fillet of beef with saffron glazed potatoes*

FILLET OF BEEF WITH SAFFRON GLAZED POTATOES

10 medium new potatoes
300 ml (½ pt) chicken stock
pinch of saffron threads (powdered saffron
can also be used but the flavour will not be
as good)
175 g (6 oz) unsalted butter, chilled
salt and white pepper
4 × 150 g (5 oz) fillets of beef
a little oil for frying
120 ml (4 fl oz) red wine
350 ml (12 fl oz) veal stock
2 tsp wholegrain mustard
50 ml (2 fl oz) double cream
sprigs of dill (optional)

Turn the potatoes into barrel shapes about 4 × 1 cm (1½ × ½ inch) making two from each potato. Bring these to the boil in the chicken stock, along with the saffron, 15 g (½ oz) of the butter and a little salt. Boil until the potatoes are just cooked. Remove the potatoes from the stock and reserve; reduce the stock until only 2 tbls remain; set aside.

Season the fillets with a little salt and

Below: *Quartet of lamb with basil and tomato*

pepper. Heat the oil in a frying pan then add 15 g (½ oz) of the butter and sauté the fillets until cooked. Remove the fillets from the pan and leave in a warm place; pour off the fat from the pan and, over a high heat, add the red wine and reduce until it has almost all gone. Add the veal stock, return to the boil, whisk in the mustard and reduce the sauce over a high heat until it thickens.

Reheat the fillets in a hot oven for about 1 minute. Meanwhile, return the saffron stock to the boil, add the cream then gradually add the remaining butter, whisking continuously until it has all melted. Return the potatoes to this and keep warm (do not allow to boil).

To serve, pour a circle of the mustard sauce into the middle of each plate, leaving at least 2.5 cm (1 inch) between it and the rim of the plate. Divide the potatoes evenly around this, then pour the saffron sauce around to create a dark inner circle surrounded by a pool of bright yellow. Place a fillet in the middle of each plate and, if you wish, finish off with small sprigs of dill placed on each potato.
Serves 4

ROAST FILLET OF MONKFISH WITH ROASTED CLOVES OF GARLIC AND A RICH RED WINE SAUCE

2 × 1 kg (2 lb) monkfish tails
2 tsp oil
25 g (1 oz) unsalted butter
salt and white pepper
20 cloves garlic
250 ml (8 fl oz) red wine
350 ml (12 fl oz) fish stock
350 ml (12 fl oz) veal stock
a few sprigs of chervil

Preheat the oven to 230°C/450°F/Gas Mark 8.

Fillet the monkfish and remove any dark meat. Heat the oil in an ovenproof sauté pan and when hot add the butter. Season the monkfish and seal in the fat. Add the garlic and place the pan in the oven for about 5 minutes. Turn the fish once during cooking.

Remove the fish and garlic from the pan (if the garlic is not quite cooked return the pan to the oven until it is). Pour off the excess fat, add the red wine and reduce until it has almost all gone, then add the fish stock and reduce until only about a quarter remains. Add the veal stock and reduce until thickened. Return the fish to the oven for 1 minute and reheat, and meanwhile strain the sauce and pour on to the plates. Cut each fillet into 12 slices and arrange on the plates with the garlic and sprigs of chervil.
Serves 4

Above: *Roast fillet of monkfish with roasted cloves of garlic and a rich red wine sauce*

SAUTÉED VEAL STEAK WITH A SAUCE OF PINK GRAPEFRUIT

2 pink grapefruit
120 ml (4 fl oz) sugar syrup
50 g (2 oz) caster sugar
a little oil for frying
225 g (8 oz) unsalted butter, chilled
salt and white pepper
4 × 150 g (5 oz) veal steaks, cut from the
loin, or two veal fillets weighing 275 g
(10 oz) each
85 ml (3 fl oz) dry vermouth
350 ml (12 fl oz) chicken stock
120 ml (4 fl oz) double cream
a few sprigs of chervil

Peel and segment the grapefruit, saving the peel from one and all of the juice. Remove the pith from the reserved peel. Bring the sugar syrup to the boil and plunge in the peel; boil for about 3 minutes. Drain the peel and roll it in the sugar, then leave in a warm place to dry slightly before cutting into thin strips.

Heat the oil in a frying pan and when hot add 15 g (½ oz) of the butter. Lightly season the steaks and gently sauté in the pan until they are cooked but still slightly pink in the centre. Remove from the pan and keep warm. Pour off the fat and, over a high heat, add the vermouth. Reduce this until it has almost gone. Add the chicken stock and the reserved grapefruit juice and reduce by three-quarters.

To serve, reheat the veal steaks in a hot oven for about 1 minute. Bring the stock to the boil, add the cream and return to the boil. Gradually add the remaining butter, whisking continuously until it has all melted, then strain the sauce through a fine sieve or muslin. Scatter about five segments of the grapefruit on to each plate and pour two-thirds of the sauce over them. Slice each steak into six pieces and arrange around the plate; pour the remaining sauce over. Scatter the grapefruit peel over the meat and sauce then garnish with a few sprigs of chervil.
Serves 4

Right: *Sautéed veal steak with a sauce of pink grapefruit*

CHOCOLATE CUP FILLED WITH AN ALMOND CREAM AND POACHED APRICOTS, WITH AN APRICOT PUREE

225 g (8 oz) dark chocolate
1 kg (2 lb) small apricots
300 ml (½ pt) sugar syrup
juice of ½ lemon
50 g (2 oz) ground almonds
150 ml (¼ pt) double cream
25 g (1 oz) icing sugar
Amaretto, to taste
4 mint leaves
a few toasted almond flakes
a little extra double cream (optional)

Using cotton wool, polish the insides of four metal moulds about 7.5 × 5 × 4 cm (3 × 2 × 1½ inches). This is to prevent the chocolate from sticking.

Cut the chocolate into small pieces and melt in a bowl over hot water; do not allow the chocolate to go above blood heat. Using a clean dry brush, brush the insides of the moulds with a thin layer of the melted chocolate and allow to set. Once set pour chocolate into each mould, one at a time, filling them up then tipping the chocolate out again. This will leave a thin layer of chocolate in the mould. Leave to set in the refrigerator for at least 30 minutes.

Put four nice apricots to one side. Cut the rest into eighths and poach in the sugar syrup until soft. Drain, reserving the liquor and about 40 pieces of apricot. Purée remaining apricots in a blender or food processor with the lemon juice until smooth. Rub through a sieve. If you feel the sauce is too thick, thin it down with a little of the cooking liquor.

Poach the four reserved apricots in the cooking liquor so that they are just cooked. Allow to cool then remove their skins.

Sprinkle the ground almonds on to a baking tray and brown under the grill until toasted. When they are cold, whip the cream and the icing sugar, fold in the almonds and add Amaretto to taste. Gently remove the chocolate cups from their moulds and half fill each with the almond cream. Fill the rest of the cup with the pieces of apricot.

To serve, place a chocolate cup slightly off-centre on each plate, pour a little of the sauce next to it and place a whole apricot on a mint leaf to the side. Sprinkle a few toasted almond flakes on the plate. If wished feather the sauce with a little extra double cream. Serves 4

Above: *Chocolate cup filled with an almond cream and poached apricots with an apricot pureé*

DAVID ADLARD

'Are you Mrs Adlard?' I enquired of the lady who had greeted us and who seemed to be in charge. 'No,' she replied, 'she's upstairs feeding the baby.' Moments later a wiry, feverish, Woody Allen figure with gold-rimmed spectacles emerged from the kitchen to bid a brief welcome to his guests before shuffling briskly back to his stoves. At the end of the evening, Mrs Adlard did appear. Fresh-faced, pink-cheeked and smiling, she sat down at our table looking a million dollars in a warm woolly dressing-gown with a pair of fluffy bedroom slippers on her feet. After 15 minutes her husband joined us, similarly shod. He was looking more relaxed now, the tension which had seared his brow earlier dissolved into relief and an air of modest satisfaction. It had been a good evening and the benign eccentricity of the scene had made the occasion one of the most memorable that my wife and I could recall. We had dined on fare worthy of the Connaught, Adlard's culinary alma mater, but in circumstances more akin to a family gathering around the kitchen table.

This was my first encounter with the Adlards in their Wymond-ham premises – the tiny butcher's shop-turned-bistro with its flagstoned floor and rickety pine furniture – before they moved up the road and up-market to Norwich. There the style of the restaurant in Upper St Giles Street is more obviously in tune with the manner of the *patron*'s cuisine. Walls covered in an emerald green suede-soft fabric and hung with pastoral watercolours illuminated by brass shaded picture lights exude a suitable balance of dramatic impact, warmth and clubbable good taste. The informality and easy friendli-ness that were the Adlards' trademark in Wymondham remain unaffected by the polish of professional interior design and owe much to the natural vivacity of Mary, who provides the electricity in the room and the support for a man whose singleminded absorption in his kitchen hides a sensitive, almost vulnerable character. Thirteen years

his junior, she is endearingly protective and proud of him although he gives her all the credit for his success: 'If I had not met Mary, I would never have opened my own restaurant,' he admits.

Certainly this would appear to be the case. Like David Wilson at the Peat Inn, Adlard discovered his passion for cooking relatively late in life and it was only after he had met his future wife that he finally mustered enough confidence to hang his eponymous sign above the front door. By then he was already 39 years old.

David Adlard was born and bred a citizen of Norwich. His father managed a bank and could comfortably afford to send his son to Greshams where, on paper and on the breast pocket of his blazer, David displayed the future promise of a Nobel prize and a neck-load of Olympic gold medals. He gathered more GCEs than there are months in the year and narrowly missed scholarships to both Oxford and Cambridge because of his addiction to running four-minute miles. In 1963, when he was 19, he walked into Sussex University and, three year later, walked out again carrying off an honours degree in chemistry before joining Alcan in London as a budding production manager and putative captain of industry.

However, as Adlard progressed up the lower rungs of the corporate ladder, the appeal of the boardroom faded and he came to dislike the games that company men play. In his mid-twenties, he began to buy *Family Circle* and the *Cordon Bleu* magazines and, in the peace of his Hampstead flat, cooking gradually became a medium to salve his discomfort with the outside world. The familiar surround-ings of the university lab metamorphosed into a kitchen, recipes were as formulae and the ingredients for his dishes came together like chemical compounds.

While the solace of the domestic stove brought a measure of fulfilment to his life, it was not until the age of 30 that Adlard made

DAVID ADLARD

the break from big business. His middle-class, conservative upbringing dictated that a change of career would just be too great a shock to the system. However, eventually the sheer tedium and misery of his job drove him to Kilburn Polytechnic, where he enrolled on a government retraining scheme – a course of instruction from which he emerged 'with a qualification' but as ignorant about catering as when he started.

Although the born-again David Adlard had long nursed a vague and romantic notion of starting up on his own, it took him longer still to make any serious effort to realize his dream. Now that he had been freed from the corporate yoke, he determined to have some fun with work directly linked to the principal pastimes of sailing, surfing and sex. For two years he drifted in and out of jobs which assisted his pursuits but which taught him nothing in the kitchen other than how *not* to do it. He may have been ignorant, but he had a natural instinct for the craft and an obsession about doing things meticulously; in the meantime he had to suffer the sight of proprietors picking through

swill bins to recycle leftovers into pâté, chefs making cottage pies out of canned mince and Cadbury's Smash and crème brulées made from a béchamel base, topped with caster sugar and glazed with a cigarette lighter.

Eventually the itinerant playboy, who was now hitting his middle 30s, came to his senses and landed a junior's job at the Connaught in London where Michel Bourdin, forgiving Adlard his prodigality, sensed that beneath the naïveté there lay a mature student with the attitude and will to become an accomplished cook. Knowing his ultimate ambition, Bourdin made Adlard promise to work at the Connaught for a minimum of six months. In the event he stayed put for three and a half years and in that time he mastered the essentials of top drawer classical cuisine which, to this day, are the fundamental strengths and attractions of his food. 'We made wonderful stocks,' he says. 'The butchery was good and all kitchen practices were precise and drummed into you.'

Bourdin was a disciplinarian of the old school with a type-cast temperament which could break like a thunderclap, but Adlard saw him as a 'very generous and loveable guy'. On one occasion, when Adlard had overcooked a fillet of beef, the *maître chef* swept the dish off the hotplate and on to the kitchen floor in a fit of blind rage. After the service, the contrite apprentice went to apologize. Bourdin embraced him and told him that he was making good progress.

Time passed and Adlard continued to ruminate about a place of his own. He rehearsed his dream by throwing dinners for his friends at home, charging them £10 for a meal which would have cost £50 at the Connaught. He learned about wine and scored a distinction in his exams for the Wine and Spirit Education Trust's Higher Certificate. He grew herbs, hunted wild mushrooms and amassed hundreds of

cookery books. At last, in 1981, he bade Michel Bourdin farewell. But while his mind was made up, the heart was still faint. Until, that is, he met Mary, the lawyer's daughter from Worcester, Massachusetts.

Having trod water for a year in his native East Anglia – at Le Talbooth in Dedham – he had taken himself off to Boston where he served as *maître d'* in the kind of restaurant which likes to pour flaming alcohol into coffee cups from a great height. Boy met girl. And girl followed boy back across the Atlantic, where love blossomed over tea at the Ritz. 'I knew he was Mr Right the moment I saw him. He arrived wearing bell-bottomed trousers, platform shoes, a polka-dot shirt with a rounded collar and a big kipper tie,' she croons. And this was 1982.

It took the best part of another year for the couple to find their humble Wymondham restaurant and the £50,000 to buy it. They opened in August 1983 but no sooner had they found their feet when Adlard was hit by a stroke which rendered him speechless – except for a short vocabulary of four-lettered expletives. 'Our only form of communication took place in the marriage bed,' he confides.

Adlard soon recovered and in the five years that followed he laid the foundations for their nine-mile removal to Norwich in early 1989, collecting a Michelin star on the way. His greatest battle was the lamentable supply situation – a problem which he tackled in much the same way as some of the other far-flung chefs in this book. To his credit, a number of raw materials now available in the area still would not exist were it not for his dogged efforts to seek out local producers who were prepared to accede to his demands.

At first, he could not even find a butcher to supply him with veal bones for his beloved stock pot. He had to instruct greengrocers on haricot verts and mangetout and he never allowed them to deliver, preferring to 'shop like a housewife' until they understood his definitions of perfection. Fresh herbs were unheard of, so Adlard grew his own on an allotment five miles away and he provided Mary with a book illustrating the different varieties to help her identify what to pick. One of their waitresses was inveigled into growing salad leaves for the restaurant in her own kitchen garden.

As word of Adlard spread, the tables began to turn and eager suppliers, hearing about the tricky restaurateur in Wymondham, saw an opportunity of enhancing their own reputations by association with his. A fishmonger agreed to act as Adlard's broker at Lowestoft

Left: *Waiting for the first customers to arrive. The lonely figure of the patron standing expectantly at the door of his restaurant in Upper St Giles Street.*

Far left: *'If I had not met Mary, I would never have opened my own restaurant.'*

market. Norfolk pigeon from Clayton Vernon, now recognized as one of the best squab rearers in the country, appeared on the menu and a reliable producer of quail's eggs was found.

Now that he and his family are agreeably billeted in Norwich with the problem of his stock-in-trade licked, Adlard's energies have allowed him to refocus even more keenly on his cooking. His style is conservatively modern, his themes are undeviatingly seasonal and his executions are underwritten by basic preparation work which is painstaking in its precision. The result is a finished product shining with finesse and clarity of flavour. He eschews fuss and the traps of gastronomic pyrotechnics in favour of food cooked perfectly in its most simple, undisguised state. For Adlard is not so much the creative chef as the superb technician whose final presentations are formulaic rather than arty. Each set piece, be it fish, meat or game, arrives with its own interesting little side-show which not only complements the main act but also injects a dash of brio on to the plate. Hence a tart with a soft-boiled quail's egg lies beside generous slices of warm smoked salmon, an aubergine gâteau beside a rack of lamb, pasta with venison and so on.

However, the keynote to Adlard's cooking is his saucing. He fusses over his stocks like a manic witch-doctor casting spells on a magic potion. The consistency of his sauces is not achieved entirely by reduction, which avoids that caramelly tackiness that can often paralyse the palate. If the resultant liquid is too thin, he will thicken it with a little arrowroot and finish the sauce with a knob of unsalted butter to produce a beautifully balanced lubricant which points up the true flavours of the produce.

Puddings also display the same conservative precision and care in preparation. There is no flashiness, no desire to indulge in culinary fantasy. To Adlard, the thoroughbred cook, spontaneity is not the name of the game but getting it right is and for this reason, notwithstanding the pressures of a busy service, customers are sometimes kept waiting. 'Occasionally, it can be a problem,' says Mary. 'But that customer may be a Michelin inspector,' he replies. 'Each dish that goes out must be the very best that I can do.'

To watch Adlard at work in his kitchen is to see a man utterly absorbed in his own world. Still like the boffin adjusting the apparatus in his laboratory, he darts about the range checking a sauce, peeking under the salamander, peering intently into an oven, a permanent expression of anxious concentration written across his face. Even off duty, his obsession with culinary exactitude is rarely given a break. At his daughter Lucy's christening party, he insisted on passing the eggs for the sandwiches through a kitchen sieve. But then perhaps he suspected the priest of being in the pay of the Michelin Guide.

A LITTLE SAVARIN OF FISH MOUSSE WITH SEAFOOD AND LOBSTER COULIS

200 g (7 oz) white fish, such as lemon sole
plaice or whiting, cleaned
50 ml (2 fl oz) egg white
salt and pepper
1 large shallot, finely diced
a little unsalted butter
3 white button mushrooms, caps finely
diced
50 ml (2 fl oz) dry white wine
300 ml (½ pt) double cream or 250 ml
(8 fl oz) double cream and 50 ml (2 fl oz)
crème fraîche
cayenne pepper
24 large spinach leaves, blanched and
refreshed

For the sauce
1 tbls corn oil
shells from a 450 g (1 lb) lobster, crushed
(from the fish garnish)
¼ onion, chopped
¼ stick celery, chopped
a sprig of fresh parsley
a sprig of fresh fennel
1 tbls tomato purée
50 ml (2 fl oz) brandy
200 ml (7 fl oz) dry white wine
2 tomatoes, deseeded
750 ml (1¼ pt) fish stock
500 ml (18 fl oz) double cream

For the fish garnish
450 g (1 lb) Dover sole, filleted
450 g (1 lb) monkfish, filleted
450 g (1 lb) cooked lobster, shelled
12 scallops, shelled
sprigs of parsley

Purée the fish in a food processor with the egg white and salt. Pass the purée through a fine sieve and put into a bowl over ice. Chill in the refrigerator for 1 hour.

Sweat the shallot in butter for 3 minutes. Add the mushrooms and sweat for a further 2 minutes. Add the white wine and reduce until dry. Cool.

Butter six savarin moulds, 9–10 cm (3½–4 inches) in diameter, twice, hardening

the first layer in the refrigerator before applying the second. Make discs of buttered greaseproof paper and foil to cover moulds.

Beat 50 ml (2 fl oz) of the cream into the fish purée, add the cold shallot and mushroom mixture and beat thoroughly for at least 5 minutes with a wooden spoon until the mixture is smooth and glossy. Add nearly all the remaining cream, beating continuously. Season with salt, pepper and cayenne pepper and test the consistency by making a small quenelle and poaching it gently in simmering water. Adjust with more cream if the mousse is too solid. Check the seasoning.

Lay the spinach in the base of the moulds, leaving an overlap around the edge. Fill the moulds with the mousse, using a piping bag. Bang on a hard surface to settle the mixture and smooth it level with the edge of the moulds. Fold the spinach over the mousse. Rest in the refrigerator for 1 hour.

To make the sauce, heat the oil in a frying pan and sauté the shells, vegetables and herbs (do not burn the shells). Add the tomato purée and cook for 4–5 minutes, stirring.

Flambé with a little brandy. Add the white wine and tomatoes and reduce until nearly dry. Add fish stock to cover and reduce again until nearly dry. Add cream to cover and cook gently for 10 minutes. Pass the sauce through a sieve pressing all the juice through and keep warm.

To finish the dish, cover each mould with a greaseproof and a foil disc, securing with string. Steam the mousses gently for about 5 minutes until firm. Rest for 3–4 minutes. Cut up the Dover sole, monkfish and lobster to appropriate sizes and steam the white fish for 4–5 minutes until just firm and white. Heat the lobster by steaming with the scallops for 2 minutes. Remove wrappings, then unmould a mousse on to each plate. Pour the sauce around the outside. Arrange the fish decoratively and finally garnish with parsley.
Serves 6

Above: *A little savarin of fish mousse with seafood and lobster coulis*

DAVID ADLARD

WARM SMOKED SALMON WITH CHERVIL BUTTER SAUCE GARNISHED WITH A TART OF SOFTLY BOILED QUAIL'S EGG

4 quail's eggs
100 g (4 oz) puff pastry
¼ side of smoked salmon (use the centre cut)
salt and pepper

For the mushroom purée
½ onion, finely diced
15 g (½ oz) unsalted butter
200 g (7 oz) button mushrooms
200 ml (7 fl oz) red wine
1 tbls double cream

For the sauce
2 large shallots, finely diced
150 ml (¼ pt) dry white wine
50 ml (2 fl oz) white wine vinegar
1 tbls double cream
350 g (12 oz) unsalted butter
salt and pepper
a bunch of chervil

Plunge the quail's eggs into rapidly boiling water and cook for exactly 2 minutes. Plunge into iced water. When they are cold, peel them carefully. They should be soft. (They are delicate – you will probably need spares.) Put them in cold water and store in the refrigerator.

Roll out the pastry very thinly and line four 4 cm (1½ inch) tartlet cases. Rest in the refrigerator for 1 hour. Preheat the oven to 180°C/350°F/Gas Mark 4, and bake blind the pastry cases.

To make the mushroom purée, sweat the onion in the butter until soft, then work in a food processor with the mushrooms. Put into a dry, heavy, wide pan, add the wine and heat slowly to evaporate all the liquid.

Trim the salmon of bones and remove the dry outer layer. Cut diagonally into 12 slices, 5 mm (¼ inch) thick. Overlap each portion on buttered foil.

To make the sauce, reduce the shallots, wine and vinegar until dry. Add the cream, bring to the boil and whisk in the butter in small quantities over a low heat. Season and keep warm. Chop the chervil and add to the sauce, reserving some to garnish.

To finish off the dish, warm the mushroom purée with the reserved double cream. Warm the tarts. Warm the salmon by steaming for 2 minutes so it is cooked to a delicate pink on the surface but remains deep pink in the middle.

Place a chip basket in a pan of nearly boiling water. Plunge in the quail's eggs for 30 seconds. Drain and season.

Fill the base of the tarts with mushroom purée and put them on the plates. Rest the eggs on top. Arrange the salmon on the plate, fanning the slices and exposing the deep pink in the middle. Pour the sauce on the egg, not the salmon and garnish with the chervil.
Serves 4

Below: *Warm smoked salmon with chervil butter sauce garnished with a tart of softly boiled quail's egg*

NORFOLK SQUAB WITH ITS OWN SAUSAGE COATED WITH SESAME SEEDS

4 squabs
a little pork back fat
salt and pepper
1 dessertspn Madeira
4 tsp corn oil
sesame seeds
a little caul fat

For the sauce
4 shallots, finely sliced
1 tsp unsalted butter
200 ml (7 fl oz) Malmsey Madeira
500 ml (18 fl oz) sauce demi-glace, made
with squab stock
25 g (1 oz) unsalted butter

To prepare the sausages, remove the innards from the squabs and reserve the heart and liver. Cut off the legs and remove the meat. Mince the leg meat and offal finely with an equal weight of pork back fat. Season and add the Madeira. Make a small 'hamburger' and fry in 1 tsp of the oil, to check the taste. Shape the mixture into 4 sausages. Roll them in sesame seeds so they are completely covered and wrap them in caul fat.

To prepare the sauce, sweat the shallots in the butter for 3 minutes and deglaze the pan with the Madeira. Reduce by two-thirds. Add the demi-glace and reduce until syrupy. Keep warm in a bain marie.

Preheat the oven to 220°C/425°F/Gas Mark 7. Brown the squab breasts on either side in the remaining oil, then cook in the oven on one breast for 3 minutes and on the other breast for 2 minutes. Turn the birds on to their backs, baste and cook for a further 4–6 minutes, the breasts should be pink. Remove from the oven and rest.

Grill the sausages and keep warm. Warm the squabs and whisk the butter into the sauce. Take the skin off the breasts and remove them from the carcases. Cut the sausages diagonally into five or six pieces. Arrange on the plates and pour the sauce around. Serve with a selection of three or four vegetables.
Serves 4

ROAST PARTRIDGE WITH AN ENVELOPE OF BROWN LENTILS

100 g (4 oz) brown lentils
½ onion, spiked with 4 cloves
1 small bay leaf
150 ml (¼ pt) sauce demi-glace, made
with partridge stock
1 Savoy cabbage
4 young Norfolk partridges
4 squares 5 × 5 cm (2 × 2 inches) pork
back fat
1 tbls corn oil

For the sauce
1 tsp butter
4 shallots, finely chopped
¼ stick celery, finely sliced
5 peppercorns, crushed
100 ml (3½ fl oz) red wine vinegar
200 ml (7 fl oz) red wine
500 ml (18 fl oz) sauce demi-glace, made
with partridge stock
25 g (1 oz) unsalted butter

Soak the lentils overnight in cold water. Drain, wash in cold water and cook in salted water with the onion and bay leaf for 30 minutes, until almost tender. Drain, add the demi-glace and reduce until the taste is good.

Meanwhile, throw away the outside leaves of the cabbage and lightly cook eight dark inside leaves. Refresh and dry. Line four 7.5 cm (3 inch) timbale moulds using two leaves per mould. Spoon in the lentils and fold the leaves over to enclose them.

Preheat the oven to 220°C/425°F/Gas Mark 7. Cover the breasts of the partridges with the squares of pork back fat and truss them. Brown the birds in the oil on both sides, lay the birds breast side down and put the pan in the oven. After 3 minutes turn them on to the other breast for 3 minutes. Turn on to their backs, baste the breasts and cook for another 9 minutes. Take the back fat off 4 minutes before the end and baste again. Rest in a warm place for 5 minutes.

To prepare the sauce, melt the butter and sweat the shallots, celery and peppercorns for 3 minutes. Add the vinegar and reduce until dry. Add the wine and reduce again until dry. Add the demi-glace and reduce to a light syrup, then keep warm in a bain marie.

To serve, warm the partridges and lentil moulds in the oven and stir the butter into the sauce. Cut the breasts and legs off the partridges and arrange symmetrically at the top of each plate. Invert a lentil mould on each plate and pour the sauce around.
Serves 4

Above: *Roast partridge with an envelope of brown lentils*
Left: *Norfolk squab with its own sausage coated with sesame seeds*

COLLOPS OF VENISON WITH CRANBERRY SAUCE, TAGLIATELLE AND BACON

250 g (9 oz) piece green back bacon
500g (1¼ lb) loin of venison, trimmed of
excess fat
1 tbls corn oil
parsley sprigs to garnish

For the sauce
1 tsp butter
4 shallots, finely sliced
100 g (4 oz) cranberries
25 g (1 oz) granulated sugar
100 ml (3½ fl oz) ruby port
500 ml (18 fl oz) sauce demi-glace, made
with venison stock
grated zest of ½ orange
25 g (1 oz) unsalted butter

For the pasta
250 g (9 oz) semolina or strong plain flour
2 eggs
1 egg yolk
salt and pepper
1 tbls corn oil

Above: *Strawberries with fine sablé biscuits with orange and lemon syllabub*
Below: *Collops of venison with cranberry sauce, tagliatelle and bacon*

To make the sauce, melt the butter and sweat the shallots for 3 minutes. Add the cranberries and sugar and sweat for a further 3 minutes. Deglaze the pan with the port and reduce by two-thirds. Add the demi-glace and orange zest and reduce to a light syrup. Pass through a fine sieve and keep warm.

Make the pasta by combining all the ingredients except the oil, to form a smooth dough. Beat hard to work the dough. Rest for 30 minutes. Roll out very thinly and cut into thin strips. Plunge into boiling salted water until the strips float to the surface. Drain and rinse with cold water. Toss lightly with the oil and store in the refrigerator.

Preheat the oven to 220°C/425°F/Gas Mark 7. Cut the bacon into batons, blanch and refresh. Brown the venison in 2 tsp of the oil on both sides and cook in the oven for 8 minutes, turning once. The meat must be rare. Remove and rest in a warm place.

Meanwhile, sauté the bacon in the remaining oil and whisk the butter into the sauce. Warm up the pasta gently in boiling water. Drain, season and add the bacon.

To serve, cut the venison into collops and arrange in a half circle to enclose the pasta. Surround with sauce. Garnish with parsley.
Serves 4

STRAWBERRIES WITH FINE SABLE BISCUITS WITH ORANGE AND LEMON SYLLABUB

750 g (1½ lb) strawberries
icing sugar, to taste
50 ml (2 fl oz) Grand Marnier

For the rich shortcrust pastry
100 g (4 oz) plain flour
75 g (3 oz) unsalted butter
40 g (1½ oz) caster sugar
½ tsp grated lemon zest
2 egg yolks

For the syllabub
50 g (2 oz) caster sugar
½ wine glass sherry
juice and finely grated zest of ½ orange
juice and finely grated zest of ½ lemon
300 ml (½ pt) double cream

To make the pastry, mix the flour, butter, sugar and lemon zest and rub until the mixture resembles breadcrumbs. Add the yolks and mix together. Rest in the refrigerator. When the consistency is hard enough, roll out thinly and cut eight biscuits with a fluted 7.5 cm (3 inch) cutter. Preheat the oven to 200°C/400°F/Gas Mark 6 and cook the biscuits for 8 minutes. Cool.

To make the coulis, hull 225 g (8 oz) of the strawberries; purée with some icing sugar and the Grand Marnier in a food processor. Check for taste. Adjust if necessary and pass through a sieve. Hull and, if necessary, halve the remaining strawberries, reserving two with their stalks. Cut in half through the centre of the stalks.

To prepare the syllabub, combine the sugar, sherry and orange and lemon zest and juice. Whisk the cream to soft peaks and add the sherry mixture. Beat until stiff.

To serve, put some coulis on to each plate. Put one biscuit on each plate and add a spoonful of syllabub in the middle. Enclose the syllabub with strawberries. Place the second biscuit on top of the strawberries. Sieve some icing sugar over, to decorate. Glaze the reserved half strawberries with a little strawberry coulis and put one in the middle of each biscuit.
Serves 4

WARM WINTER TART WITH SPICED APPLE AND A CALVADOS SABAYON

4 dessert apples, peeled, cored and diced

For the pastry
240 g (8½ oz) plain flour
65 g (2½ oz) ground almonds
175 g (6 oz) butter
1 egg
150 g (5 oz) caster sugar
½ tsp vanilla essence

For the almond paste
75 g (3 oz) unsalted butter, softened
150 g (5 oz) granulated sugar
½ vanilla pod
¾ tsp ground cinnamon
100 g (4 oz) blanched almonds, chopped

For the Calvados sabayon
2 egg yolks
1 tbls caster sugar
1 dessertspn Calvados
6 tbls dry white wine

To make the pastry, place the flour, ground almonds and butter in a bowl. Work these ingredients in as for shortcrust pastry. Beat the egg, sugar and vanilla essence in another bowl until the mixture is very pale. Add the egg mixture to the flour mixture and rapidly combine. Finish on the table by kneading gently until the pastry is evenly combined. Wrap in cling film and rest in the refrigerator for about 2 hours.

Roll the pastry out 3 mm (⅛ inch) thick and line a 20 cm (8 inch) flan ring. (If the pastry is too hard leave it at room temperature for 15 minutes.)

To make the almond paste, cream the butter and sugar, add the vanilla seeds scraped from the pod and beat in the cinnamon and chopped almonds.

Preheat the oven to 200°C/400°F/Gas Mark 6. Fill the pastry case with the diced apple and press out a circle of almond paste to cover the apples. Bake for about 40 minutes, when the top should be golden brown and the pastry cooked.

To make the sabayon put the ingredients in a large, heatproof, round bowl. Whisk to amalgamate. Put the bowl over a saucepan of simmering water. Whisk vigorously for 3–4 minutes until the mixture is light and white, forming a thick mousse.

To serve, warm the tart and then divide into six portions. Serve the sabayon around and on top of the tart.
Serves 6

Below: *Warm winter tart with spiced apple and a Calvados sabayon*

ALASTAIR LITTLE

There was a moment when a notable commentator was moved to observe that Alastair Little received more press attention than the Princess of Wales. He may not have been the first of the young turks to hit the headlines in the Eighties but in the popular imagination Little has been adopted as the foodie world's favourite son. Certainly, he is the leading symbol of the kitchen revolution's youth movement and although the guide books are wildly divided in their opinions of his food (a signal of the confusion in their priorities more than any failure of judgement) he was the first of the new breed to put the boot into *nouvelle cuisine* and, for good measure, he debunked the trend for swanky decor and its associated props as prerequisites of fashionable dining. Little is a trailblazer and an iconoclast and, not unimportantly in a trade which has become serious show business, he has what it takes to charm both media and public alike – star quality laced with bags of sex appeal.

In an age of Thatcherite extravagance, Little's eponymous Soho premises are aggressively ascetic. Serried ranks of miniature strip lights hang like glistening daggers from the ceiling. The tables are black and bare. The chairs are black and slatted. The floor is bare wood and the white walls are bare too, save for three curious paintings which, perhaps, proffer an equally bare statement of Little's intention: food, fire and entertainment. Drew Smith described the place as 'the finest café in the country'. It is a neat and polite description for a restaurant which enjoins the shock of first impression with the unexpected joy of wholesome and nourishing food masterfully prepared in a manner which looks carefree on the plate but which is executed with great thought and precision.

Little is another example of the great self-taught cooks of the modern era. In the kitchens that have employed him, he has never been anything other than the head chef, leaving him unencumbered by the doctrines and prejudices of college or apprenticeship. This freedom has allowed him to evolve an eclectic style which he has made intensely personal but which developed out of a voracious appetite for both the contents of vast numbers of cookery books and the menus of other people's restaurants. At heart he is still an unrepentant poacher, but as the man who is principally responsible for leading the field in culinary eclecticism after breaking away from the *nouvelle* herd, today he is wearing the clothes of a much loved and admired head gamekeeper.

Almost from the moment he was born – in the Lancashire town of Colne in 1950 – Alastair Little learned to exercise his sharply inquisitive palate. Like all good babies at that time of rationing, he was weaned on cod liver oil and rather enjoyed it. When he was eleven, his parents started to take him on continental holidays and from that time on he lived for his next good meal. His earliest gastronomic memory was the taste of a homemade chicken broth with noodles in Limoges: 'It was a distinct experience, quite different from any restaurant I had been to in England,' he recalls. In Spain he ate paella and fried squid, and in Provence he watched a big Italian mama making *soupe au pistou*, eggplant fritters, ratatouille and *coq au vin* while her husband made his own pastis in the cellar of their house.

Back at his boarding school, poor Alastair's gustatory sensibilities suffered appallingly. By nine in the morning he felt sick from the smell of the cabbage being cooked for lunch. At table he lined his pockets with the empty envelopes of his mother's letters and quietly scooped the foul stuff into them.

When he went up to Cambridge to read archaeology and anthropology, he found the grub at Downing College marginally more up-market but equally disgusting. To survive he became a frequent patron of the town's Cypriot, Italian and Indian restaurants,

running up a huge overdraft which took him all of eight years to pay off. His studies also began to include a number of extramural texts – in particular those of Elizabeth David and Julia Child – and this encouraged him to throw a regular round of dinner parties at the superior digs he had acquired in his final year.

Little left Cambridge in 1972 with the vague notion that he might become a film editor. He started as a messenger boy around Soho earning a pittance which he supplemented at night as a waiter at Small's, a fashionable Knightsbridge café, where he made more money in one evening than the sum total of his weekly wage packet. Consequently, he turned to waiting full time. By 1976 he was back in Soho working at the Old Compton Wine Bar and when the chef walked out in a huff, he leapt into the breach and took over.

His cooking did not pass unnoticed. One day a strange, hairless man with bulging eyes and a big fur coat came in for some lunch and offered Little a partnership in a restaurant in Suffolk. Little accepted. By this time *nouvelle cuisine* was firmly in the ascendant and the

illustrated recipes of Michel Guérard and les Frères Troisgros swept like stardust through the young chef's mind. He started making vegetable terrines and placed them daintily on red puddles called coulis. However, Little's artistry did not wash with the folk in East Anglia, whose ideas of good food were confined to a grilled Dover sole or fillet steak. So John Lincoln, Little's partner, sold up and reinstalled his chef in a small, 28-seater restaurant in Putney where the vegetable terrines, fish mousses, *feuilletés* and noodle dishes were received with great enthusiasm by Fay Maschler and the readers of her column in London's *Evening Standard* but where Little himself failed to settle his partnership agreement. When John Lincoln died suddenly it was time to move on.

In 1981 Nick Lander employed Little to run the kitchens at L'Escargot, only to find that he had hired an intense and scholarly cook rather than a chef with the organizational nous it takes to lead a large brigade cooking for two hundred. Nevertheless, Little survived a year before dissolving into a brief state of limbo, re-emerging as

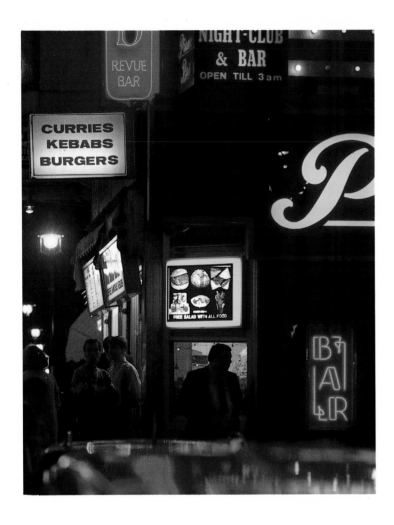

thinking on menu composition by suggesting a basic working structure which Little still uses as his blueprint today. Simplicity was the key and the formula had to include good soups, a big salad, fresh fish and some offal, chicken and dark meat. Puddings featured, *inter alia*, a nice tart and some homemade ice creams. Moreover, the menu had to be rewritten both for lunch and dinner according to the availability of supplies which were purchased daily.

Little responded immediately to the creative and intellectual demands imposed by Mackintosh's brief. He gave up vegetable terrines as a bad job and started to drift away from the *nouvelle* mode. He saw that there was a bolder, more universal, more laid-back side to food which deserved as much attention and he also saw that it was possible to serve good food fast. 'There is no need for people to wait hours while some chef thumbprints everything and saturates it all with his own personal bacteria,' he says.

Like 192, Alastair Little the restaurant works much as a neighbourhood canteen although the rise and rise of Alastair Little the cook has made him a victim of his own success, with his customers sometimes taking the experience of a visit more seriously than he ever intended them to do. He dislikes the élitism and formality of restaurant protocol at the best of times and, if he had his way, another practice he would love to abandon is the habit of accepting table reservations. As it is, he is not too fussed if late evening bookings are kept waiting for their tables even if the clients get sniffy about the delay. In his words, his restaurant 'is not the Connaught Hotel'.

In the kitchen, Little's offerings are directed by his own catholic tastes, controlled by the disciplines of his menu's framework and modulated by the produce of the day. Unschooled he may be but his ways with food are applied like the concise chapters of a definitive textbook. On buying, he insists on keeping faith with the natural seasons of his raw materials – a lesson he learned from Jane Grigson. On saucing, he criticizes the classical kitchen for being over-obsessed with passing, sieving and reductions. Where most chefs will cook a piece of fish as soon as an order is received, he waits until the table is cleared of its last course. Where others blanch their green vegetables in advance, he cooks to order. On garnishes, his ideas are as minimalist as his decor and if a sauce dribbles up the edge of a plate, he leaves it. 'There's too much wiping,' he says. 'It's better that the customer gets the food freshly cooked and hot.'

chief cook at 192 in Kensington Park Road, a new post-modernist meeting place for the literati and art fraternity of the district.

192 was the father that begat 'Alastair Little' of Soho. These were happy days. It was at 192 that Little met and fell in love with Kirsten Pedersen, his future partner and wife, and shortly afterwards the two became best pals with Mercedes André-Vega to complete the triumvirate which was to open in Frith Street in the autumn of 1985.

Little's ideas as a restaurateur were already well advanced by the time he was cooking in Putney in the late Seventies. He hated the pernicious and furtive extra charges which often crept on to restaurant bills and he banished a number of well-established practices. Out went the cover charge and additions for service, and he stopped charging extra for vegetables. However, it was Tony Mackintosh, one of the proprietors of 192, who influenced his

Little's thoughts on his cooking make plain good sense but they provide only part of the answer to the sublimity of its execution and the individuality of its style. His academic background, a variegated career free of grand hotel dogma and his own gastronomic curiosity equipped him with the means to embrace a peripatetic cuisine which he has bound into a kind of federated whole. The unity is evident because he is not hidebound by his eclecticism. He is also an adventurer who is not afraid to bend the rules to suit his setting, the circumstances and, not least, his own imagination. All his dishes are researched meticulously but never at the cost of invention.

In Japan tataki is traditionally served with finely sliced spring onions and lemon juice. Little prefers to marry the dish with broccoli or some other greens. English loin of lamb may come with polenta but this northern Italian staple reasserts itself with the addition of chopped cabbage, onion, celery and carrot like some Venetian rendition of bubble and squeak. Carpaccio is customarily presented as wafers of raw beef but Little ignores the custom and slices the meat like sirloin. However, a *bollito misto* is made by the book (essentially to Marcella Hazan's recipe) although even this is reworked into a soup if, at the end, there is a surfeit of stock and not enough meat.

In British cuisine's hall of fame, Little is more than just another remarkable talent. He broke the mould and reached beyond the ephemera of fashion to establish something fresh, different and substantial. He had none of the support mechanisms sometimes associated with a rise to stardom – big money, power patronage, lush premises and the like – but he succeeded in touching just the right nerve in metropolitan opinion at a time when it was beginning to get bored with food as an egocentric art form. He created a new awareness of style and theme which has brought him to the verge of becoming an institution, if he is not already one, and both his stature as a chef and his outlook as a restaurateur have assumed an aura not dissimilar to that of a modern George Perry-Smith. When the social historians of the next century come to reflect on these times, my guess is that Alastair Little will figure.

Left: *It's been a hard day's night!*
Far left: *Soho's neon cuisine where some like it hot, fast and on the hoof. Nearby others prefer Alastair Little.*

Rehydrate the seaweed if using.

Mix the soy sauce with the lemon juice. Mix the Japanese mustard with water, as for English mustard.

Arrange some broccoli on each plate and sprinkle with a little soy mixture. Slice the tuna into 24 neat pieces across the grain and arrange next to the broccoli. Sprinkle the fish with the spring onions and the broccoli with sesame seeds, if using and serve with more soy in dipping plates.

Note: All the Japanese ingredients should be available in oriental supermarkets (many Chinese and Thai shops have a small Japanese section). This dish should be eaten with chopsticks.

Serves 6

STEAMED TURBOT FILLET WITH MUSTARD AND DILL SAUCE

salt and pepper
2 × 225 g (8 oz) fillets of turbot or brill
a little groundnut oil
3 tbls white wine
1 shallot, finely chopped
2 tbls strong Dijon mustard mixed with 2 tbls double cream until thick
a small bunch of fresh dill, chopped
50 g (2 oz) unsalted butter
thinly sliced cucumber, marinated in a little salt and sugar for 2 hours then squeezed out

Season the fillets of turbot or brill and place

Left: *Tataki of tuna with broccoli, soy and strong Japanese mustard*
Right: *Breasts of chicken wrapped in Savoy cabbage and pancetta*
Below: *Steamed turbot fillet with mustard and dill sauce*

TATAKI OF TUNA WITH BROCCOLI, SOY AND STRONG JAPANESE MUSTARD

salt and pepper
500 g (1¼ lb) very fresh tuna, cut from a middle section in one piece
450 g (1 lb) broccoli or 1 pkt dehydrated wakame seaweed
8 tbls soy sauce
2 tbls lemon juice
Japanese mustard (substitute English if unavailable)
2 spring onions, very finely sliced, or sesame seeds (optional)

Season the tuna thoroughly and heat a ribbed grill pan as hot as possible. Prepare a container of iced water in which to immerse the tuna after cooking.

Pan fry the tuna on all sides for 1 minute each. Immediately plunge into the iced water to arrest the cooking process. Remove from the water as soon as the tuna is cold, pat dry and refrigerate.

Blanch the broccoli in boiling water until just cooked and then plunge into the iced water. Drain and dry using kitchen paper.

on a plate with a little oil and water. Heat your steamer.

Turn the fish over on the plate to ensure a thin, even coating of oil and water. Steam the fish on the plate for about 5 minutes – it will render a little water when it is done.

Meanwhile reduce the wine and shallot in a sauté pan. Off the heat, add the mustard and cream mixture, the dill and the cooking juices from the fish. Whisk in the butter.

Carefully transfer the fish fillets to two plates. Half coat with the sauce and garnish with the marinated cucumber.
Serves 2

BREASTS OF CHICKEN WRAPPED IN SAVOY CABBAGE AND PANCETTA

8 inner leaves of Savoy cabbage
8 thin slices pancetta, about 100 g (4 oz)
100 g (4 oz) unsalted butter
4 large breasts of free-range or corn-fed
chicken, pheasant or guinea fowl
salt and pepper
300 ml (½ pt) chicken stock or water
50 ml (2 fl oz) double cream

Preheat the oven to 230°C/450°F/Gas Mark 8.

Blanch the cabbage leaves for 1 minute in boiling water. Drain, cool and remove any tough stalks.

Arrange two leaves each on four 25 cm (10 inch) square sheets of aluminium foil then cover with the pancetta slices. Spread a knob of butter on each then place the chicken breasts in the centre. Season with salt and more heavily with pepper. Wrap up so the foil loosely encloses the breasts.

Place the stock or water in a roasting tin, add the chicken parcels and any remaining butter. Cook in the oven for 25 minutes.

Remove from the oven and tip any juices trapped in the chicken wrappers into the roasting tin. Place over a medium heat, add the cream and simmer until a good sauce consistency is reached.

Meanwhile slice the chicken and arrange on four plates. Pour the sauce around and serve immediately.
Serves 4

FILLET OF LAMB WITH GRILLED POLENTA

salt and pepper
1 pair best ends of lamb, chined and the
eye of the meat removed
a little groundnut oil

For the sauce
lamb bones from the best ends, trimmed of
all fat, chopped and roasted until brown
1 onion, diced
1 carrot, diced
2 sticks celery, diced
a little vegetable oil
1 tbls brown sugar
2 tbls balsamic vinegar
½ bottle red wine
2 sprigs of fresh thyme
a sprig of fresh rosemary
1 clove garlic
300 ml (½ pt) tomato passato
2 tsp potato flour

For the polenta
225 g (8 oz) polenta
15 g (½ oz) unsalted butter
1 onion, sliced into rings
2 cabbage leaves or the heart of a small
Savoy, sliced

To make the sauce, place the browned, chopped lamb bones in a wide, shallow pan, add the vegetables and sauté in a little oil until the vegetables are browned. Add the sugar and balsamic vinegar and cook until the vegetables are caramelized. Add the red wine and cook until nearly evaporated, then add enough water to cover the bones. Bring to the boil, turn down to a simmer and skim. Cook for 1½ hours, topping up with water as necessary and skimming. After 1 hour add the thyme, rosemary, garlic and tomato passato.

Pass through a sieve into another wide, shallow pan, pressing firmly on the bones and vegetables to extract as much flavour as possible. Reduce gently for a further 30 minutes, skimming often, until reduced by half. Thicken by beating in the potato flour dissolved in a little water. You may continue to cook the sauce *very gently* or allow it to cool and reheat when necessary.

Pour the polenta into a large pan containing 600 ml (1 pt) of boiling water. Remove from the heat and whisk. Return the pan to a low heat and, stirring continuously, simmer until cooked, taking care it doesn't burn or stick. This should take about 10 minutes.

In a small pan, melt the butter and sauté the onion until cooked. Blanch the cabbage in boiling water for 2 minutes, then refresh immediately in cold water. Mix the onion, drained cabbage and polenta and check the

Below: *Fillet of lamb with grilled polenta*

seasoning – be careful with this as polenta is very easily oversalted. Transfer to a buttered dish 5 cm (2 inches) deep and allow to cool.

Season the lamb generously and heat a cast iron frying pan until very hot. Brush the lamb with a little oil and sauté briskly on all sides until quite crisp – this will take about 10 minutes. Keep in a warm place for 10 minutes. Cook for 5 minutes longer if you require it medium and 10 minutes longer for well done.

To serve, cut four 2 cm (¾ inch) thick slices of polenta and cook under a hot grill for 2 minutes each side – do not attempt to turn until the 2 minutes have elapsed and then be decisive about turning them over.

While the polenta is grilling, slice the lamb, add any juices to the sauce and heat through. Arrange the slices of lamb beside the polenta on each plate and pour the sauce around.

Serves 4

SAUTEED SWEETBREAD WITH CARAMELIZED SHALLOTS

1 calf's sweetbread
225 g (8 oz) shallots
175 g (6 oz) unsalted butter
4 tbls balsamic vinegar
2 tbls demerara sugar
½ bottle red wine
150 ml (¼ pt) veal stock
seasoned flour

Soak the sweetbread in several lots of fresh water for 3 hours to clean out the blood. Then place in a saucepan, cover with fresh cold water and bring to the boil slowly. Remove from the heat and allow to cool, then drain and carefully pull off the outside skin, membranes and nodules of fat.

Dip the shallots in a saucepan of boiling water for 1 minute then run under cold water until cool; peel.

Melt 50 g (2 oz) of the butter in a heavy-based pan, wide enough to hold the shallots in a single layer. Cook the shallots over a low heat for 30 minutes until golden brown. Add the vinegar and sugar and boil vigorously until the shallots are glazed. Remove the

Above: *Sautéed sweetbread with caramelized shallots*

shallots from the pan, pour in the red wine and reduce rapidly by four-fifths. Add the veal stock and reduce a little, then simmer very slowly until needed.

Slice the sweetbread and dip in seasoned flour. Melt 50 g (2 oz) of the butter in a pan and sauté the sweetbread slices for 2 minutes on each side (do not overlap in the pan).

Add the shallots in their cooking liquor and simmer together for 1 minute, swirling in the remaining butter which will amalgamate with the sauce, thickening it slightly and giving a glaze. Serve immediately.

Serves 2

BOLLITO MISTO

1 whole shin of beef (ask your butcher to
bone it and tie it and chop the bones)
1 best end of veal, chined, rolled and tied,
bones chopped
1.5 kg (3 lb) carrots, trimmed, reserve
trimmings
1 stick celery, trimmed, reserve trimmings
2 leeks, trimmed, reserve trimmings
1 calf's foot
2.75 kg (6 lb) capon
4 whole onions
1 zampone, prepared by an Italian
delicatessen
1 ox tongue (buy ready-cooked from your
local butcher)

Preheat the oven to 160°C/325°F/Gas
Mark 3.

Place all the bones in a roasting dish and
brown in the oven for 30 minutes. Add the
reserved vegetable trimmings. Brown for a
further 20–30 minutes. Place in a large
saucepan. Cover with water, boil and skim.

Meanwhile place the calf's foot in a
saucepan, cover with cold water and bring to
the boil. Skim, turn down and simmer for 20
minutes then drain, discarding the water.

Add the calf's foot to the stock, add more
water to cover, boil, skim and turn down to a
gentle simmer. After 1 hour, add the beef;
after a further 1½ hours add the veal, the
capon and vegetables (each time returning
the stock to the boil, skimming and if
necessary adding water). Cook slowly for 1
hour more. Remove from the heat and cool.

Carefully remove all the meat and vegetables from the stock. Keep the flesh from
the calf's foot but discard the bones. Pass the
stock through a sieve into another pan and
reduce by half, skimming often.

Cut all the meat, including the zampone,
into chunks and reheat with the vegetables in
the broth. Slice the ox tongue and in a
separate pan heat in a little stock. Add to the
rest of the ingredients in the broth when hot.
Note: When this dish is finished any left over
meat and vegetables can be diced and sim-
mered with the remaining stock for 10
minutes to make a hearty broth.

Serves 10–15

PRUNE AND ALMOND TART

450 g (1 lb) best prunes or ripe fresh figs
a little armagnac
275 g (10 oz) puff or shortcrust pastry
crème fraîche, Jersey cream or ice cream,
to serve

For the almond paste
4 eggs
100 g (4 oz) ground almonds
100 g (4 oz) caster sugar
50 g (2 oz) plain flour
50 g (2 oz) unsalted butter

Soak the prunes in a little water and the armagnac overnight, then poach for 10 minutes. If using figs there is no need to soak them overnight. Allow to cool then halve and stone. Roll out the puff pastry thinly and line a 25 cm (10 inch) flan tin with it. Freeze.

Preheat the oven to 230°C/450°F/Gas Mark 8.

To make the almond paste, place all the ingredients in a food processor and blend until well combined.

Take the pastry case out of the freezer at the last minute and put the almond paste into it. Gently push the prune halves into the almond paste.

Bake in the oven for 10 minutes until the pastry rim shows signs of firming up then turn the oven down to 200°C/400°F/Gas Mark 6 and bake for a further 20 minutes. Finally turn down to 120°C/250°F/Gas Mark ½ and cook until the almond paste in the centre is done.

Serve warm with crème fraîche, Jersey cream or ice cream.
Serves 8

Left: *Bollito Misto broth*

Right: *Prune and almond tart*

SIMON HOPKINSON

In November 1987 the restaurant Bibendum opened with enough media hyperbole to inflate the jolly Michelin man into a balloon the size of the dome of St Paul's Cathedral. The difference on this occasion was that the razzle-dazzle had substance. Here was a place that added a new dimension to the accepted assumptions and definitions of what constitutes top-drawer eating out in London.

For a start, one shibboleth to be dismantled was the synonymity of decor and designer-food. Ambiance was removed from the plate and returned to the walls and furnishings in a manner that has re-energized the luxury restaurant by burying the clichés of swags and festoons, pastels and pomp. Sir Terence Conran's design is modern and invites fun rather than gastronomic worship, while, at the same time, maintaining a scrupulous and inventive sympathy with historical roots. The ubiquitous presence of Monsieur Bibendum is reflected with wit on stained glass, vases, decanters and ashtrays. However, Conran's singular achievement lies in the translation of his natural grasp of what good restaurants need to provide for the enjoyment of good food beyond a unique environment. He understands the importance of comfort, space and light. At Bibendum the ceilings are high and the atmosphere up-beat but the tables are cut low and you sink into moulded armchairs which embrace you with bonhomie.

The only point of contact between design and cuisine, the only tangible clue to culinary expectation – saving the menu – are the plates laid at each table setting. These are large, white and deep as satellite TV dishes. They promise generosity, satisfaction and contentment. And this is precisely what Simon Hopkinson dishes up from his big, brassy repertoire of old-fashioned bistro favourites like *tête de veau*, or snails which come jumping and sizzling to the table or fresh fish served on the bone. The irony of Bibendum's success is that

modern chic has lit the stage for the return of traditional, wholesome nosh to fashion and acceptability in the upper echelons of foodie society. Bibendum has allowed Hopkinson to rehabilitate steak and chips, and where once *dégustation* was the polite response at table, he is making salivation respectable again. He wants people to savour their food, not merely to taste it. For him, the mousses, purées and boneless servings of meat and fish espoused by the *nouvelle* school too often minimalize the identity and natural juiciness of the raw ingredients. Moreover, by mobilizing the faculties of teeth, jaws, tongue, as well as palate, he is reviving the pleasure of chewing as an essential part of the enjoyment of eating. Whereas in the recent past finesse, subtlety, aesthetics and invention were the hallmarks of sophisticated dining, Hopkinson is reinvesting in culinary heritage and restoring the gastronomic status of the old values of honesty, gutsiness and flavour with a big F.

Simon Hopkinson's route to the professional kitchen was charted – albeit unconsciously – from a very early age. He has always loved his food. Born in 1954, he grew up in Bury, Lancashire, where his father practised as a dentist and his mother taught. Both parents ate out and cooked with some enthusiasm and their young son relished the prospect of starting his day with a hearty breakfast of lamb's balls or beef kidneys on fried bread. He had no idea what he was eating but 'it was absolutely delicious'. At the age of eight, Simon won a choral scholarship to St John's, Cambridge, where he was nicknamed 'Hoggy' by his chums. This, in turn, moved his maths master to write a play about a bunch of sailors shipwrecked on a Caribbean island with Hoggy cast as 'Seaman Keating who was over-fond of eating'.

When he graduated to his public school in Derbyshire, his gustatory adventures continued with regular outings to local steak houses led by his music tutor, who introduced him to the joys of

drinking Mateus Rosé. And the kitchenette at the end of his study corridor provided a useful, if sometimes hazardous, laboratory for his early culinary experiments. On one occasion he exploded a haggis.

At home he dipped into the Cordon Bleu magazines and rehearsed their recipes on his mother's Aga, and on Mediterranean holidays he learned to eat squid, mussels and octopus. So it was no surprise to his family when, at seventeen, he left school to join the kitchen of Yves Champeau, the mercurial *patron* of the Normandie in nearby Birtle – a restaurant ranked highly by the *Good Food Guide* in the Sixties and Seventies. Simon was an anxious, shy young man and the experience was more akin to a baptism by fire than an apprenticeship. 'I was in tears once a week,' he confesses. Champeau was tougher on him than any of the other boys in the brigade, which was as much a reflection of the man's personality as his instinct that Simon was destined for the first division. Although Simon only stood twelve months of Champeau's regime, the Normandie's style of bourgeois and regional French cooking made a seminal impression which is evident on the

menu at Bibendum. The *steak au poivre* served with an Everest of *frites* is the classic example.

The next six years were a period of drift. Apart from a rising swell of excitement about his craft, Hopkinson has never been bitten by grand ambition. His genial, roly-poly schoolboy looks hide a frame taut with the angst of day-to-day pressures, but he has never planned his future and there has been no great sense of mission as with some of his contemporaries. 'Things just happened,' he says disarmingly, although his one regret is his failure to muster enough self-assurance to work in France.

From the Normandie he went to another *Good Food Guide* favourite, the Hat and Feather in Knutsford, Cheshire, where the kitchens lacked Champeau's professionalism but introduced him to the ideas of Elizabeth David and Robert Carrier. The owners then sent him to their hotel in Wales, which led to a succession of jobs around the coastal towns of the Dyfed peninsula. Confidence soon followed experience and in May 1975, a month before his twenty-

seductively on his gastronomic instincts. When he was offered a job as an Egon Ronay inspector, he could not believe his luck: 'I was actually being paid to eat out – to do the very thing I enjoyed doing most.' The next two and a half years saw a series of intensive bouts of critical indulgence around the best places in Britain, spiced with a number of extramural attractions which included Ronay's survey of transatlantic airlines and a report on twenty-one New York hotels. However, the penalty for his effort was a seriously expanded waistline and his final project – reviewing the cheaper eateries of London suburbia's outer reaches – finished him off. Besides, he longed to return to the stove.

At first he was too timid to face the fire of the front line. He needed to play himself in gently and so he went into private service as chef to some well-heeled residents of Cheyne Walk for three years until Alan Crompton-Batt, the restaurant consultant and noted epicure and an old comrade-inspector from his days with Ronay, helped to install him at Hilaire – a new restaurant in Old Brompton Road opened by Kennedy Brooks in the autumn of 1983.

Hilaire was the making of Simon Hopkinson. After a long absence from the heat of the commercial stove, he began nervously but soon grew into the cook that he is today. He tested his way in and out of a variety of culinary texts with a menu of cultural alternatives. He began to be noticed and before long the good and the great rolled in to pass judgement. Georges Blanc came from Vonnas and found a clear Thai soup ruinous on his palate while the taste buds of Paul Levy and Fay Maschler coped admiringly. Roger Vergé came from Mougins and ate a *steak au poivre* with deep satisfaction. And Terence and Caroline Conran became enthusiastic regulars.

From these early beginnings a friendship was struck between chef and future benefactor. They both loved France, they shared similar appetites and Simon visited the Conrans in Provence where they cooked rabbits with olive oil, herbs and wine on an open fire. At Hilaire one evening, a napkin was sent down to the kitchen. By the side of a sketch of Monsieur Bibendum, Conran had written the words, 'I've got it!' Many months later, Hopkinson moved into Michelin House and he is now an equal partner with Sir Terence and Paul Hamlyn holding the other two corners of the golden triangle.

Fashion and celebrity have been the coincidental by-products of Hopkinson's success. He only cooks what he enjoys eating himself, which may sound like a truism but tends to be the exception rather

first birthday, his father lent him £1,000 to set up on his own in a tiny restaurant called The Shed in Dinas, just east of Fishguard. The *Good Food Guide* applauded the effort but business was thin and he recalls one bleak November when he did not cook for a single customer in six days. Two years later he threw in the ovencloth and accepted an offer to rearrange the first floor of the Globe Inn in Fishguard. He named his new restaurant Hoppy's but the deal he struck with the landlord – trading profits on his drink sales for those on the pub's bar snacks – was a naïve misjudgement and nine months later he quit with losses of £2,000. Nevertheless, he left his mark on Egon Ronay, who awarded him a star in the 1978 guide, thus establishing him as the youngest chef to receive the decoration.

By now Hopkinson had tired of Pembrokeshire and, anyway, for some years the glamour of the London restaurant scene had played than the rule in a trend-sensitive trade. Moreover, his time with the Ronay organisation demonstrated just how badly some of his favourite dishes were being treated and this in itself planted the urge to drag these honourable themes from the doldrums and raise them to a new state of the art.

The source of the cooking is strongly Parisian but not exclusively so. *Daube de boeuf* and rabbit conjure the powerful fragrances and sunshine of Provence. A baked aubergine with pesto is redolent of Elizabeth David, and there is a nod to the genius of Michel Guérard in a *pithivier au chocolat*. But the main thrust of Hopkinson's menu is inspired by his love of the brasseries and bistros of Paris – places like La Coupole and Bofinger, or L'Ami Louis with its legendary reputation for roasts of poultry and game, *pommes allumettes*, snails and frogs' legs. Offal too is given a fair crack on the carte at Bibendum. A salad of calves' brains comes with a *sauce ravigote* which begs to be scooped up with a crust.

Bibendum's food is tactile and sensual – appealing to the heart rather than the mind – and, like the Sirens, it has won over the pundits. The culinary laurels are shared with a setting which eschews the labels of generic definition because it is unique, although the spirit of the place – with its bustle and banter, *joie de vivre* and cachet of cosmopolitan vogue – is more brasserie than restaurant. However, the Conran-Hopkinson potion adds up to much more. Sir Terence has done the British eating-out scene a great service by providing Simon Hopkinson with a highly polished platform for the attention he has received and the recognition he has deserved. Somehow I doubt it could have happened in Dinas or Fishguard. Hopkinson himself has had the confidence and conviction to cook what pleases him, not what impresses the guide books. If he were a man of a more ambitious disposition with ideas of seeing his name in neon lights, he might have pursued a very different track. As it happens, both integrity and critical acclaim have ended up sharing the neon bill. But the greatest compliment of all rests with Elizabeth David. Bibendum has become her favourite.

Left: *Temple of gastronomy. The Michelin building in Fulham Road, one of London's great architectural landmarks.*

Far left: *'Nunc est bibendum' (now is the time to drink), commands Monsieur Bibendum from his stained glass Communion table – his famous curves echoed in vases, decanters and even the multi-tiered service point.*

GRILLED AUBERGINE WITH PESTO

1 large aubergine
salt and pepper
a generous handful of fresh basil
2 cloves garlic
2 dessertspn pine kernels
olive oil
2 tbls freshly grated Parmesan

Split the aubergine in half either lengthways or crossways. Score the flesh about 1 cm (½ inch) deep in a criss-cross fashion with a sharp knife. Salt the surface liberally and drain, cut surface down, on a wire rack for about 1 hour so that the bitter juices can run away.

Meanwhile, put the basil, garlic, pine kernels and salt and pepper in the food processor. Grind until you achieve a paste. Add enough olive oil to produce a loose textured purée similar to a thick vinaigrette. Stir in the Parmesan cheese, which will stiffen the mixture.

Preheat the oven to 220°C/425°F/Gas Mark 7.

Bake the aubergine halves in the oven for about 20 minutes. Remove from the oven and spread the surface with the pesto mixture. Place under a very hot grill until golden and bubbling. Serve immediately.
Serves 2

Above: *Salad of calf's brain with sauce ravigote*

SALAD OF CALF'S BRAIN WITH SAUCE RAVIGOTE

1 calf's brain, cleaned of blood and nerves

For the court bouillon
1 carrot
1 leek
1 stick celery
a sprig of thyme
1 bay leaf
4 peppercorns
dash of vinegar
salt
600 ml (1 pt) water

For the sauce ravigote
1 tsp Dijon mustard
1 dessertspn wine vinegar
salt and pepper
1 dessertspn capers, coarsely chopped
a sprig of tarragon, finely chopped
1 dessertspn flat-leaf parsley, finely chopped
1 dessertspn finely chopped onion
120 ml (4 fl oz) peanut, sunflower or vegetable oil

Cook all the court bouillon ingredients together for 30 minutes. Strain into a clean pan.

Poach the brain for about 10 minutes until firm to the touch. Leave to cool in the liquid, then drain.

To make the sauce ravigote, mix together the mustard, vinegar and salt and pepper until well blended. Add the capers, herbs and onion. Whisk in the oil gently as if you were making mayonnaise. (If the sauce separates, briskly whisk in a tablespoon of boiling water.)

Slice the brain thinly and arrange in one layer on a large plate. Gently spoon the sauce over the surface of the brain and if liked, garnish with sprigs of tarragon and leaves of parsley.
Serves 2

BONED LEG OF RABBIT AND BACON WITH MUSTARD SAUCE

1 good farmbred rabbit
50 g (2 oz) unsalted butter, softened
1 small clove garlic, chopped
1 tbls chopped tarragon
salt and pepper
10 rashers streaky bacon
tarragon leaves, to garnish

For the mustard sauce
1 shallot, chopped
150 ml (¼ pt) white wine
1 tbls concentrated chicken stock
150 ml (¼ pt) double cream
1 tbls Dijon mustard
salt and pepper

Preheat the oven to 200–220°C/400–425°F/ Gas Mark 6–7.

Take the hind legs off the rabbit and remove the thigh bones. Use the rest of the rabbit for another dish. Mix together the butter, garlic and tarragon. Season with salt and pepper. Pack into the cavities left by the thigh bones and wrap each leg neatly in five rashers of bacon. Roast the legs in the oven for about 10 minutes and leave to rest in a warm place (e.g. the oven, with the door ajar) for a further 10 minutes.

Above: *Boned leg of rabbit and bacon with mustard sauce*
Far left: *Grilled aubergine with pesto*

Meanwhile, make the sauce. Put the shallot, the white wine and the chicken stock in a small saucepan. Reduce briskly over a high heat until syrupy. Add the cream and simmer until the consistency has thickened. Whisk in the mustard and strain through a sieve into a clean pan. Keep warm but do not boil again.

Correct seasoning.

Slice the thighs into three and arrange on two plates. Sit the drumstick part flat side down, with the bone standing vertically proud. Pour the sauce around the meat and garnish with a few tarragon leaves.
Serves 2

STEAK AU POIVRE

1 dessertspn white peppercorns
1 dessertspn black peppercorns
2 × 165 g (5½ oz) fillet steaks, trimmed
salt
1 tbls olive oil
50 g (2 oz) unsalted butter
a good slug of cognac
meat glaze or roasting juices (optional)

Grind the peppercorns *coarsely* in a pestle and mortar, or in a coffee grinder. Tip the pepper into a sieve and shake well until all remnants of powder have been dispersed.

Season the steaks with salt and firmly press the peppercorns into the surface of each steak. Heat the olive oil and 25 g (1 oz) butter in a frying pan. When golden brown, lay the steaks in the frying pan. Cook gently until each is done to your taste. Try to resist turning too often – the aim is to produce a good crusty coating on each surface. Remove steaks to warmed plates.

Add the cognac to the pan and whisk together with the juices. Add the remaining butter and optional meat glaze. Boil until well amalgamated. Pour over the steaks and serve immediately.
Serves 2

Above: *Crème renversée à l'orange*
Left: *Steak au poivre*

CREME RENVERSEE A L'ORANGE

finely grated zest of 6 oranges
1 litre (1¾ pt) milk
185 g (6½ oz) caster sugar
3 eggs
9 egg yolks
julienne of orange soaked in sugar syrup, to decorate

For the caramel
200 g (7 oz) caster sugar
water, to cover the sugar in the pan

Place the orange zest, milk and sugar together in a saucepan and bring gently to the boil. Cover and infuse for 2 hours.

Place the eggs and egg yolks in a bowl and gently pour on the orange milk. Mix lightly together, but don't allow the mixture to become frothy. Strain through a chinois, pressing down well on the orange zest to extract all the flavour. Skim the surface.

Preheat the oven to 150°C/300°F/Gas Mark 2.

To make the caramel, place the sugar in a heavy-based saucepan or copper pan with the water and cook to a rich brown caramel. Pour into a square container approximately 13 × 15 cm (5 × 6 inches) and 6 cm (2½ inches) deep.

When the caramel has set, gently pour on the milk mixture. Place in a bain marie and cook in the oven for approximately 2 hours or until the mixture is set. Remove from the bain marie. Place in the refrigerator until completely cold. Turn out on to a tray and serve cut into squares. Decorate with orange julienne soaked in sugar syrup.
Serves 8

CHOCOLATE PITHIVIER

225 g (8 oz) unsalted butter, softened
225 g (8 oz) caster sugar
3 eggs
225 g (8 oz) ground almonds
100 g (4 oz) cocoa powder
½ tbls dark rum
225 g (8 oz) plain chocolate, chopped
350 g (12 oz) puff pastry
beaten egg, to glaze
icing sugar

For the crème pâtissière
500 ml (18 fl oz) milk
1 vanilla pod, split
6 egg yolks
150 g (5 oz) caster sugar
40 g (1½ oz) plain flour

First make the crème pâtissière. Place the milk in a saucepan with the vanilla pod and heat gently to boiling point. Whisk together the egg yolks, sugar and flour. Pour on the hot milk and whisk lightly together. Return to the saucepan and gently cook the mixture until it thickens and coats the back of the spoon. Continue cooking until the mixture tastes not in the least bit floury. Pour through a sieve, discard the vanilla pod and chill.

For the pithivier mixture, place the softened butter and sugar together in a bowl and beat together until the mixture is light and fluffy. Add the eggs and beat together. Next add the ground almonds and cocoa powder and beat together lightly. Then add the rum and crème pâtissière and finally fold in the chopped chocolate. Chill.

Preheat the oven to 200°C/400°F/Gas Mark 6.

Roll out the puff pastry to approximately 3 mm (⅛ inch) thick. Cut out 8 squares 10 × 10 cm (4 × 4 inches) and 8 larger squares 15 × 15 cm (6 × 6 inches). Place the smaller squares on a floured board and place a scoop of the chocolate mixture in the centre, using a large ice cream scoop. Brush the pastry with half the egg. Place the larger square of pastry on top and press down firmly around the mixture to extract all the air.

Place a 10 cm (4 inch) round pastry cutter over the mixture and cut out a circle. Press

Above: *Chocolate Pithivier*

the edges together with a fork. Brush the pithiviers with the remaining beaten egg and dust lightly with icing sugar.

Place on a greased baking tray and cook in the oven for approximately 15–20 minutes until the pastry is well risen and golden brown. Remove from the oven, dust lightly with some more icing sugar and serve hot with thick cream.
Serves 8

CHRIS OAKES

There is an ancient beech wood in the Slad Valley which would make a perfect spot for a murder. The trees like bunched masts of a galleon fleet lilt gently to the wind – their trunks dressed in a coat of rich green ivy. The dense undergrowth is softened by a deep moss carpet and the web of rough tracks running through the forest is lined by low banks of earth, stone and exposed root half-hidden by a riot of wild strawberry bushes and blackberry bramble. This is the country of Laurie Lee, Slad's lyrical hero, whose childhood tales of skulduggery in the valley are told in *Cider With Rosie*.

The exact location of these woods must remain a secret but, mercifully, for no evil purpose today. For this is where Chris Oakes gathers the ceps and chanterelles for his kitchen. On the July afternoon we joined him, we even found a shaggy ink cap, a rude fungus which moved Martin Brigdale to liken it to some primitive condom.

Oakes's communion with the mushroom is almost symbolic in its devotion – indeed it forms the motif on the cast iron name-plaque fixed to the outside wall of the pretty Cotswold stone house which is his restaurant. He is a man of the soil and the sea, his heart still tethered to the bucolic and maritime traditions of his upbringing in the marshy lowlands between Felixstowe and Aldeburgh. The pace of his career, like the way of life in rural England, has been cautious, thoughtful and unrushed. It is a philosophy which has served him well as his first entry in the 1988 edition of the *Good Food Guide* proved. He came in with a score of 16/20 which placed Oakes firmly amongst the country's top chefs and Drew Smith's observation that he is 'perhaps the most controlled of the modern British chefs' holds true to the character of the man.

Chris Oakes was born and bred a native of East Anglia. His parents kept a public house in the village of Hollesley and the family lived over the shop. This was a pub of the old order. Mr Oakes's customers were the local farmers and their dogs. The bar would hang heavy in a static veil of khaki-grey tobacco smoke, and a ploughman's lunch of a wedge of cheese, a raw onion and half a loaf of bread – a ritual since anaesthetized by the big breweries – was eaten with a penknife.

Chris went to school five miles away in the neighbouring village of Butley, where he was a very average pupil until his last year when the headmaster, in a fit of anti-sexist zeal, decided that the girls should be instructed in woodwork and that the boys should practise cookery. At the end of the autumn term the young cooks were required to make, ice and decorate a Christmas cake for a critical panel of judges drawn from the school's staff and, for the first time in his life, Oakes came top of the class. He lapped up the recognition, persevered and continued to excel in his new-found talent.

Then tragedy struck the family. In 1970, just before Chris's fifteenth birthday, his father died of cancer. He had been unwell for some time and had long since quit the pub to take on a less demanding job as a nightwatchman. Nevertheless, the death was traumatic and dramatically changed the family's circumstances. They moved to a council flat and Chris left school to help support his mother.

Without a thought for his future, Chris accepted any job he could find. He worked on building sites. He delivered milk. And he drew the dole. Eventually, a family friend encouraged him to apply for an apprenticeship at Seckford Hall, a country house hotel in nearby Woodbridge. The head chef, Malcolm Long, liked what he saw, took the young 16-year-old on and had his first impressions rewarded by his protégé's good progress. After Long had left to take up an appointment as a chef-tutor at Colchester Technical College, Chris stayed on and began to settle down a mite too comfortably on his weekly wage packet of £25. He needed a judicious prod and he

received it from his old chef who had detected a promising future in a gentle youth too green to see it for himself.

Without Chris's knowledge, Long arranged an interview at Le Talbooth, a lovely Tudor-timbered house on the banks of the river Stour near Dedham which its ebullient owner, Gerald Milsom, had made into East Anglia's most famous restaurant. Long then called Chris, presented the date of his interview as a *fait accompli* and instructed him to wear his Sunday best. Chris obliged by turning up in a pair of bright orange trousers — a sartorial gesture which more than compensated for his shyness.

In September 1973, Chris Oakes began a seven-year association with the Talbooth and the various catering offshoots which comprised Milsom's mini-empire. There were two spells away from the home turf — the first in the Swiss resort of Davos and the second at Gleneagles in Scotland and the Plough at Clanfield in Oxfordshire. But these were essentially useful sabbaticals to support an experience which laid the first foundations on his path to success as a top-flight chef. Above all, Gerald Milsom's potent cocktail of a personality — one part taskmaster, one part Dutch uncle, one part fairy godmother — gradually instilled in Oakes a self-confidence and an awareness of his own ability which had always been lacking.

By the end of 1980, and now 25, Oakes had completed almost three years as second-chef at the Pier, Milsom's new fish restaurant in Harwich. At last it dawned on him that there was life after 'Mr Gerald' and he sought promotion to a senior league. There was more to learn and for the first time the camaraderie of the brigade which had bound his loyalty was overtaken by the sting of ambition. But he was not ready to be chef. What he wanted was a kitchen led by a first-division player of the *nouvelle vague* and he found his goal at the Castle in Taunton, my own hotel, as understudy to John Hornsby, who had been Anton Mosimann's *sous-chef* at the Dorchester. Over the next two years the Castle's reputation soared while Oakes absorbed his new chef's teachings like honey on warm bread. However, early in 1983 Hornsby left abruptly.

Like Malcom Long and Gerald Milsom before me, I had come to admire in Oakes an innate talent and an unusual dedication to his craft. Without a moment's hesitation, I called him to my house and offered him the job of head chef. He refused it, believing still that he was 'not ready'. Eventually, we compromised on the title of acting head chef until I could find a replacement for Hornsby. It was a search that I made with little vigour. Six months later Chris Oakes assumed full control and in 1984 he earned the Castle its first Michelin star.

Amongst the young kitchen revolutionaries of the '80s, Oakes, like Ian McAndrew, was one of the first chefs to begin to take serious advantage of the improving supply situation. He did not like using the established London suppliers but preferred to seek out his own local contacts who were cajoled into producing the goods and the quality he demanded. Fed up with the state of British poultry, he and I mounted a campaign for 'real chicken' in the local press which persuaded a canny smallholder to rear the birds we wanted from his eccentric hideout on a redundant World War II RAF station in the Blackdown Hills. An emerald-fingered GP who spent more time tending his Edwardian walled garden than the patients in his surgery began to produce fruits, vegetables and herbs exclusively for the Castle. Our cheese trolley became a celebration of the cows, ewes and goats of the West Country. Our fish was landed in Brixham or Lyme Regis. The game was Exmoor. And, of course, the mushrooms were Oakes-picked from the Quantocks.

Good suppliers are a chef's best friend and Oakes recognized their value by printing an honours list of those most highly favoured on the first page of his menu – a courtesy he has maintained in Stroud and one which Gary Rhodes has continued in Taunton.

In June 1984, Oakes married my secretary, Caroline Scott – a vibrant, quick-witted redhead who provided the ideal counterpoint to a partnership which led from *le lit d'amour* to a family business. The reluctant bud came into bloom and in 1986 Oakes mustered simple logic to realize his dreams: 'If I can work successfully for someone else for 15 hours a day, I can do the same for myself. It seemed the natural next rung on the ladder.'

Oakes's eponymously christened restaurant opened on Guy Fawkes night with a party which was more poetic than pyrotechnic. Laurie Lee was there and when Chris emerged to face his audience at the end of the performance, the author turned to me and whispered: 'Look at him. Pale, pleased and exhausted. He's given birth.'

The history of that birth is remarkable for its courage and the faith of Caroline's parents in their son-in-law. Nowell Scott resigned his

Right: *Oakes Restaurant, an early 19th-century Cotswold stone house overlooking the lush green slopes of the Slad Valley.*

Far right: *With only two assistants to support him, Chris Oakes's tiny kitchen is already overcrowded. Here he prepares the mixture for his cinnamon soufflé.*

directorship in a light engineering company and he and his wife, Jean, sold their comfortable Hampshire home to buy the house in Slad – an old primary school run by two elderly sisters. They borrowed £100,000 from the bank and – save for the heavy building work – the family performed a do-it-yourself miracle to transform the house into a restaurant. Nowell spent six weeks reconstructing the floor. Fifty chairs and 15 tables, bought second-hand from a Berni Inn steakhouse, were stripped and revarnished. The interior was redecorated and the wilderness behind the house was cleared to create a garden and, most importantly, the chef's fruit and veg plot.

The early days were tough and the nights were filled with sleeplessness and visions of vampires dressed as bank managers. There were evenings when only one table was occupied and that was by the family playing Trivial Pursuit. If a car did draw up outside, there was the thrill of slamming the board shut and looking lively. But word spread and Stroud's location at the crossroads to the Midlands, South Wales and the West Country soon brought the restaurant a gathering tide of enthusiastic callers.

Oakes's themes in the kitchen reflect the down-to-earth honesty, singlemindedness and restraint of his temperament. He does not like fuss. His preference is for clean, bold flavours and simply-matched textures prepared and arranged in the modern idiom without any of the contrived prettiness. It looks like real food for people with an appetite to tuck into: hearty food that is nevertheless balanced by the care and technical confidence of a serious craftsman. Scallops, seared on top of a scrubbed stove, are served whole to conserve their juiciness; so much better than slicing the little things. A salad of duck breast is presented with the skin and fat left on the fowl. An apple, orange and sultana chutney is a perfect foil for his chicken liver parfait. And the marriage of red mullet with braised onion and rösti potato is vintage Oakes – a signature dish and a classic example of his style.

In many ways Chris Oakes's life reminds me of the fable of the hare and the tortoise – a cautionary tale which is largely ignored by the young turks of the British culinary scene, hell-bent on instant stardom. Despite the limitations of a tiny kitchen which frustrates his creative development, Oakes is still in no rush. He would like to expand, perhaps into premises with a few bedrooms, but for the moment he has put his chef's ego in his pocket because his natural wisdom dictates that he prove his ability to run a successful business.

For the time being culinary growth remains on hold although he knows that he has much more to give. Meanwhile, the country lad-made-good has no intention of selling his soul and his livelihood for a bag full of stars which might not pay the mortgage.

Above: *Salted sea trout*

SALTED SEA TROUT

1 × 1.5 kg (3 lb) side fresh salmon trout,
all bones removed
approx 350 g (12 oz) rock or sea salt
approx 75 g (3 oz) Dijon mustard
50 g (2 oz) fresh dill, finely chopped
50 g (2 oz) fresh parsley, finely chopped
15 sprigs of fresh dill

For the sauce
2 tsp caster sugar
450 g (1 lb) natural yoghurt
2 tbls chopped fresh dill
100 g (4 oz) cucumber, trimmed of skin
and seeds and finely diced
salt and pepper

Make sure all the bones are removed from
the trout but leave the skin on. Cover the fish
completely with the salt and leave in the
refrigerator for 24 hours.

Wash the fish thoroughly and then dry it
with absorbent paper. Spread the mustard
over the fish. Mix the chopped dill and
parsley together and sprinkle over the mustard, then press them in to ensure they stick.
Cover and store in the refrigerator for up to
four days.

To make the sauce, mix the sugar into the
yoghurt until a sauce consistency is reached.
Add chopped dill and cucumber and season
to taste.

To serve, slice the salmon trout as thinly as
possible, starting at the tail end. Arrange on
plates and pour the sauce around. Garnish
with a sprig of dill.

Note: If a smaller fillet of salmon trout is used,
then accordingly less time is needed for
salting it.

Serves 15

CHICKEN LIVER PARFAIT SERVED WITH HOMEMADE CHUTNEY AND BRIOCHE

2 medium onions, roughly chopped
225–275 g (8–10 oz) pork back fat, thinly
sliced
750 g (1½ lb) chicken livers, trimmed
900 ml (1½ pt) double cream, lightly
whipped
salt and pepper

For the brioche
15 g (½ oz) fresh yeast
25 g (1 oz) caster sugar
150 ml (¼ pt) warm water
225 g (½ lb) unsalted butter
450 g (1 lb) strong plain flour
10 g (¼ oz) salt
4 eggs

For the chutney
1 orange
5 Granny Smith apples
50 g (2 oz) sultanas
a pinch of mixed spice
salt and pepper
1 glass red wine
120 ml (4 fl oz) red wine vinegar

Preheat the oven to 160–180°C/325–
350°F/Gas Mark 3–4. Heat a large frying pan.
Fry the onion in the dry pan and leave until
'burnt'. Stir occasionally.

Meanwhile, line a terrine mould 25 ×
7.5 cm (10 × 3 inches) with the pork back
fat (the slices should be no more than 1 mm
(¹⁄₁₆ inch) thick). Overlap the slices slightly
and leave enough fat overhanging the terrine
to cover the top.

When the onions are ready, place in a food
processor and turn on for 30 seconds. Then
add the livers and process until the mixture is
a purée. Pass through a fine sieve. Combine
the liver purée, lightly whipped cream and
seasoning. Pour the mixture into the lined
terrine and place the overhanging fat over
the top. Cover with foil and the lid.

Cook the terrine in a water bath in the
oven for approximately 1 hour. To test if
cooked, remove the lid and press the edges
gently with your fingers. If firm, replace the

CHRIS OAKES

A SALAD OF SLICED DUCK BREAST, MIXED LETTUCES AND PINE KERNELS SERVED WITH A RED WINE DRESSING

a few leaves of radicchio, curly endive,
lollo rosso, oak leaf lettuce and purslane
3 tbls walnut oil
salt and pepper
a few toasted pine kernels
4 boneless breasts of duck
1 tbls vegetable oil
25 g (1 oz) unsalted butter

For the dressing
2 shallots, finely chopped
1 glass dry red wine
25 ml (1 fl oz) red wine vinegar
120 ml (4 fl oz) grapeseed oil
salt and pepper

Wash and pick over all the salad leaves. Toss in walnut oil and season. Divide between four plates and sprinkle the pine kernels on top.

Fry the seasoned duck breasts in the oil and butter, leaving them pink. Slice each warm duck breast into five thin slices and arrange on top of the lettuces.

To make the dressing, reduce the shallots and red wine by half. Add the vinegar and reduce until almost all the liquid has evaporated. Whisk in the oil slowly and season. Pour the warm dressing over the duck and lettuces. Serve immediately.
Serves 4

Above left: Chicken liver parfait served with homemade chutney and brioche

Below: A salad of sliced duck breast, mixed lettuces and pine kernels served with a red wine dressing

lid, remove from the oven, cool and then place in the refrigerator for 24 hours.

To make the brioche, cream the yeast and sugar and dissolve in the warm water. Leave in a warm place to start fermenting.

Cut the butter into small cubes. Place the flour and salt in a mixing bowl and add the yeast mixture and eggs; work to form an elastic dough. Gradually incorporate the cubes of butter. Cover with cling film and prove in a warm place until the dough has doubled in size.

Knead the dough again, cover and place in the refrigerator. Leave for four hours before using.

Shape and place into a lightly greased 20 × 10 cm (8 × 4 inch) loaf tin, cover with oiled polythene and prove in a warm place until double the volume.

Preheat the oven to 220°C/425°F/Gas Mark 7 and bake the brioche for 35 minutes. Leave to cool before serving.

To make the chutney, segment the orange and peel and core the apples. Cut into eighths. Place all the ingredients in a saucepan and gently simmer until the chutney is of the correct consistency.
Serves 10.

FILLET OF RED MULLET BAKED WITH BRAISED ONION, TOMATO AND THYME AND SERVED ON A ROSTI POTATO WITH A CREAM SAUCE

2 × 450 g (1 lb) red mullet
vegetable oil
4 large onions, finely sliced
salt and white pepper
2 tomatoes
sprig of fresh thyme
300 ml (½ pt) fish stock
175 ml (6 fl oz) dry white wine
300 ml (½ pt) double cream
50 g (2 oz) unsalted butter
2 large new potatoes

Scale and fillet the red mullet, leaving the skin on, but making sure all the bones have been removed, and place in the refrigerator.

Put a heavy-based pan on a high heat and add just enough vegetable oil to cover the bottom of the pan. Add the onions and stir. Reduce the heat to moderate, place a close-fitting lid on the pan and leave to stew for about 5–10 minutes. Take off the lid; the onions should have started to caramelize. Add a little cold water and mix into the onions, taking up any sediment in the pan. Repeat this action until the onions are very soft and brown in colour and most of the liquid has evaporated. Add salt and pepper to taste. Remove the pan from the heat and keep to one side.

Blanch, refresh and peel the tomatoes. Scoop out the seeds and neatly dice the flesh. Pick off the leaves of thyme and add to the diced tomato. Put to one side.

Boil the fish stock down gently until it has reduced by three-quarters. Add half the white wine and reduce further by three-quarters. Add the double cream and gently reduce again by three-quarters. Take off the heat and whisk in the butter until emulsified. Season with a little salt and ground white pepper. Keep warm.

Preheat the oven to 220°C/425°F/Gas Mark 7.

Peel and grate the potatoes on a cheese grater and dry in a clean tea towel. Place a small, heavy-based frying pan over a moderate heat and add enough vegetable oil to coat the bottom of the pan. Put in a quarter of the grated potato and spread evenly to cover the bottom of the pan. Gently fry until golden on each side. Repeat with the remaining potato to make four potato cakes. Keep warm.

Arrange the braised onion, in four equal portions, in a heavy-based, shallow-sided roasting tin. Place a fillet of fish on top of each portion and sprinkle each with a little of the tomato and thyme mixture. Season with salt and pepper and add the remaining white wine to the pan (there should be enough liquid to just cover the bottom). Cover completely with kitchen foil and place in the oven for about 10–12 minutes. Take out when cooked and keep warm.

To serve, place a warmed potato cake in the middle of each warmed plate. Using a fish slice, scoop up the fish and onions and put on top of the potato. Pour the sauce around the fish and serve immediately.

Note: The fish stock can be replaced by adding 120 ml (4 fl oz) of dry vermouth to the white wine when making the sauce. Increase the butter by a further 50 g (2 oz).

Serves 4

Below: *Fillet of red mullet baked with braised onion, tomato and thyme and served on a rösti potato with a cream sauce*

SLICED LOIN OF ROE DEER WITH WOOD MUSHROOMS, BACON AND SPRING ONIONS

1.5 kg (3 lb) saddle of roe deer
1 bottle red wine
2 shallots, chopped
sprig of fresh thyme
sprig of fresh marjoram
100 g (4 oz) ceps
100 g (4 oz) chanterelles
75 g (3 oz) unsalted butter
salt and pepper
4 rashers bacon, cut into strips
vegetable oil
4 spring onions, chopped

For the stock
bones and trimmings from the deer
1 carrot, roughly chopped
1 onion, roughly chopped
1 leek, roughly chopped
sprig of fresh thyme
sprig of fresh marjoram
1 clove garlic
2 bay leaves
6 peppercorns
2.25 litres (4 pt) water

Remove the loins from the saddle and trim off all fat and sinew. Bone, and set the bones and trimmings aside for the stock. (This can always be done by the local butcher.)

Marinate the loins in one-third of the bottle of red wine, with the shallots, thyme and marjoram. Cover and leave in the refrigerator for 24 hours.

Wash, trim and slice the mushrooms. The trimmings may be put in the stock.

To make the stock, preheat the oven to 220°C/425°F/Gas Mark 7. Roast the bones and trimmings until they start to colour, then add the vegetables and allow to brown in the oven for approximately 15–20 minutes. When ready put the bones and vegetables in a suitable saucepan. Return the roasting tray to the heat and deglaze with half the remaining red wine. Pour on to the bones and add all the remaining stock ingredients. Bring to the boil, then simmer very gently for 3 hours. Skim off any fat or scum. When ready, strain and pass through a fine sieve.

Above: Sliced loin of roe deer with wood mushrooms, bacon and spring onions

Reduce to about 600 ml (1 pt). Leave to cool and refrigerate until needed.

In a heavy-based pan melt 25 g (1 oz) butter and cook the loins of deer gently, turning occasionally to ensure even cooking. Cook for approximately 10 minutes, leaving the meat pink. Leave to rest in a warm place.

For the sauce, reduce the remaining red wine with the stock until about 300 ml (½ pt) remains. Remove from the heat and whisk in 25 g (1 oz) of the butter. Check for seasoning.

Cook the bacon strips in oil, then add the sliced mushrooms and the remaining butter. Cook for 3–4 minutes. Add the spring onions at the end.

To serve, slice the loins, arrange on hot plates with the mushroom garnish and pour the sauce around.

Serves 4

SCALLOPS SERVED IN A PASTRY CASE WITH A CREAM AND BASIL SAUCE

4 uncooked puff pastry rounds, 7.5 cm
(3 inches) in diameter
beaten egg yolk, to glaze
300 ml (½ pt) fish stock (2 glasses of
Noilly Prat is a good substitute if fish stock
is unavailable)
1 glass dry white wine
250 ml (8 fl oz) double cream
75 g (3 oz) unsalted butter
salt and pepper
2 strips of orange zest
4 tsp grapeseed oil
24 large whole scallops
1 medium carrot, cut into julienne
1 medium leek, cut into julienne
a few leaves of fresh basil, cut into
fine strips

Preheat the oven to 220°C/425°F/Gas Mark
7. Glaze and bake the puff pastry rounds in
the oven for 10–12 minutes until brown.
Leave in a warm place to dry out thoroughly.

Reduce the fish stock by three-quarters.
Add the white wine and reduce further. Add
the double cream and simmer for 2–3
minutes. Remove from the heat and whisk in
50 g (2 oz) of the unsalted butter. Season if
necessary. Leave in a warm place.

Trim any pith from the strips of orange
zest. Slice very finely and blanch in a little
water for 30 seconds. Refresh in cold water.

To serve, heat a heavy-based pan, add the
oil and quickly fry the scallops (approximately 2 minutes). Add seasoning, the remaining butter, the carrot, leek and orange
zest. Cut the pastry rounds in half horizontally and place on plates with 6 scallops on
top of each pastry base. Spoon strips of
vegetables and orange over the scallops. Add
the basil to the sauce at the last minute and
spoon around the scallops. Place the pastry
lids on top and serve.
Serves 4

Above: *Scallops served in a pastry case with a cream and basil sauce*

CINNAMON SOUFFLE WITH DRAMBUIE CREAM

625 g (1 lb 6 oz) pears, roughly chopped
1 tsp cornflour
1 tbls water
3 tbls gound cinnamon
300 ml (½ pt) whipping cream
15 g (½ oz) sugar
Drambuie, to taste
5 egg whites
75 g (3 oz) caster sugar
a little unsalted butter
a little icing sugar

Place the pears in a saucepan, barely cover
with water and cook until soft. Liquidize and
pass through a sieve. Return to the stove
in a clean pan. Simmer until thick, stirring
occasionally (approximately 10 minutes).

Mix the cornflour and water together.
Whisk into the pear mixture and leave on a
low heat for approximately 10 minutes until
it has thickened. Add the cinnamon powder
and whisk again. This mixture can now be
used immediately or alternatively kept in the
refrigerator for later use.

Whip the cream until it peaks. Add sugar
and Drambuie to taste.

To make the soufflé, preheat the oven to 220°C/425°F/Gas Mark 7. Warm the pear mixture gently in a bain-marie. Whisk the egg whites in a copper bowl until they peak. Add the sugar a little at a time. Mix a spoonful of whites into the pear mixture, then fold in the rest.

Butter and sugar the inside of four ramekin moulds. Spoon in the soufflé mixture until it is 2.5 cm (1 inch) above the rim. Smooth off around the edge at a 35 degree angle with a palette knife, then level the centre of the mixture. Place on a baking sheet in the oven for approximately 10–12 minutes.

Dust with the icing sugar and serve immediately with the Drambuie cream in a separate dish.

Note: Apples may be used with the same method but, obviously, leave out the cinnamon.

Serves 4

Below: *Cinnamon soufflé with Drambuie cream*

HONEY PARFAIT SERVED WITH HAZELNUT BISCUITS AND ARMAGNAC FLAVOURED PRUNES

15 egg yolks
25 g (1 oz) caster sugar
50 ml (2 fl oz) water
175 ml (6 oz) clear honey, slightly warmed
600 ml (1 pt) double cream, lightly whipped

For the biscuits
6 egg whites
165 g (5½ oz) caster sugar
40 g (1½ oz) plain flour
35 g (1¼ oz) unsalted butter, melted to blood heat
100 g (4 oz) hazelnuts, very finely chopped

For the decoration
slice of honeycomb
sliced prunes soaked in armagnac and a little caster sugar

Whisk the egg yolks until they are pale and fluffy. Dissolve the sugar and water together, then boil until they reach the soft ball stage on a sugar thermometer. Combine the yolks and sugar mixture and whisk over a double boiler until the ribbon stage is reached. Remove from the heat and stir in the honey and fold in the cream. Pour into moulds, either individual or terrine moulds, (it helps if the moulds are lined with cling film) and freeze for 24 hours.

To make the biscuits, preheat the oven to 150°C/300°F/Gas Mark 2. Whisk the egg whites and add the sugar to make meringue. Fold in the flour. Add the melted butter and hazelnuts. Using a 5 mm (¼ inch) wide plain nozzle pipe on to silicone paper (any shape but approximately 3 mm (⅛ inch) thick). Make sure the nozzle is very close to the paper; this will produce very thin biscuits. Bake for 10 minutes, or until brown, in the oven.

Decorate each mould with a slice of honeycomb and sliced prunes soaked in armagnac and caster sugar. Serve with the biscuits.

Serves 16

GARY RHODES

His strategy was uncompromising. He began with a major assault on the palate by offering my friends and me a pimiento bavarois on brioche toast as an *amuse gueule* which, at the time, struck me as an appetizer designed to excite our taste buds rather than merely to amuse them. This was serious stuff. He wanted our attention before demonstrating the breadth and subtlety of his cooking but, first off, he was signalling his principal dictum of celebrating – even magnifying – the true flavours of his raw materials. The menu continued with a salad of calves' sweetbreads, shallots and thyme; a scallop mousse on braised cabbage and leeks with a champagne sauce; and a loin of lamb with a confit of tomato and garlic. For his finale he produced what has now become a classic on his menu: a wafer-thin apple tart covering the entire surface of a large plate and served with an apple sorbet – a dish inspired by his spell at Lameloise in Chagny, the three-star shrine in the heart of Burgundy.

This was March 1986 and my first introduction to the cooking of Gary Rhodes. Three weeks earlier I had met him in the lounge of London's Inn on the Park for an interview which developed into an absorbing four-hour gossip about good food – an occasion I shall remember as fondly as his magnificent test meal in Taunton before he took command of the Castle's kitchen in succession to Chris Oakes.

Born in 1960 in South London, young Rhodes grew up in Kent. When he was six years old, and just after the birth of his sister Cheryl, his father deserted the family.

By the time he had turned 13, and with his mother out at work, simple necessity obliged him to take over the responsibility of feeding himself and his younger sister. In spite of all the old clichés about chefs and their mothers, it is nevertheless a fact that Mrs Rhodes was a proud cook. Her son profited handsomely from her influence and, not least, her insistence on using fresh produce. Before long, he was cooking the family's Sunday lunch, baking cakes and making steamed sponges and upside-down pudding. Mum approved of Gary's cuisine and by his fifteenth birthday he had already decided to become a chef.

He enrolled at Thanet College and, from the start, he was an impatient student driven by a ravenous will to be best. His bible was *Le Répertoire de la Cuisine*, which he carried with him at all times and dipped into in every spare moment. In the classroom, it was always his hand that shot up first to answer a question. He began to shine and, one suspects, impressed his tutors so much that occasionally they felt obliged to restrain their bright young puppy to avoid his success and enthusiasm being soured by arrogance.

His three years' schooling was marked by a succession of prizes, including College Chef of the Year and Student of the Year. But once he had entered his final year, his mind turned to the future. He wrote to the Roux brothers and to Michel Bourdin at the Connaught, all of whom turned him down. Further petitions to Bocuse, Guérard, the Troisgros and the rest of the good and the great in France all failed. Finally, he accepted a job at the Amsterdam Hilton in the hope that this might provide the springboard for his career.

He arrived in Holland in August 1979. Twelve days after starting work, he was knocked down by a van and rushed to hospital. His distraught mother flew to Amsterdam immediately but received little hope from the doctors who had had to operate on his brain. However, they did not know their patient. Rhodes gradually fought his way back to health and four months later he returned to his station on the buffet section in the Hilton's banqueting kitchen.

Within a matter of weeks, he was pestering his chef for a transfer to the restaurant kitchen and as if this was not good enough, he pitched for the job of *commis saucier*. He got it and, six months later, just in sight of his twenty-first birthday, he was elevated briskly to

chef saucier – an important rank within the traditional kitchen hierarchy which would have delighted most cooks in their middle to late twenties.

Rhodes remained in Amsterdam for another year then, in February 1982, he returned to England and an 18-month wilderness of his own making. While his youthful impatience fuelled his early success, it also clouded the route he had planned for himself to learn from some of the best chefs in Europe. Stupidly, he withdrew his acceptance of an offer to work at Lenoir's two-star *hostellerie* at Auvillers-les-Forges in the Ardennes. Instead, a friend persuaded him to help open a new restaurant in Bournemouth. Within two months he had quit. Once again, he wrote to Michel Bourdin at the Connaught and this time he received a firm offer of a job as a first *commis*, which he promptly refused in favour of the grander title of *sous-chef* at the Reform Club – a move he came to regret. 'Who is going to want to take me on after working here' he was heard to confide eleven months later.

Nevertheless, his frustration was partially relieved by a brief spell as head chef of a struggling restaurant called Winston's in Bloomsbury, where his natural talent was given a free rein. It worked. In the eight months of his stewardship of the kitchen he attracted attention and filled his tables in spite of the fact that, at the time, he did not win the approval of Fay Maschler, the influential food critic of the *Evening Standard*.

However, Rhodes was still an unsettled, discontented man. At 23, he knew he had the ability to succeed but he had only proved it to himself superficially. He was still on the fringe – a gadfly, an attractive but aimless kitchen playboy. What he now needed was the endowment of substance and patronage of the kind which only a highly-respected chef in a well-established restaurant could provide. His benefactor turned out to be a man called Ivor Robbins, his vegetable supplier, who brought Brian Turner, head chef of the Capital, to dine at Winston's one evening. Turner was impressed and in October 1983 Rhodes returned to cooking's fast lane as the

Capital's senior *sous-chef*, where he stayed put for the next 18 months with a short break of work experience at Lameloise.

By 1985, Rhodes's confidence and maturity as a chef were more securely cast. Now he wanted to be master of his own kitchen and he moved to Whitehall, a new country house hotel in Broxted, Essex, where he created an immediate impact and was received enthusiastically by the guide books. However, his tenure of office was brief and unhappy and in January 1986 Brian Turner took him back at the Capital until his move to the Castle later in the year.

It would be too easy to suggest that the ups and downs of Rhodes's career betray a volatility of character – although there were moments when he appeared to behave like a blind kangaroo. From the start, it became apparent that he was blessed with a remarkable natural gift matched by a single-minded determination to make the top. Certainly, he shows that independence of spirit which is the hallmark of modern chefs, who are no longer constrained by the strict disciplines of Escoffier and the classical repertoire. But these characteristics of freedom and independence are valueless unless they can be harnessed to a sound understanding of the basic principles of good cooking and, of course, real talent – all qualities which Rhodes has in abundance. And so, if he has made mistakes, there is little to

suggest that his career has suffered by them. Indeed, he refuses to concede any error of judgement in deciding to take on the kitchens of Winston's and, later, Whitehall, where he enjoyed the freedom to express himself, develop his style and experiment.

In spite of the formality of his culinary education, therefore, there has been an element of self-tutelage in his progress. At Whitehall, he perfected his stocks and sauces: 'Good saucing is for me the essence of cooking,' he says. He used to clarify his stocks with egg whites. Not any more. 'If you make a good stock, there is no need to clarify it because it should come out like consommé anyway. It's just in the method of cooking.'

This desire to learn and develop from within provides the clue to his favourite heroes and, not least, to some of the sources of his inspiration. He has a deep admiration for Raymond Blanc and Nico Ladenis because they are both self-taught, self-motivated and passionately dedicated. He also admires their ability to create robust combinations of flavours from their raw materials.

However, while Rhodes's central preoccupation is with flavour and texture, he also has a well-developed sense of presentation – but not in the geometrically precise form so often associated with *nouvelle cuisine*. Michel Guérard's books *Cuisine Minceur* and *Cuisine Gourmande*

Right: *From Gary with love. The final touch to his roast best end of lamb with a fresh mint and green peppercorn crust – a rich sauce with poached currants.*

Far right: *The Castle at Taunton. Once part of the Norman fortress, the hotel has been welcoming travellers to the town for over 300 years.*

have been a particular influence on his style: 'There is no prissiness about Guérard's dishes. They look naturally beautiful, with a quality that might almost be described as rustic. It's very clever.'

Rhodes's dishes often reflect this style. A prime example is his fillets of John Dory, cooked in hazelnut oil and served with spring vegetables and saffron potatoes. It looks simple, natural and colourful but it requires considerable skill to compose. The same approach is adopted with a salad which may look naturally tossed when it is presented but, to achieve the effect, each leaf is positioned carefully and precisely on the plate.

Another distinct influence on Rhodes's cooking today has been his immediate environment. His move from London opened his eyes to new sources of fresh produce of a quality he had not expected. The fertile pastureland of Somerset, and Taunton's location at the centre of the south-western peninsula, introduced him to local suppliers of excellent meat, fish, poultry, vegetables and dairy produce. He uses them to good effect and it has encouraged him to rediscover and reinterpret traditional favourites like braised oxtail, boiled leg of mutton with caper sauce, beef stew with carrots and savoury dumplings, and boiled bacon with split peas. Less fashionable vegetables like cabbage have also been resurrected and reworked – memories, perhaps, of his childhood: 'On Sundays, my mother would give us shredded cabbage with a little butter, onion and bacon. It was crunchy and packed with flavour.' He now goes further and he will often use reduced cabbage liquor in some of his saucing.

However, while his arrival at the Castle reawakened the cooking of his adolescence and led him to develop a repertoire of hearty British dishes – satisfying current foodie fashion as much as the appetites of the good burghers of Taunton – his style and his inspiration still owe more to France and the great masters of modern cuisine.

The creative process works in a mysterious way and for Gary Rhodes it can often be agonizing. Occasionally my own visits to France stimulate his thoughts as I feed him with menus and recipes gathered along the way. A notable composition on his current menu consists of thin slices of salmon and a sea bass mousse layered between crisp puff pastry and spinach floating on a champagne and butter sauce. The dish bears no resemblance to Louis Outhier's *mille-feuille de saumon au cerfeuil* but the idea sprang straight from L'Oasis in La Napoule on the Côte d'Azur.

As for the future, Rhodes is not seduced by the fashionable urge to become a *chef-patron*. Of course, it may come one day but his overriding preoccupation is his growing stature as a *cuisinier* which, he realizes, can blossom by pinning his colours to one mast. At the Castle, he has found a home and the platform he has sought to build his long-term reputation. Meanwhile, as impatient as ever, he is chasing a second Michelin star.

FILLET OF RED MULLET WITH A CORIANDER AND OLIVE OIL DRESSING

2 × 400 g (14 oz) red mullet, filleted, with
all small centre bones removed
50 g (2 oz) unsalted butter

For the dressing
300 ml (½ pt) extra virgin olive oil
25 g (1 oz) coriander seeds, crushed
2 cloves garlic, roughly chopped
2 tsp chopped shallot
bunch of tarragon
salt and pepper

For the garnish
1 tsp chopped tarragon
2 tomatoes, peeled, deseeded and cut into
small dice
3 green olives, pitted
2 medium carrots
2 medium courgettes

To make the dressing, take the extra virgin olive oil and add the coriander seeds, garlic, shallot, tarragon including leaves and stalks, and salt and pepper. This dressing should be made one week in advance so that all the flavours infuse into the olive oil. This will come through as a nice tarragon and coriander dressing with the garlic and shallots just adding a little fire to the flavour.

Gently fry the fillets of red mullet in the butter. Cook skin side down to begin with for 1 minute. Turn on to the flesh side and continue to cook for a further 2 minutes. Leave to one side and keep warm.

For the garnish, take the tarragon, the tomatoes and olives (sliced lengthwise and then sliced into small half moon shapes). For the carrots and courgettes you will require a printanier cutter which is a very small melon-baller about 5 mm (¼ inch) across. Peel the carrots and make small balls using the cutter. Leave the skin on the courgettes and make small balls of courgette. These should both be blanched separately, the carrots for 2 minutes, the courgettes for 30 seconds.

To serve, strain off some of the olive oil dressing through a tea strainer and add the garnish ingredients. Mix well and check the seasoning. Lay the red mullet fillets on to four separate plates and, with a dessertspoon, lightly cover each fillet with the garnish and oil. This dish should be served immediately. Serves 4

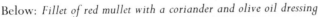

Below: *Fillet of red mullet with a coriander and olive oil dressing*

PIMIENTO BAVAROIS

1 small shallot, chopped
1 clove garlic, chopped
a good pinch of fresh thyme chopped
10 g (¼ oz) unsalted butter
1 bay leaf
750 g (1½ lb) red peppers, cored and cut
into small dice
2 tbls dry white wine
3 tbls red wine vinegar
150 ml (¼ pt) double cream
1 leaf gelatine
salt and pepper to taste
lemon juice to taste

Sweat the shallot, garlic and thyme in butter over a moderate heat with the bay leaf and red peppers until the peppers become tender. Add the dry white wine and red wine vinegar and reduce until all the liquid has evaporated. Remove the bay leaf and liquidize all of the mixture then press through a sieve until all the flesh has gone through. Place in the refrigerator to cool.

Whip the double cream until firm and soak the gelatine in a little cold water. Add the pepper mix to the cream and lightly fold in. Season with salt and pepper and add lemon juice to taste (a few drops will do). Remove the gelatine from the water and warm in a pan over gentle heat to dissolve, then whisk very quickly into the pepper cream mixture. Leave in the refrigerator for 1–2 hours before serving.

To serve, using 2 spoons shape into quenelles and serve with toast.
Serves 6

SALMON AND SEA BASS MILLE-FEUILLE

225 g (8 oz) puff pastry
225 g (8 oz) sea bass flesh, minced through a fine mincer twice
salt and pepper
1 egg white
300 ml (½ pt) double cream
16 thin slices wild salmon
225 g (8 oz) spinach
25 g (1 oz) unsalted butter
a pinch of grated nutmeg
50 ml (2 fl oz) fish stock

For the sauce
2 glasses champagne
300 ml (½ pt) fish stock
150 ml (¼ pt) double cream
75 g (3 oz) unsalted butter
salt and pepper

Preheat the oven to 230°C/450°F/Gas Mark 8. Roll the puff pastry out as thinly as possible, place on a large baking tray and cook in the oven until crisp and golden, approximately 10 minutes. To prevent it from rising too much in the oven, roll it at intervals during cooking. This will give a very light but crisp pastry. Using a pastry cutter cut out 12 circles about 7.5 cm (3 inches) diameter. Reduce the oven temperature to 180°C/350°F/Gas Mark 4.

Take the minced sea bass flesh and add salt and pepper to taste. Add the egg white and

Above: *Salmon and sea bass mille-feuille*

beat until the mixture becomes very firm. Gradually add the cream. This should then come up to a light consistency and should just hold its own weight when dropped from a spoon. Check for seasoning and consistency – some more cream may be needed. Place in a piping bag with a 5 mm (¼ inch) plain nozzle and put to one side.

Take eight buttered squares of greaseproof paper. Dip the pastry cutter into some oil to grease it then cut out a round from each piece of salmon. Place a round of salmon in the cutter itself, pipe on the mousse and cover with another round of salmon. Lift the cutter from this and you will have a small sandwich of salmon and sea bass mousse. Place on a buttered square of greaseproof paper. Repeat this method until all the salmon rounds and mousse have been used.

To make the sauce, reduce the champagne with the fish stock until it reaches a syrupy consistency, add the cream and cook until the consistency will just coat a spoon. Add

the butter in small knobs and whisk in. Check for seasoning and consistency, if it is a little thick just add a touch of water.

Cook the spinach leaves in the butter, then season with salt, pepper and a touch of nutmeg.

Cook the salmon and sea bass sandwiches in the preheated oven with the fish stock, which should just cover the bottom of the pan to create a steaming effect. This will take about 6 minutes. When they are cooked, place a little of the spinach on to one of the puff pastry rounds, lay one of the salmon and sea bass sandwiches on to this, cover with more spinach and another pastry round. Then add another layer of spinach, salmon and sea bass sandwich, more spinach and end with a pastry round. If liked, for a final touch grill mark the top pastry round using a skewer which has been heated.

Put on a plate, pour some of the sauce around and serve immediately.
Serves 4

Above: *Fillets of John Dory*

salt, pepper and lemon juice if needed. This sauce should be of a thin soup consistency.

Quickly blanch all of the vegetables, apart from the julienne of leek, the wild mushrooms, the spring onions and the potatoes, for about 1 minute. Refresh immediately in iced water. Boil the potatoes in water flavoured with the saffron threads.

Place the hazelnut oil in a hot frying pan with 25 g (1 oz) butter. Season the John Dory fillets with salt and pepper and place in the pan, presentation side down. While the John Dory is cooking, heat 15 g (½ oz) butter in a separate pan and toss the wild mushrooms, leek and spring onions for about 30 seconds. Reheat the blanched vegetables then toss in the remaining butter with salt and pepper.

Turn the fillets of John Dory over and cook for a further minute, then arrange them in the centre of the plate. Place the saffron potatoes around the outside of the John Dory, sprinkling the wild mushroom, spring onion and leek on top. Arrange the remaining vegetables around and on top of the John Dory. Warm the butter sauce and spoon over the fish. Serve immediately.
Serves 4

FILLETS OF JOHN DORY

20 small barrel shaped pieces of carrot
20 small barrel shaped pieces of courgette
20 small barrel shaped pieces of cucumber
4 asparagus tips, cut into 3 mm (⅛ inch) slices
1 stick celery, cut into julienne
20 small barrel shaped pieces of potato
a generous pinch of saffron threads
1 tbls hazelnut oil
50 g (2 oz) unsalted butter
salt and pepper
12 small fillets John Dory, skinned
100 g (4 oz) small pleurotes and girolles
1 leek, cut into julienne
8 spring onions, finely cut diagonally

For the sauce
300 ml (½ pt) fish stock
2 glasses champagne
150 ml (¼ pt) double cream
100 g (4 oz) unsalted butter
2 tbls hazelnut oil
salt and pepper
lemon juice to taste

To make the sauce, reduce the fish stock with the champagne by fast boiling and when it has almost evaporated, add the double cream. Cook this to a sauce consistency and then over very gentle heat add the butter in small knobs, whisking all the time. Remove from the heat and add the hazelnut oil and whisk vigorously to emulsify the sauce. Season with

BEST END OF LAMB WITH A MINT AND GREEN PEPPERCORN CRUST SERVED WITH A CURRANT SAUCE

2 racks of lamb, French trimmed but without the fat
50–75 g (2–3 oz) unsalted butter
a little Dijon mustard

For the crust
100 g (4 oz) fresh white breadcrumbs
20 green peppercorns, crushed
½ bunch of mint, chopped
salt
50 g (2 oz) unsalted butter, melted

For the sauce
1 glass dry white wine
50 g (2 oz) currants, poached in water
1 glass brandy
600 ml (1 pt) lamb stock reduced to 300 ml (½ pt)
25 g (1 oz) unsalted butter, softened

To make the crust, take the breadcrumbs and add the peppercorns and chopped mint. Season with salt. Add the melted butter and mix to a paste. Using a rolling pin press the mixture between 2 sheets of greaseproof paper to make a thin crust.

For the sauce, reduce the white wine with 25 g (1 oz) of currants and the brandy by fast boiling to half its volume. Once reduced, add the lamb stock and cook for about 10–15 minutes. Pass through a sieve, pushing through all of the currants. Add the softened butter and place on one side.

Preheat the oven to 220°C/425°F/Gas Mark 7.

Sauté the racks of lamb in the butter then cook in the oven for 8–9 minutes. Remove from the oven (they should be cooked medium rare). Brush the meat with a little Dijon mustard.

Place the breadcrumb mix across the meat, covering all the rack. Lay this under a preheated grill until you have a nice golden-brown breadcrumbed crust on the lamb.

Slice the lamb, allowing three cutlets per portion. Arrange neatly on a plate, add the remaining currants to the sauce and reheat. Pour the sauce around the lamb and serve.
Serves 4

BRAISED OXTAIL

2 tbls vegetable oil
2.75 kg (6 lb) oxtail, chopped and excess fat removed
2 carrots, chopped
1 onion, chopped
1 leek, chopped
2 sticks celery, chopped
2 glasses dry white wine
1 tbls tomato purée
2 litres (3½ pt) oxtail stock (see below)

For the stock
3.5 kg (8 lb) oxtail, chopped and excess fat removed
4 carrots, chopped
2 onions, chopped
2 leeks, chopped
½ head celery, chopped
4 peppercorns
1 bay leaf
6 tomatoes, chopped
1 clove garlic

For the garnish
2 carrots, very finely diced
1 onion, very finely diced
2 sticks celery, very finely diced

1 leek, very finely diced
50 g (2 oz) unsalted butter
2 tomatoes, peeled, deseeded and cut into small dice
small bunch of parsley, chopped

To make the stock, place the oxtail pieces in a frying pan over a high heat and brown well on all sides. Add all the other ingredients and stir until they are slightly coloured. Remove from the pan and place in a saucepan. Cover with cold water, remove any sediment left in the frying pan and add to the stock. Bring to the boil then reduce the heat and cook gently for at least 8 hours. When ready, allow to cool slightly, pass through a fine sieve and set aside. Do not allow the stock to reduce to a sauce consistency; you will need a stock consistency to cook the oxtail.

To braise the oxtail, heat the oil in a pan on top of the stove, add the oxtail and brown on all sides. Place in a colander so that any remaining fat will drain off. Put the vegetables in the pan and cook to a light brown colour. Place in the colander with the oxtail. Pour the white wine into the pan to soften any residue and keep to one side.

Preheat the oven to 200°C/400°F/Gas Mark 6. Transfer the oxtail to a braising pan and place the vegetables and residue on top. Add the tomato purée and oxtail stock. Bring to the boil on the top of the stove; skim off any fat. Cover with a lid and cook in the oven for 2 hours.

When the oxtail is tender, remove from the stock. Pass the liquor through a fine sieve and reduce by fast boiling to a sauce consistency.

To make the garnish, sweat the carrots, onion, celery and leek in butter until tender.

When the stock has reduced check the seasoning and add the oxtail. Allow to simmer for 10–15 minutes for the oxtail to absorb all the flavours, then add the sweated vegetables and tomato. Sprinkle with parsley and serve immediately.
Serves 6

Below: *Best end of lamb with a mint and green peppercorn crust served with a currant sauce*

APPLE TARTS WITH APPLE SORBET

For the sorbet
450 g (1 lb) caster sugar
600 ml (1 pt) water
8 Granny Smith apples
4 slices green apple, to decorate

For the tart
225 g (8 oz) puff pastry
8 Granny Smith apples
50 g (2 oz) unsalted butter
4 tsp caster sugar
4 tbls apricot jam, sieved and warmed with
2 tbls water to make glaze

To make the sorbet, dissolve the sugar in the water and bring to the boil. Boil for five minutes. Peel, core and roughly chop the apples and place in the pan with the sugar syrup. Bring to a simmer and cook until tender.

Purée in a liquidizer or push through a sieve. Cool, then freeze the mixture in a sorbet machine. If you don't have one, spread the purée on to a plastic tray and place in the freezer; when at setting point whisk in a food processor, repeat this several times to give a good consistency. When the sorbet is made freeze until required. This can be made the day before.

To make the tart, roll out the pastry very thinly and leave to rest. Cut out four rounds of pastry (approx 20 cm (8 inch) diameter) and place on baking trays. Peel, quarter and then slice the apples. Place the slices on to the pastry rounds, overlapping all the way around until the pastry is totally covered.

Preheat the oven to 220°C/425°F/Gas Mark 7. Dot a few knobs of butter on to the tarts and sprinkle with the caster sugar. Bake in the oven for 10–15 minutes until the pastry is crisp and the apples start to colour.

To serve, lightly brush with warmed apricot glaze and put on to warm plates. Shape the sorbet between two tablespoons into an oval and arrange on separate plates. For colour, take a slice of green apple and place on top of each serving of sorbet.
Serves 4

TOFFEED STRAWBERRIES

For the strawberries
450 g (1 lb) granulated sugar
50 ml (2 fl oz) glucose syrup
42 strawberries

For the lemon sauce
3 egg yolks
40 g (1½ oz) caster sugar
300 ml (½ pt) milk
juice and zest of 2 lemons

For the sponge
75 g (3 oz) unsalted butter
60 g (2¼ oz) caster sugar
2 eggs
20 g (¾ oz) plain flour
10 g (¼ oz) cornflour
75 g (3 oz) ground almonds

For the mousse
100 ml (3½ fl oz) sugar syrup
200 ml (⅓ pt) of strawberry coulis
2–3 leaves gelatine, soaked in a little cold water
150 ml (¼ pt) double cream, lightly whipped

For the glaze
150 ml (¼ pt) raspberry coulis
1 leaf gelatine, soaked in a little cold water

To make the toffeed strawberries, put the sugar and glucose syrup in a saucepan and add enough water to just cover the sugar. Bring this to the boil and allow to cook until the sugar reaches a very light golden colour.

Below: *Apple tart*

Above: *Toffeed strawberries*

Put a cocktail stick into the end of each strawberry and dip into the hot sugar, allowing any excess to drop off. Place on a lightly oiled tray.

To make the lemon sauce, beat the egg yolks and sugar together. Bring the milk to the boil, pour on to the egg mixture and cook in a double boiler over a moderate heat until it reaches a thick consistency. Add the lemon juice and zest to taste and pass through a fine sieve. Allow to cool.

To make the sponge, preheat the oven to 200–220°C/400–425°F/Gas Mark 6–7. Cream the butter and sugar in a food processor, add the eggs and then the flour, cornflour and ground almonds. Spread the mixture on to a buttered tray about 5 mm (¼ inch) in depth and bake in the oven until golden brown, approximately 10–15 minutes.

To make the mousse, warm the sugar syrup, add the strawberry coulis and the soaked leaves of gelatine and stir until dissolved. Chill until setting point is reached, then fold in the whipped cream.

Cut a square out of the sponge 15 × 15 cm (6 × 6 inches) and place in either a lined loose bottomed mould or a mould made from some cardboard and lined. The cardboard mould is preferable as it will have a closer fit. Pour the strawberry mousse over the sponge to a depth of 2.5 cm (1 inch). Allow this to set in the refrigerator.

To make the glaze, warm 2 tbls of the raspberry coulis and add the gelatine; stir until dissolved. Add to the remainder of the coulis and pour on to the top of the set mousse. This will leave about 3 mm (⅛ inch) of jelly on top.

To serve, pour some lemon sauce on to each plate to form a circle, put seven strawberries around. Remove the mould from the outside of the bavarois, cut off six small squares and serve separately.
Serves 6

JOHN BURTON-RACE

John Burton-Race has never believed in making life easy for himself or anyone else around him. He is a driven man. His close-cropped curls, taut athletic build and handsome features conjure up an image of a Greek charioteer charging up the most perilous tracks of Mount Olympus, churning vast dust clouds in a fruitless search for the gods. He knows that he will never find them but the effort is glorious. There are no ultimate prizes because the chase in itself becomes the mission – a kind of unrelenting voyage of gastronomic exploration. Unlike most other great chefs he is not content to come to rest, find his plot on a side of the mountain and cultivate his perfect olive grove. Frustration is the fire in his belly: 'Even if I live to a hundred, I shall die knowing nothing. You can only scratch the surface. It is impossible to be a master of such a vast subject.'

Whatever view he might have of himself – and he is obsessively self-critical – the pundits have wreathed him with laurels and they have already crowned him one of the culinary princes of the 1990s. While the eulogies are deserved, foodie commentators have an awful habit of putting chefs they admire into tidy little boxes and labelling them neatly with a two-word appellation which typecasts their *cuisine* for the instant illumination of the less discerning punter. Burton-Race has suffered from this branding syndrome – which is meaningless because it is quite impossible to put his cooking into a stylistic straitjacket. His creative output, his technique and his artistry are evolving so furiously that no-one can really predict his final destination. The recipes and pictures on these pages are no more than a snapshot of where he was along the trail in the summer of 1988. Still in his early thirties, he has a long way to go.

John Burton-Race's early years were nomadic. Born in Singapore in May 1957, he followed his parents around Africa and the Far East until, at the age of 12, they sent him away to school a short drive from the family's Hampshire home on the south coast near Southampton. His father was a high-flying consultant civil engineer and his mother expected equally great things of her son. But life was never quite that simple with young John. At school he was 'very rebellious, bloody lazy and a general pain in the arse' and three weeks after he had started his 'A' level course at a sixth form college he dropped out. Mother administered a sound thrashing, father took the next flight out of Senegal and the 17-year-old son and heir was asked what precisely he planned to do with himself. When he suggested art college, his parents were not impressed: 'Only three types of people do art – hippies, drug addicts and queers.'

Eventually, a peace formula was struck with cooking cast as the instrument of appeasement. John had always loved dining in the grand hotels of the Orient, his mother was highly competent in the kitchen and regarded cooking as an honourable trade and father prayed that the drudgery of the work might just knock enough sense into his son to bring him back to academe.

The next few years were hardly a signal of future greatness. For the sake of a quiet life at home and to try his luck, Burton-Race took the first job he was offered – an apprenticeship, coupled with college training on day-release, at the Wessex Hotel in Winchester, a modern red-brick in the shadow of the cathedral. But the angels were smiling and he was on his way. He scored no marks for good behaviour and the chef put up with his cheek because he saw a glimmer of talent, ambition and a will to get on. Two years later Burton-Race was sent to Quaglino's in London but because his CV lacked the gloss of a professional stamp he soon left, having persuaded his tutors in Hampshire to allow him to sit his exams without the tedium of attending a two-year full-time course. He returned to college for three months and passed his finals with distinction.

Armed with his new credentials his career gathered steam and in 1977 he went to one of Britain's most celebrated country house hotels, Chewton Glen in New Milton, which had just been awarded Egon Ronay's Gold Plate as 'Hotel of the Year'. Twelve months later, a young, soft-eyed and pretty French management trainee joined the staff. This was Christine, John's future wife and a woman who in time would prove to be a decisive influence on him and a safe harbour for his mercurial temperament. However, the prospect of marriage at the age of 21 rekindled old parental anxieties. Nevertheless, on this occasion, love triumphed over logic and they were wed.

Happiness at home now coincided with boredom at work. In two good years Burton-Race had taken from Chewton Glen all that he wanted and he went in search of new adventure. The young couple found Oliver's, a new restaurant converted from an old chapel in Midhurst, which they ran for a London businessman. The experiment was short-lived because they soon learned that the owner was selling out beneath their feet. However, they were there long enough to be

discovered by an Egon Ronay inspector and the 1980 guide praised the chef's 'imaginative dishes' and 'immense care in the kitchen'.

While the guidebook's notice boosted his youthful ego for a moment, it did little to promote his restless ambition. Oliver's was a silly mistake and he felt that his career was losing its impetus. Once again he turned to his tutors, who put him and Christine in touch with André Chavagnon, *chef-patron* of La Sorbonne in Oxford, a well established restaurant noted for its classical and regional French cooking. Burton-Race did predictably well and Chavagnon rewarded him with promotion, but after two years he knew it was time to move on – a decision which caused his employer some agitation.

Meanwhile, by the turn of the decade, the accomplishments of Raymond Blanc at Les Quat' Saisons in Banbury Road were beginning to strike a fever of excitement on serious palates up and down the country. In 1982, Burton-Race went to see Blanc for a job. Unable to take him immediately, Blanc installed him and Christine as private chef and housekeeper on a 350-acre estate in North Oxfordshire

his master soon recognized a rare ability in him: 'I felt something different about John. I pushed him hard and he took it in his stride. He learned quickly and understood what I was trying to do.'

Blanc's gift to Burton-Race was to teach him a frame of mind about cooking: to be curious, not to be timid, to have the passion and the will to develop dishes to their extreme and not to be content with what has been achieved before.

When, in 1984, Blanc left Oxford to open Le Manoir au Quat' Saisons at Great Milton, he put John and Christine in charge of the Banbury Road premises which were rechristened Le Petit Blanc — a new restaurant conceived as a first-rate bistro in town to complement the country grandeur 12 miles down the road.

However, Blanc's sensible marketing stratagem was soon diluted by Burton-Race's burgeoning impatience to make his mark. Having been seduced by the charisma of his teacher's cooking, he found it difficult to change tack and as the cost of wages and raw materials soared, so did the prices on the bills and the hyperbole in the press. By 1986, Burton-Race had won his first Michelin star and Le Petit Blanc was beginning to look like Le Manoir's culinary clone.

It was time to up sticks again, and, thanks only to the quiet but firm counsel of Christine, John turned down a number of tempting offers and began to consider his own restaurant. There seemed little point in delaying the agony which now had to be exorcized and he decided to call on Sir David Napley, the distinguished solicitor and his greatest fan at Le Petit Blanc. Honouring a promise he had made one lunchtime in Oxford, Sir David went to work and, in early October 1986, Burton-Race moved into the kitchens of the Old Vicarage, Shinfield as Nico Ladenis moved out to fulfil his second coming in London. It was a deal which took ten frantic days to conclude and on the opening night L'Ortolan was still £40,000 short of the money required to make the business remotely viable. But as people began to leave at the end of the evening, their last customer handed Christine an envelope. When she opened it and saw the contents she stared in disbelief and rushed into the kitchen to show John. It contained a cheque for £38,500. Three months later, in January 1987, L'Ortolan was accorded its first Michelin star. At the church next door, the angels were still smiling on John Burton-Race.

The menus at L'Ortolan are highly descriptive and change almost monthly. The force of evolution is astonishing. While Burton-Race used to be soaked up by the style of Blanc, he is now establishing his

belonging to a property developer who was a devoted regular client. A year later John joined the brigade at Les Quat' Saisons.

Blanc's effect on the outlook of his new recruit was like a bolt of high-voltage electricity. At last the rebel had found his cause. He was no longer bored. Suddenly, he was fired with an enthusiasm and a buzz which until now had been absent. Burton-Race was on a high and own culinary roots and the early blossoms of the new shoot are technicoloured and kaleidoscopic: 'I simply can't do the same things again and again. I am looking for excitement and I want different flavours and sensations on the palate.'

The distinguishing marks vary from dish to dish. A presentation of lightly roasted pigeon breast is encased by a smooth mousse made from the bird's leg and wrapped in cabbage to deliver a symphonious contrast of colour and texture. The sliced pieces come on the pigeon's natural juices, flecked with truffle to accentuate the brilliant shine and translucence of the saucing. Coulis on pudding plates bear the same wonderful luminosity. Other dishes belie their complexity by appearing and tasting rustic and gutsy. A roasted guinea fowl with a ballottine of its leg in a pig's trotter is plain earthy. Similarly, a terrine of sea bream and langoustines is generous, chunky and uncontrollably piscine.

In total contrast, Burton-Race is capable of amusing flights of fantasy, beautiful presentations and off-beat marriages of ingredients. A raw quail's egg perched atop his délice of salmon encourages a moment of audience participation. A turbot and lobster pâté is nouvellishly pretty. And the conjunction of Aberdeen Angus fillet with snails sandwiched in puff pastry is faintly over the top.

Perhaps, in the end, Raymond Blanc's supreme gift was to pass on the secret of the artist — a secret which Burton-Race learned instinctively as he acquired the courage, flair and imagination to go beyond the limits of current knowledge and to break new ground in culinary understanding.

Burton-Race has a deep urge to satisfy his own creative impulses in spite of the strain on his kitchen and irrespective of the *gloire* of Michelin stardom; but ultimately, his future status as a chef will be measured by his ability to harness and direct his amazing creative output. As he matures and comes to terms with his great talent, there is little doubt that he will achieve the harmony that has to be balanced with the agony of invention.

Blanc himself has said that Burton-Race 'will be one of the great chefs of the Nineties'. Meanwhile, and with Christine as its quiet navigator, he is like a Titan rocket which has lifted off, burning vast quantities of fuel to propel itself into space. It will not be long before he breaks through the Earth's atmosphere.

Left: *The Old Vicarage at Shinfield, now L'Ortolan. Tucked away just off the busy M4 motorway at exit 11, the restaurant is only 50 minutes from Hyde Park Corner.*

Right: *The frenetic atmosphere of Burton-Race's kitchen is steadied by the calming presence of his wife, Christine. 'Without her, I would be nowhere,' he confesses.*

A DELICE OF SALMON WITH CHIVE AND PEPPER CREAM

175–225 g (6–8 oz) fillet of fresh salmon,
skinned and cut into 5 mm (¼ inch) dice
2 small shallots, finely chopped
1 tsp chopped dill
2 tsp chopped chives
small amount of crushed garlic to taste
salt and pepper
juice of ½ lemon
4 large thin slices of smoked salmon
a little vinaigrette flavoured with tarragon

For the chive and pepper cream
2 small bundles of fresh chives, coarsely
sliced
300 ml (½ pt) soured cream
1 tsp freshly grated horseradish
2 tbls natural yoghurt
½ Granny Smith apple, grated
½ yellow pepper, skinned
½ red pepper, skinned
salt and pepper

For the garnish
8 half slices of lemon
8 salmon caviar eggs
strips of chive
½ tsp Beluga caviar (optional)
1 tomato, peeled, deseeded and cut into
small dice, seasoned and sharpened with
lemon juice
8 small sprigs of fresh chervil
4 quail's eggs
a little cayenne pepper

To prepare the chive and pepper cream, mix all the ingredients except the peppers together, cover, and place in the refrigerator for at least 24 hours, stirring it now and then. When ready to use, pass through a fine sieve into a small basin and reserve about 2 dessertspoons to finish the dish.

Take the peppers and cut into small dice then blanch them in boiling water for 30 seconds. Dry them on kitchen paper. Whip the cream mixture until it forms soft peaks then fold in the peppers. Season with salt and pepper and keep in the refrigerator.

Arrange two half slices of lemon on each plate and garnish with the salmon eggs and strips of chive. Then, using a teaspoon dipped in boiling water, spoon out two small oval quenelles from the chive and pepper cream and put on the plate. Place a small heap of Beluga caviar on top, if using. Place the tomato dice in two small heaps and top each with a sprig of chervil.

Prepare the salmon as close to serving as possible. In a small bowl, place the raw diced salmon, then add the shallots, dill, chives, garlic, seasoning and lemon juice.

Line four 5 cm (2 inch) ramekins with cling film, then line again with the slices of smoked salmon. Place the raw salmon mixture into the ramekins and fold the smoked salmon back over the filling to encase the 'délice'. Turn this out on to your prepared plates and brush with the vinaigrette to give a shine.

Make a small indentation in the top of each 'délice' and insert a raw quail's egg, still in its shell but with its top cut off and a little cayenne pepper sprinkled into it. Then spoon a small amount of the reserved cream mixture on to each plate.

Serve each portion with a slice of warm brioche.
Serves 4

FILLET OF BEEF WITH MILLE-FEUILLE OF SNAILS AND RED WINE SAUCE

100 g (4 oz) puff pastry
50 g (2 oz) girolles
50 g (2 oz) bone marrow, cut into 5 mm
(¼ inch) dice
1 small bulb fennel, cut into fine dice
75 g (3 oz) large, canned snails, halved
1 clove garlic, crushed
25 g (1 oz) clarified butter
small glass of Pernod
4 tournedos weighing 150 g (5 oz) each
salt and pepper
a little garlic butter
25 g (1 oz) fresh parsley, chopped
chopped chives
3 tomatoes, peeled, deseeded and diced

For the red wine sauce
75 g (3 oz) unsalted butter
225 g (8 oz) shallots, thinly sliced
2 cloves garlic, thinly sliced
sprig of fresh tarragon
175 g (6 oz) button mushrooms, sliced
½ bottle red Burgundy
600 ml (1 pt) chicken stock
65 ml (2½ fl oz) meat glaze
truffle juice, optional

For the shallot purée
8 shallots, roughly chopped
1 clove garlic, roughly chopped
25 g (1 oz) unsalted butter
salt and pepper
a little lemon juice
50 ml (2 fl oz) water

For the shallot confit
8 shallots, sliced
25 ml (1 fl oz) water
25 g (1 oz) unsalted butter
salt and pepper
a little lemon juice

Preheat the oven to 220°C/425°F/Gas Mark 7.

Roll out the puff pastry to make a thin square approximately 10 × 10 cm (4 × 4 inches), place on a lightly greased baking sheet and prick all over. Put aside to relax, in a refrigerator if possible, for 15 minutes, then bake for 10 minutes. Should the pastry start to rise in places it can be lightly pressed with a cloth while cooking. When evenly golden brown, remove from the oven, slide gently on to a wire tray and set aside to cool down.

Meanwhile, prepare the sauce: in a large pan, melt 25 g (1 oz) butter, add the shallots, garlic and the tarragon and allow to soften. Add the mushrooms and increase the heat, stirring all the time, until the moisture from the mushrooms has evaporated. Add the Burgundy and reduce until almost dry, pour in the chicken stock and meat glaze, bring to the boil, remove any scum and simmer for 10 minutes. Pass through a fine sieve and reserve.

Clean the girolles by scraping the stalks and gills off and wash thoroughly to remove any traces of dirt. Cut into quarters if they are large and mix with the marrow. Keep cool.

Mix the diced fennel with the snails and the crushed garlic. Heat the clarified butter in a large frying pan, put in the fennel, snails and garlic, and stir rapidly for 1 minute. Pour the Pernod over, let it flame then tip the snails out on to a plate to cool down.

To make the purée, mix the chopped shallots and garlic in a saucepan and add the butter, salt, pepper and lemon juice. Add the water and bring to the boil, then let it gently simmer until very soft. Liquidize and pass through a fine sieve, check seasoning and keep warm. Cover with a butter paper.

To make the confit, place the sliced shallots in a pan with the water, butter, salt, pepper and lemon juice. Bring to the boil and simmer gently, covered with a lid, until just cooked but still crunchy. Keep warm.

To serve, cut the puff pastry into 8 small rectangles 5 × 2.5 cm (2 × 1 inches) and gently warm. Bring the red wine sauce to the boil, remove any scum and begin to reduce rapidly by fast boiling to half its volume. Season the tournedos and seal in a hot heavy-based pan. Cook for 3–4 minutes for pink meat, remove from the pan and allow to rest for 4 minutes. Meanwhile, reheat the snails in a little garlic butter and add chopped parsley. Heat a heavy-based pan, with no fat, until very hot. Add the diced marrow and the girolles, toss rapidly for 30 seconds, add the chives and turn out on to kitchen paper immediately to drain the fat.

On each large warmed plate place one piece of the puff pastry. Top with the shallot confit, then the hot snails, one spoon of shallot purée and finally a pastry lid. In the middle place the tournedos and pour over the reduced red wine sauce which has been enriched with the remaining 50 g (2 oz) butter and a little truffle juice, if using. Place the girolle and marrow mixture around the tournedos and sprinkle the diced tomato on top. Eat immediately.

Serves 4

Right: *Fillet of beef with mille-feuille of snails and red wine sauce*

GRILLED FILLETS OF RED MULLET WITH CAVIAR AND PEPPER COULIS

4 × 200–250 g (7–9 oz) red mullet
salt and pepper
a dash of lemon juice

For the marinade
200 ml (7 fl oz) virgin olive oil
sprig of fresh basil
⅓ bay leaf
sprig of fresh thyme
1 clove garlic, sliced
2 shallots, sliced
2 strips lemon zest, blanched
a few black peppercorns, crushed

For the caviar cream
25 g (1 oz) unsalted butter
3 shallots, sliced
1 star anise
2 leaves basil
1 clove garlic
sprig of fresh thyme
⅓ bay leaf
100 ml (3½ fl oz) Noilly Prat
200 ml (7 fl oz) dry white wine
mullet bones
150 ml (¼ pt) water
100 ml (3½ fl oz) whipping cream
a dash of lemon juice
2 tbls Beluga caviar

For the pepper coulis
juice of 1 orange
1 piece of orange zest
4 tbls virgin olive oil
1 red pepper, cored and diced
3 shallots, finely sliced
sprig of fresh thyme
⅓ bay leaf
sprig of tarragon
sprig of fresh basil
salt
white peppercorns, crushed
1 tbls tomato purée
450 g (1 lb) ripe tomatoes, peeled, deseeded and diced
1 clove garlic, crushed
150 ml (¼ pt) clear fish consommé

For the garnish
a little clarified butter
salt and pepper
mullet livers
4 garlic croûtons
cooked baby fennel (optional)
4 spirals of pasta, cooked (optional)

To prepare the marinade, combine all the ingredients together in a large flat dish.

Scale and clean the mullet (keep the livers for garnish) then fillet them. Save the bones to make stock for the caviar cream and put the fillets in the marinade, ideally leaving overnight.

Preheat the oven to 200°C/400°F/Gas Mark 6.

To make the caviar cream, melt the butter in a pan that may be used in the oven. Add the shallots, star anise, basil, garlic, thyme and bay leaf. Cook but do not colour. Deglaze the pan with the Noilly Prat. Reduce the liquid by fast boiling until almost dry.

Add the white wine and reduce by half. Add the red mullet bones and moisten with the water. Bring to the boil, removing all scum that rises to the surface. Cover with some butter paper or foil and put a lid on top. Place in the oven and cook for approximately 10 minutes.

Remove the stock from the oven and strain the liquid through a conical sieve, then through a muslin cloth. Pour the stock into another pan and reduce the liquid by fast boiling to a light syrup consistency. Add the whipping cream, boil and reduce by half by fast boiling. Correct the seasoning.

Acidulate the cream by adding a few drops of lemon juice, then finally add the Beluga caviar. Keep warm but do not allow it to boil as this will cause the sauce to split and the caviar to congeal, giving the cream a bitter and unpleasant taste.

To make the pepper coulis, boil the orange juice and remove any scum which rises to the surface to clarify it. Reserve on the side. Blanch the orange zest in boiling water then refresh it in ice cold water. Strain and repeat this process twice.

Heat the olive oil in a saucepan and add the pepper, shallots, thyme, bay leaf, tarragon, basil, salt and peppercorns. Add the tomato purée and cook for approximately 5 minutes. Moisten with the orange juice and add the tomatoes, garlic and orange zest.

Add the fish consommé, bring the liquid to the boil and skim. Correct the seasoning and simmer for a further 30 minutes.

Liquidize and return the coulis to the stove. Boil again and skim off any scum. Pass through a conical sieve and keep warm.

Remove the fillets of mullet from the marinade and put them on a tray under a moderate grill for approximately four minutes. Season and sprinkle with a little lemon juice.

To prepare the garnish, heat a little clarified butter in a small sauté pan and fry the seasoned red mullet livers for approximately 10 seconds. Turn out the livers on to kitchen paper to absorb and eliminate excess fat, then place them on the garlic croûtons. As an option you can use cooked fennel or pasta as a garnish.

Arrange the red mullet on the plate and pour a cordon of the pepper coulis one side of the fillets and the caviar cream on the other. Top with a prepared croûton to finish.
Serves 4

Left: *Grilled fillets of red mullet with caviar and pepper coulis*

PIGEON BREAST WRAPPED IN CABBAGE WITH MADEIRA

2 Norfolk squab pigeons
50 g (2 oz) fresh foie gras de canard
4 shallots, coarsely sliced
2 cloves garlic, halved
2 sprigs of thyme
⅓ bay leaf
a little madeira
a little ruby port
a little dry white wine
120 ml (4 fl oz) chicken stock
salt
300 ml (½ pt) double cream
a little clarified butter
4 savoy cabbage leaves, 15 cm (6 inches) in
diameter, blanched until tender then dried

For the sauce
2 pigeon carcases, chopped in small pieces
a little clarified butter
4 shallots, chopped
1 clove garlic
sprig of thyme
¼ bay leaf
2 tbls white wine vinegar
4 tbls vintage dry madeira
450 ml (¾ pt) clear chicken stock
100 g (4 oz) button mushrooms, sliced
1 tbls meat glaze
a little fresh truffle, finely diced
25 g (1 oz) unsalted butter

For the garnish
a little clarified butter
175 g (6 oz) assorted wild mushrooms
¼ clove garlic, chopped
1 tsp chopped chives
1 shallot, finely chopped
25 g (1 oz) unsalted butter
salt and pepper
4 small puff pastry cases shaped as
saucepans

Remove the breasts and legs from the pigeons, retaining the carcases for making the sauce. Skin the breasts and put them to one side.

Bone the legs and place them with the hearts and livers from both birds in a small bowl. Add the foie gras de canard, shallots, garlic, thyme sprigs and bay leaf. Then add 2 tsp of madeira, port and dry white wine. Leave to marinate for 12 hours in the refrigerator.

When marinated, place the meat in a colander set over a small pan and catch the juices. Bring them to the boil, removing all the scum and impurities which surface. Reduce the juices over a medium heat until syrupy, add the chicken stock and reduce by fast boiling to half the volume. Strain and leave to cool.

Remove the shallots, thyme, garlic and bay leaf from the meat and discard.

Place the flesh from the legs, hearts, livers and foie gras in a food processor, add 2 good pinches of salt and purée until very fine (approximately 1 minute). This must then be chilled, which can be done in a freezer for about 15 minutes, before working in the cream to give a thick mousse. Check the seasoning and pass the mousse through a fine sieve. Finally add the reduced juices from the marinade and leave the mousse in the refrigerator until required.

To make the sauce, fry the pigeon carcases in the clarified butter until sealed and golden brown.

Add the shallots, garlic, thyme and bay leaf and fry together for 2 or 3 minutes. Deglaze the pan with the white wine vinegar and cook until dry. Add the madeira and reduce the liquid by half by fast boiling. Moisten with the chicken stock then bring the liquid to the boil and skim off the impurities. Turn down to a simmer, add the mushrooms and cook for 1 hour.

Strain the stock into a pan and bring it to the boil again, skimming off the impurities. Reduce by fast boiling until a light syrupy consistency is achieved. Enrich the sauce with the meat glaze, check the seasoning and consistency and keep warm.

To assemble the pigeons, heat a little clarified butter in a small frying pan and seal the seasoned pigeon breasts for 30 seconds on each side. Leave to cool.

Lay out the cabbage leaves on the table and spoon a small amount of mousse on one half of the leaves. Place the pigeon breasts on top and spoon the remaining mousse over the breasts, smoothing it with a palette knife. To enclose the breasts completely, fold the remaining part of the leaf over the top. Press down on the edge. Trim away the overlapping cabbage.

Wrap each parcel in cling film, ensuring the package is totally airtight. Cook in a saucepan of water at boiling point for about 10 minutes.

To prepare the garnish, heat the clarified butter, throw in the wild mushrooms, garlic, chives, shallot and 15 g (½ oz) of butter and cook over a vigorous heat. Season. Remove from the heat and fill the warm puff pastry cases with the mixture.

To finish, remove the pigeon breasts from the boiling water and carefully unwrap them. Slice each into five pieces and arrange them into a semi-circle on the plates. Place a puff pastry saucepan at the top of each plate.

To finish the sauce, add the diced truffle and whisk in the butter a little at a time. Spoon the sauce round the pigeon. It is now ready to serve.

Serves 4

Right: *Pigeon breast wrapped in cabbage with Madeira*

JOHN BURTON·RACE

HOT GRAND MARNIER SOUFFLE WITH ORANGE SALAD

grated zest of 4 oranges
4 tsp Grand Marnier
2 tsp fresh orange juice
4 tbls crème pâtissière
8 egg whites
4 tsp caster sugar
icing sugar, to dust

For the orange salad
2 oranges
a dash of Grand Marnier

To make the orange salad, remove the peel from the oranges and finely slice into julienne. Segment the flesh and squeeze any remaining juice into a bowl. Add a dash of Grand Marnier to the juice and marinate the orange segments in the mixture. Drop the julienne of orange zest into boiling water for 10 seconds. Remove and refresh in cold water immediately.

Preheat the oven to 240°C/475°F/Gas Mark 9.

Grease the inside of 4 individual soufflé dishes about 10 cm (4 inches) in diameter.

Add the zest, Grand Marnier and the orange juice to the crème pâtissière and set aside. Whisk the egg whites until stiff and as they begin to peak add the caster sugar, a spoonful at a time beating well to incorporate. Fold the egg whites into the crème pâtissière quickly and evenly. Divide the mixture between the soufflé dishes making sure you fill them to the top, level off with a spatula.

Place in the oven for 10 minutes to cook. Halfway through cooking, quickly loosen the edges of the soufflés with a palette knife to allow them to rise evenly.

When cooked, remove the soufflés from the oven and dust with icing sugar. Place the orange segments on a side plate with a little of the juice and serve immediately.
Serves 4

GENERAL INDEX

ACKNOWLEDGEMENTS

The last page seems hardly the most appropriate place to offer a note of profound thanks to the many people who have assisted me with this book. However, thank you all for your patience, time and wisdom. Firstly to my eighteen chefs, their spouses, partners and teams who cooked for me, talked and gave so freely of their magnificent hospitality. To Martin Brigdale whose beautiful photography enlivens these pages and who has become a good friend. To Elizabeth David, Derek Brown, Richard Binns, Drew Smith, George Perry-Smith and Heather Crosbie with whom I spent many stimulating hours debating the state of British gastronomy. To Joe Hyam of *Caterer and Hotelkeeper*, Frank Kelly, Alistair Hankey and Bedford Pace of the British Tourist Authority, and John Petersen and David Rodin of American Express for their invaluable support. To Anne Snead-Cox for introducing me to Octopus Books and to Isabel Moore, my publisher, who had the confidence to commission a complete stranger. To my editor, Isobel Greenham, who mustered the fortitude of Boadicea and the kindliness of a saint to steer her argumentative author to a safe harbour. To my great friends Kevin and Fran Loftus who supplied me with the wherewithal for my manuscript. And to my valiant secretary, Gill Whatmore who, with her understudy Jacqui Gifford-Bennett, gladly undertook the labour of typing, filing and proof reading.

    Lastly, I want to thank my dearest parents, Peter and Etty Chapman, for their wonderful encouragement and enthusiasm in my task. And, above all, I shall never forget the love and steadfast support of my wife, Louise, who sustained and inspired me through many long afternoons in my study at home.

REFERENCES

I would like to acknowledge the following sources which provided me with useful background information for this book:

Good Food Guides: 1961–1989

Egon Ronay Guides: 1962–1989

Michelin Red Guides: 1974–1989

British Gastronomy, by Gregory Houston Bowden
    (Chatto and Windus, 1975)

The British at Table 1940–1980, by Christopher Driver
    (Chatto and Windus. The Hogarth Press, 1983)

Food in History, by Reay Tannahill
    (Penguin, 1988)

British Food Finds 1989, edited by Henrietta Green
    (Rich and Green, 1989)

The Good Food Directory, edited by Drew Smith and David Mabey
    (Consumers' Association, 1986)

Good Things, by Jane Grigson
    (Michael Joseph 1973)